ANIMAL CONVENTIONS IN ENGLISH RENAISSANCE NON-RELIGIOUS PROSE (1550-1600)

WILLIAM MEREDITH CARROLL

ANIMAL CONVENTIONS
IN
ENGLISH RENAISSANCE
NON-RELIGIOUS PROSE
(1550-1600)

BOOKMAN ASSOCIATES   NEW YORK

Copyright, 1954, by William M. Carroll

MANUFACTURED IN THE UNITED STATES OF AMERICA

TO MY FATHER AND MOTHER

Sweet are the uses of adversity;
Which, like the toad, ugly and venomous,
Wears yet a precious jewel in his head:
And this our life exempt from public haunt
Finds tongues in trees, books in the running brooks,
Sermons in stones and good in every thing.
—WILLIAM SHAKESPEARE, *As You Like It*, II, i, 12-17

Preface

CONVENTION AND REVOLT AGAINST CONVENTION ARE PHENOMENA THAT may be noticed in any age of literature and art. Adherence in modern times to Greek and Latin classical literary models is a following of conventions established in ancient times and either perpetuated through the Middle Ages or revived in the Renaissance. It is the purpose of this dissertation to affirm the existence, even in pre-literary times, of an ocean of animal lore whence came into ancient Greek, Latin, and Oriental literature many ideas that became conventional and persisted as conventions in the later literature of western Europe and to show how and why the chief writers of English prose in the latter half of the sixteenth century continued to follow these conventions in their works. The magnitude of such an undertaking makes it advisable to limit the investigation of the subject to the study of conventional ideas about animals in the principal non-religious prose writings of England in the period 1550-1600.

The exposition of this subject must first characterize the general background that gave rise to animal conventions in the literature of western Europe and then show how these ideas about animals were perpetuated in medieval literature on the Continent and transmitted to England, where precedents became established for their subsequent employment in Elizabethan prose. It is hoped that this study will shed some more light upon the character and significance of the animal lore in Elizabethan non-religious prose literature and upon at least one aspect of the English Renaissance in relation to ancient, medieval, and modern times.

The first three chapters of this dissertation have been written in order to survey the background against which the animal conventions in the English non-religious prose of the period 1550-1600 are to be studied. The material of these chapters is, for the most part, available elsewhere; and no pretense to originality in the handling of it is made here. My indebtedness to such works as Percy A. Robin's *Animal Lore in English Literature,* Thomas Wright's *A History of Caricature and Grotesque in Literature and Art,* Professor Lynn Thorndike's *A History of Magic and Experimental Science,* Professor Rupert Taylor's *The Political Prophecy in England,* Professor Arthur B. Leible's *Conventions of Animal Symbolism and Satire in Spenser's Mother Hubberds Tale,* and other sources is acknowledged in the footnotes and the text. I have been guided in these chapters by Professor Leible's work perhaps more than the footnotes indicate.

A list of the animals, birds, reptiles, and other creatures with the conventional ideas pertaining to them is given in the Appendix, where also are to be found the page references to their occurrence in the natural histories of Aristotle, Pliny, and Topsell and in the various Elizabethan prose writings.

I am particularly indebted to Professor Arthur B. Leible, whose criticism and advice have been most helpful, from the inception of the project to its fulfillment. I am indebted to Professor Laurens J. Mills for similar encouragement and guidance. My indebtedness to the staff of the Indiana University Library, particularly to Mr. J. W. Gordon Gourlay; to the staffs of the Harper Library of the University of Chicago and the Alderman Library of the University of Virginia; and to Miss Mayme Evans, Librarian of the University of Corpus Christi Library, for their co-operation in making available a number of rare books and other material is gratefully acknowledged.

I wish to thank Mr. Leslie E. Bliss, Librarian of the Henry E. Huntington Library in San Marino, California, for granting me permission to refer to photostat facsimiles of John Grange's *The Golden Aphroditis,* Stephen Gosson's *The Ephemerides of Phialo,* and Sir Thomas North's translation of *The Morall Philosophie of Doni.*

No less do I owe a debt of gratitude to my wife Virginia for the many helpful suggestions and the encouragement which she has given me.

WILLIAM CARROLL.

Acknowledgments

For borrowings which I have made from comparatively recent editions of some of the works discussed, I wish here to acknowledge gratefully my indebtedness to the editors and to the publishers of these editions. I desire to express thanks especially to Professor Arthur B. Leible, of Indiana University, for granting me permission to use material from his unpublished paper "The Philosophical Background of *King Lear*." For permission to quote I wish to express particular gratitude to the University of Chicago Press and to Professor Arthur B. Leible, of Indiana University, from his dissertation *Conventions of Animal Symbolism and Satire in Spenser's Mother Hubberds Tale* (Abstract published in the University of Chicago *Abstracts of Theses*, 1930); to the Columbia University Press and to Professor Rupert Taylor, of Clemson Agricultural College, from his *The Political Prophecy in England;* to the Cambridge University Press, from Professor Foster Watson's *The English Grammar Schools to 1660: their Curriculum and Practice*, Professor William Harrison Woodward's *Desiderius Erasmus concerning the Aim and Method of Education*, and Professor Albert Feuillerat's edition of Sidney's *Arcadia*; to The Clarendon Press, from Professor G. H. Mair's edition of *Wilson's Arte of Rhetorique;* to the Oxford University Press, Inc., from Herbert Hartman's edition of *A Petite Pallace of Pettie His Pleasure;* to the Harvard University Press, from A. W. Mair's translation of *Oppian, Colluthus, Tryphiodorus,* in the Loeb Classical Library Edition; to the Publishers of *Philological Quarterly* and to Professor Archer Taylor, of the University of California, from his article "The Proverb 'The Black Ox Has not Trod on His Foot' in Renaissance Literature"; and to Chatto and Windus, Ltd., from Professor C. F. Tucker Brooke's edition of *Shakespeare's Plutarch*.

W. M. C.

Table of Contents

CHAPTER ONE

The Background for the Establishment of Animal Conventions in the Literature of Western Europe

LITERARY EMPLOYMENT OF IDEAS ABOUT LIVING CREATURES OTHER THAN man presupposes the existence from time immemorial of a large stock of ideas that were accumulated and perpetuated in primitive oral tradition, which goes back ultimately to individual observation or imagination. The ideas which man has associated with other members of the animal kingdom are the product of his contemplation of the various forms of life on the earth. His long-continued association of the same ideas with the same creatures inevitably gave rise to such conventions as, for example, the foaming, furious boar; the sly, crafty fox; the ravenous wolf; the keen-sighted eagle; the gentle, constant dove; and the subtle, wicked serpent.

These and many other animal conventions that undoubtedly formed a part of the oral tradition and the mythology of pre-literary ages entered also into written literature, where they persisted in myths and fables, in the Bible, and in treatises on natural history. What in ancient times was known or thought about animals, as evidenced by these writings, was drawn largely from the store of information which was common to the peoples of nearly all parts of southwestern Asia and the Mediterranean world.

Animals, birds, reptiles, and other creatures, both real and imaginary, came to be used conventionally in literature as types of character or disposition illustrative of human nature and as subjects of similes and metaphors to portray human traits and experience.[1] Animal symbolism as a part of language itself is too well known to need specific illustration.

It would be impossible, for lack of evidence, to trace in detail the entire history or to know exactly the time or place of origin of the ideas that have become conventional as applied to various creatures; but it is safe to say that many of these ideas are almost as old as mankind and as widely distributed. Without engaging in useless speculation regarding primitive oral tradition, however, one finds in ancient writings from the time of Homer onward an extensive body of animal lore which constitutes a background sufficient to account for the establishment of the ideas about animals as conventions in the literature of western Europe.

The principal ancient writings about animals are the Aesopic and Bidpai fables and the Greek and Roman works on natural history. The Septuagint version of the Hebrew Bible (first century B.C.), with its many references to animals, brought Hebrew writings to the notice of non-Hebrew readers.[2]

The most important ancient Greek writer on natural history is Aristotle (fourth century B.C.), who is sometimes referred to as "the founder of scientific zoology," since his works on animals, especially the *Historia Animalium*,[3] contain much knowledge of living creatures obtained from actual observation.[4] But his works[5] also include a great deal of unscientific popular animal lore. The *Historia Animalium*, since it embodies most of the knowledge and popular lore concerning the animal kingdom in the time of Aristotle, is, of all his works, the most important in connection with the study of conventional ideas about animals in literature. For more than eighteen centuries writers on natural history did little more than copy, translate, or comment upon the works of Aristotle.[6]

The principal Roman writers on natural history are four: in the first century A.D., Pliny the Elder (Gaius Plinius Secundus); in the third century A.D. Oppian, Solinus (Gaius Julius Solinus), and Aelian (Claudius Aelianus). The most important one of this group is Pliny, whose *Naturalis Historia* has four of its thirty-seven books (viii-xi inclusive)[7] devoted to zoological species other than man. For his zoological knowledge Pliny relied mainly on Aristotle and Juba II, king of Mauritania.[8] Pliny's *Naturalis Historia*, like Aristotle's *Historia Animalium*, contains much unscientific popular animal lore and embodies most of what was known or thought about animals in the first century A.D. Much of Pliny's material is only a repetition of Aristotle's.

In the third century A.D. appeared four works on animals: two poems in Greek — *Cynegetica,* consisting of four books on hunting, and *Halieutica,* consisting of five books on fishing — by Oppian;[9] *Collectanea Rerum Memorabilium,* a description in Latin prose of curiosities concerning animals, by Solinus;[10] and *De Natura Animalium,* a collection in Greek prose of curious and interesting stories of animal life, by Aelian.[11] These works, however, added nothing to the store of knowledge and popular lore contained in Aristotle's *Historia Animalium* and Pliny's *Naturalis Historia.*

The same general store of information about animals was drawn upon by writers in the Middle Ages and even in the sixteenth and seventeenth centuries. Three works much read and apparently of considerable influence upon medieval writers are the *Physiologus,* a symbolic bestiary (probably stemming from a Greek original of the second century A.D.) ;[12] the Vulgate translation of the Bible (fourth century) ; and the *Etymologies* of Isidore of Seville (seventh century) . These works provided no information about animals that had not been given already by Aristotle, Pliny, and other ancient writers. Isidore forms a connecting link between Pliny and the encyclopedists of the Middle Ages.[13]

Representative examples of medieval encyclopedic works are *De Naturis Rerum Libri Duo* by Alexander Neckam, an Englishman (twelfth century) ; *De Natura Rerum* by Thomas de Cantimpré, a Frenchman; *De Proprietatibus Rerum*[14] by Bartholomew Glanvil (Bartholomaeus Anglicus) , an Englishman; and *Speculum Maius* by Vincent de Beauvais, a Frenchman — the last three written in the thirteenth century. Each of these works is a compilation in which the compiler attempted to combine the various branches of human knowledge into a single whole. Alexander Neckam's *De Naturis Rerum,*[15] for example, is not only a scientific or philosophical treatise but also a vehicle for moral instruction. The various creatures described in Neckam's work were drawn mainly from the *Physiologus* and the aforesaid works of Aristotle and Pliny, whose authority Neckam and the other medieval writers about animals followed without questioning.

The narratives of such travelers to the Far East as Marco Polo (toward the end of the thirteenth century) and Friar Odoric (early in the fourteenth century) contributed to the general store of information about animals which constitutes the background whence came the animal conventions in the literature of western Europe.[16]

As has been shown, writers on natural history, excepting Aristotle, down to the sixteenth century drew their material almost wholly from earlier writings or popular tradition; and even Aristotle cites Aesop as one of his authorities. Pliny relied on Aesop, Aristotle, and Juba II; medieval and sixteenth-century writers, mainly on Pliny and Aristotle. In the sixteenth century, however, the new spirit of exploration and direct observation that grew out of the voyages of Spanish, English, and Dutch seamen led to the beginnings of modern zoology. Modern natural history had its beginning in such works as the *Historia Animalium* (1551-1558) of Conrad Gesner (Conradus Gesnerus),[17] who is called "the German Pliny."

The works on animals printed in the sixteenth century have been rightly called a continuation and outgrowth of medieval encyclopedias and a product of further humanistic study of Aristotle, Pliny, and other classical authors.[18] Sixteenth-century writers on animals seemingly felt that nothing said by the medieval and classical authorities must be omitted, and, therefore, attempted to include all, whether true or not.

A retrospect upon ancient, medieval, and Renaissance animal lore to the end of the sixteenth century is provided by two important works in English: Edward Topsell's *The Historie of Foure-Footed Beastes* (1607) and *The Historie of Serpents, or, The Second Book of Living Creatures* (1608).[19] These works contain numerous drawings, many of which are fairly accurate, of the creatures discussed. Though Topsell made some attempt to achieve scientific accuracy in his treatment of living creatures, he mingled with whatever accurate observations he was able to make[20] much of the traditional lore which he had gathered from ancient, medieval, and sixteenth-century authorities. *The Historie of Foure-Footed Beastes* is a voluminous folio work describing "the true and liuely figure of euery Beast" and discussing fully the natural history pertaining to each. The epistle "To the Learned Readers" contains a "Catalogue of the Authors which haue wrote of Beasts," wherein are listed some 286 Hebrew, Greek, Latin, German, Italian, and French authors and works. The same folio volume also contains *The Historie of Serpents,* which in the style of its contents is much like *The Historie of Foure-Footed Beastes.*

Topsell writes, for example, that the ape is "a subtill, ironical, ridiculous and unprofitable Beast . . . made for laughter" and "capable of all humaine actions," a great imitator, "full of dissimulation, and imitation of man," especially the "Martine Munkey," a "most ingenious" imitator of men, and that the ape kills its young "by pressing it to hard."[21] The "Ape Satyres" he calls "monsters of the Desart, or rough hairy Fawnes" of "lustfull disposition,"[22] and the sphinga or sphinx a kind of ape.[23]

Of the unicorn he says that "it is questionable whether the *Monoceros,* commonly called a *Vnicorne,* the *Rhinoceros,* the *Oryx,* and the *Indian* asse be all one beast or diuers";[24] but he identifies the unicorn with the Indian ass,[25] "who in bignes equalleth a horse," being "all white on the body," but "purple headed or red (as some say,) blacke eyes, but *Volaterranus* saith blew, hauing one horne in the fore-head a cubit and a halfe long," whose upper part is "red or bay," the middle "blacke, and the neather part white," wherein the "Kings and mighty men of *India* use to drinke," holding that "all those which drinke in those hornes, shalbe freed from annoyance of incurable diseases" and "deadly poysons."[26]

Topsell asserts that the "hebrew names" in scripture "proue Vnicornes"[27] and expresses the belief that "Vnicorns aboue all other creatures, doe reuerence Virgines and young Maides" and "many times at the sight of them . . . growe tame, and come and sleepe beside them," for "there is in their nature a certaine sauor, wherewithall the Vnicornes are allured and delighted."

He denies the ancient belief that "the whelpes of bears at their first littering are without all forme and fashion,"[28] but he says that the camel troubles the water by trampling in it before drinking[29] and that "a Hart by his nose draweth a Serpent out of her hole."[30]

Topsell likewise reviews the traditional lore concerning many other four-footed beasts — lion,[31] tiger,[32] panther,[33] fox,[34] ass,[35] and wild boar[36] — and serpents, among which he includes not only snakes[37] but also the crocodile,[38] the basilisk or cockatrice,[39] the toad,[40] the bee,[41] and the caterpillar (or "Canker").[42]

Enough has been said to show the existence of an ocean of animal lore, whence the writers of the literature of western Europe drew their ideas about animals. These ideas, used over and over again by medieval and sixteenth-century authors, became conventional in literature both on the Continent and in England. A summary of this animal lore may be had from the aforesaid works of

Aristotle, Pliny, and Topsell.[43] Topsell's works include much of the animal lore which had come down to the sixteenth century, directly and indirectly, from the works of Aristotle and Pliny, and had been given literary employment by English writers in the Elizabethan period. Next must be shown the routes by which these conventional ideas came into the prose literature of England in the latter half of the sixteenth century.

CHAPTER TWO

The Channels through which Conventional Ideas about Animals came into English Prose Literature of the Latter Half of the Sixteenth Century

MOST OF THE CONVENTIONAL IDEAS ABOUT ANIMALS IN THE LITERA-
ture of the European Continent were transmitted into English literature, English prose in particular, of the latter half of the sixteenth
century through four main channels: the popular tradition of the
folk, the medieval romances, the ancient Greek and Roman works
on natural history, and the Bible.

The ideas that were transmitted through the channel of popular
or folk tradition are to be found in the popular lore consisting of
conventional ideas about creatures native to the British Isles; in the
Aesopic fables; in folk festivals, including mummers' performances,
pageants, and masques; and in the medieval beast epic, particularly
the Reynard cycle.

Any attempt to determine the exact origins of the ideas about
native British creatures that appear in Elizabethan prose literature
would be unprofitable for lack of trustworthy evidence. Such well-
known ideas, for example, as the woodcock's simplemindedness and
lack of wit;[1] the lapwing's crying ever farthest from its nest;[2] and
the two sometimes synonymous expressions — "a snake in the grass"[3]
and "a pad (paddock, toad) in the straw"[4] — are proverbial and are
to be regarded almost as parts of the English language itself, especially of Elizabethan English. It is safe to say that these and similar
ideas were drawn from a common knowledge of living creatures,
both wild and domestic, with which any observant Englishman
might be expected to have some acquaintance.

From popular tradition came conventional ideas about many other native creatures[5] besides those which already have been mentioned. It should be stated in passing that such ideas as those about the deer's antlers as the symbol of cuckoldry,[6] the hog's brutishness and wallowing in the mire,[7] the wild boar's foaming ferocity,[8] and the ideas pertaining to falconry and hawking[9] are not necessarily of English origin, though all of these ideas might have grown out of the observation of native British creatures just as easily as out of classical and Biblical animal lore. This kind of overlapping is merely an illustration of the difficulty, not to say the impossibility, of knowing where and how some of the conventional ideas about animals first came into being.

Some proverbial expressions that contain rather general allusions to birds represent a kind of conventional by-product of the same animal folklore that is behind the animal symbolism in literature: "It is a foolish bird that stays the laying salt on her tail";[10] "It is a foul bird that defiles its own nest";[11] "One bird in the hand is worth two in the bush";[12] "It is hard taking the fowl when the net is descried",[13] and "I heard a bird sing more than I mean to say."[14] To the same classification belong such ideas as the undesirability of beating the bush and letting the birds escape,[15] the futility of birds' efforts to escape from lime twigs,[16] the kinship of "birds of a feather,"[17] and the unhappiness of caged birds.[18] The expression "Bridewell birds" (jailbirds) [19] certainly implies the idea of unhappy birds in a cage.

As popular with the English folk as the animal lore which grew out of the observation of native creatures were the conventional ideas about animals found in the Aesopic fables and the fables of Bidpai. Some of the Aesopic fables had been translated into English as early as the twelfth century; but the great German collection, compiled about 1480 by Heinrich Stainhöwel, was introduced into England, through the medium of the French, by William Caxton in 1484.[20] Many of the fables which passed under the name of Aesop are identical with those of the East, particularly Bidpai's, some of which reached England in Sir Thomas North's translation from the Italian of *The Morall Philosophie of Doni* (1570) .

The Aesopic fables are either retold or alluded to time and again in English prose literature of the latter half of the sixteenth century. They were used by the writers of the period as conventional

means of expressing philosophical ideas and observations. No summary of these stories is needed, so well known are such fables as
"Androcles [and the lion]," the classic example of a lion's showing
gratitude by fawning upon a benefactor; "The Wolf in Sheep's
Clothing," the classic example of the deceptiveness of appearances;
"The Ass in the Lion's Skin," an example of the foolishness of one's
pretending to be what he is not; "The Fox and the Crow," an illustration of the folly of trusting flatterers; and "The Ant and the
Grasshopper," an illustration of the wisdom of preparing, like the
industrious ant, for the days of necessity.

The fact is self-evident that the beasts, birds, and other creatures
of the fables have the same ideas associated with them that Aristotle,
Pliny, and the other writers on natural history applied to them.
Indeed, both Aristotle and Pliny cited Aesop as one of their authorities. Both in the fables and in the *Historia Animalium* and the
Naturalis Historia the lion is noble and magnanimous, the fox
crafty and cunning, the ass dull and stupid, the serpent wicked and
subtle, and the peacock proud and vainglorious, to mention only
these few examples.

The fables of Bidpai, as such, were not so well known in England as the Aesopic fables. Some conventional ideas about animals
in Elizabethan prose literature are also found, nevertheless, in the
Bidpai fables: the impassable jungle filled with beasts of prey,
where, according to a parable in the *Maha-Bharata*, a Brahman
found himself "so beset on every hand with horribly roaring lions,
tigers, and elephants that even the God of Death would quake at
the sight";[21] the fox and the ass at the court of the lion;[22] and the
tale of the popinjay, the apes, and the glowworm, in which the
popinjay (parrot), seeing the apes mistaking the glowworm's light
for fire and trying to warm themselves, told them of their error and
was reproached for giving unsolicited advice in a matter which did
not concern him.[23]

Another part of the popular or folk tradition in which conventional ideas about animals persisted was the folk festivals, including
mummers' performances, pageants, and masques. The mimicking of
beasts in folk drama belongs to ancient tradition, which spread into
England from the Continent. In medieval England the mimicry of
beasts was a part of such performances as the horn-dance at Abbots
Bromley in Staffordshire[24] and the "riding of the George" on St.

George's day, April 23, at Norwich, Leicester, Coventry, Stratford, Chester, and York.[25] In these and other performances — the New Year revels and the *ludi domini regis,* for example — men and women wore costumes and heads in the likeness of beasts and birds.[26] The hood with ass's ears and central crest resembling a cock's comb was a well-known fool ensign, whence probably was derived the designation "coxcomb" for a foolish, vain fellow.[27] In the *ludi,* also, appeared heraldic devices with their conventional animal symbolism.[28]

The Circe myth was used in the pageants and masques of the sixteenth century.[29] Indeed, in ancient folk tradition, one of the most popular of all tales was that of the transformation of man, through the powers of witchcraft, into bestial shape. Fairy lore was full of such changes.[30]

Enough has been said to make evident the widespread conventional employment of animal imitations and animal symbols in the medieval mummers' plays and allied forms of folk festivals in continental Europe and in England. There was a continuous line of *mimi, jougleurs,* and gleemen from ancient Roman times. The fall of the Roman Empire and the overrunning of the "Eternal City" itself by barbarian hordes brought an end to the great literature and drama of Rome, but disturbed only slightly, if at all, the popular games and pastimes, which were the amusement of the common people and were either ignored or regarded as being of little importance.[31] Hence the mummers' performances and other forms of folk festivals, in which many conventional ideas about animals persisted, belong to an unbroken stream of popular tradition, which brought these ideas into England.

Widely popular on the Continent and in England during medieval times was the collection of animal stories centering in the crafty fox as their hero-villain. This collection, the Reynard cycle, arose somewhere along the border between France and Flanders perhaps as early as the fourth century A.D.[32] The stories gathered incidents from animal folk-lore and from Aesopic material. In one place is described a marvelous comb made of "the bone of a clene noble beest named Panthera . . . so lusty fayr and of colour / that ther is no colour vnder the heuen / but somme lyknes is in hym" and of such a sweet smell "that the sauour of hymn boteth alle syknessis and for his beaute and swete smellyng all other beestis folowe hym /

for by his swete sauour they ben heled of alle syknessis."[33] On the frame of a magic mirror which the fox describes to the lion are portrayed five animal fables, four of which, including "The Wolf and the Crane," are Aesopic.[34]

In England, parodies on events in the history of Reynard appear in the stone and wood carvings of churches in Hampshire, St. Martin's in Leicester, Beverly in Yorkshire, Nantwich in Cheshire, and Boston in Lincolnshire;[35] and the Reynard stories entered into English literature as well as into church architecture. Incidents from them were used by the Anglo-Norman poets Chardi and Benoit. Odo of Cherington employed them as *exempla* in his sermons and wrote fables of his own based on the Reynard tales.[36]

The great English version of these stories is that printed by William Caxton in 1481. The Caxton *Reynard* consists of a series of incidents, occurring at or near the court of the lion, which are concerned with Reynard, his coarse practical jokes constantly played upon the other animals, and his cleverness in escaping deserved punishment.

Long before the Reynard stories came to England, they contained general satire against church, court, and society, and were so understood in the Middle Ages. Poor scholars, crafty lawyers, and a corrupt clergy, the chief objects of attack by the medieval satirists, are the chief objects of ridicule in the Reynard tales.

Not only the Reynard stories but also the bestiaries and *exempla* entered into the animal symbolism which was conventional in the later Middle Ages and the sixteenth century. The bestiaries included comparatively few animals, and their symbolism was drawn almost entirely from sources which already have been considered; but they helped bring animal symbolism in literature into popular favor and served to crystallize around a few animals popular folklore beliefs.[37]

Bestiary material was a convenient source for much of the animal symbolism in medieval religious works. In a selection called "The Seven Beasts of Sin, and Their Whelps," from *The Rule of Nuns* (thirteenth century) , by Simon de Ghent, animals taken from the bestiaries are used as symbols for the seven deadly sins. The beasts are the lion of pride, the adder of envy, the unicorn of wrath, the boar of sloth, the fox of deceit, the sow of gluttony, and the scorpion of lechery. In similar symbolic terms the whelps of each beast are described; those of the lion, for example, are vainglory, indignation, hypocrisy, *presumptio,* inobedience, loquacity, blasphemy, impatience, and contumacy.[38]

Conventional ideas about animals were transmitted into English prose literature not only through the channel of popular or folk tradition but also through the medieval romances, whose popularity was widespread both on the Continent, especially in France, and in England. The romances, of which the *Romance of Sir Beues of Hamtoun* and the *Romance of Guy of Warwick* are representative examples, contained comparatively little animal lore; but, as will be shown, the conventional ideas about animals found there had a significant bearing upon Elizabethan prose literature. The romances drew their animal lore chiefly from ancient Greek and Roman mythology and from Aesopic material.

The conflict in which a knight overcame a dragon, a lion, or some other beast is well known as a conventional incident in the medieval romances. Such conflicts in the romances belong to a literary tradition which goes back to the Hebrew Old Testament and Greek and Roman mythology. One easily recalls to mind the Biblical accounts of Samson and the lion and David and the lion; the Greek and Roman myths of Perseus and the sea dragon, Hercules and the hydra, Hercules and the Nemean lion, and Hercules and the Erimanthian boar; the English legend of St. George and the dragon; and Spenser's Red Cross Knight and the dragon.

In one of the English romances (c. 1327), Sir Beues of Hamtoun in the presence of his beloved Josian killed a lion and a lioness.[39] These beasts could not harm Josian, for she was a king's daughter and a virgin:

> Iosian into *þe* caue gan shete,
> And *þe* twoo lyou*ns* at hur feete,
> Grennand on hur *with* muche grame,
> But *þ*ey ne myzt do hur no shame,
> For *þ*e kind of Lyouns, y-wys,
> A kynges douzter, *þ*at maide is,
> Kinges douzter, quene and maide both,
> *Þ*e lyouns myzt do hur noo wroth.[40]

On another occasion, Sir Beues, wearing on his helmet the image of St. George — "A nemenede sein Gorge, our leuedi kni*z*t, And sete on his helm . . ."[41] — and calling upon Christ and the Virgin Mary

for help, killed a fearful dragon.[42] In this fight, Sir Beues became
unmistakably the champion of Christendom, of goodness and right,
against the dragon, the symbol of paganism and the forces of evil.
In fact, Sir Beues is called *"þe* kniʒt of cristene lawe."[43] Hard
pressed in the fight, he took refuge at a well, whose water, by virtue
of a virgin's having bathed therein, was so holy that the dragon
would not approach it:

> Þe welle was of swich vertu:
> A virgine wonede in þat londe,
> Hadde baþede þer in, ich vnderstonde;
> Þat water was so holi,
> Þat þe dragoun, sikerli,
> Ne dorste neze þe welle aboute
> Be fourti fote, saundoute.[44]

In the *Romance of Guy of Warwick* (as a metrical romance,
probably as old as the thirteenth century),[45] Guy rescued a lion
from a dragon and the lion showed its gratitude by fawning upon
him and following him on his journeys like a gentle dog.[46] This incident of Guy and the lion is an adaptation of the Aesopic fable of
Androcles and the lion, the classic example of the lion's showing
gratitude by fawning upon its benefactor.[47]

Besides the dragon that was pursuing the lion, Guy, upon his return to England, killed another dragon that was ravaging the country in Northumberland.[48] Guy's encounters with these two dragons
are, like Sir Beues' similar encounters, examples of the conventional
incident in which a virtuous Christian knight overcame the forces of
evil in beast form.[49] More will be said in another chapter about
these incidents from the medieval romances and their bearing upon
like incidents in English prose literature of the latter half of the
sixteenth century.

Mention should be made here of Bayard, Rinaldo's horse in the
Charlemagne romances, the proverbial "blind Bayard" of Elizabethan prose literature, to be discussed in another chapter.

Of great importance as a channel for the transmission of conventional ideas about animals into the prose literature of England in
the period 1550-1600 were the ancient Greek and Roman works on
natural history — especially Aristotle's *Historia Animalium* and
Pliny's *Naturalis Historia* — of which a good deal has been said al-

ready. Although these works were not translated into English before 1600, much of their contents was available to English readers in Bartholomaeus Anglicus' *De Proprietatibus Rerum* (John de Trevisa's translation), Batman's commentary thereon (1582), and a work entitled "A Summarie of the Antiquities, and wonders of the worlde, abstracted out of the sixtene first bookes of the excellente Historiographer Plinie" (c. 1565) .[50] Pliny repeated, of course, a great deal of Aristotle's *Historia Animalium*.

But some of the writers of English prose in the period 1550-1600 were university men, who might know Aristotle in the original and certainly knew Pliny. These English writers ransacked natural history for ideas about animals to illustrate commonplace experiences and human nature.

Another important channel through which conventional ideas about animals came into the English prose literature of the latter half of the sixteenth century was the Bible[51] with its rich store of animal symbolism and metaphor. The unicorns,[52] basilisks or cockatrices,[53] and satyrs[54] in the Old Testament were so named because the translators, not knowing these creatures by their Hebrew names, substituted wrong Greek equivalents, which were translated into English.[55]

Biblical animal lore, drawn largely from the same sources as the animal lore in the Aesopic fables and in the various ancient writings on natural history, included many of the same creatures with the same ideas associated with them. The lion was fierce and courageous,[56] the wolf ravenous,[57] the fox crafty and cunning,[58] the peacock vainly proud of its fine feathers,[59] the serpent wicked and subtle,[60] the ant industrious and provident against the time of necessity.[61] The caterpillar and the moth were destructive,[62] and the owl and the raven were birds of ill omen inhabiting desolate places.[63] The scorpion's venomous sting was painful and injurious to man.[64] The "deaf adder" stopped its ear and would not "hearken to the voice of charmers."[65] The "bird of the air" was a teller of secrets.[66]

From the Bible also came the well-known allusions to Balaam's ass,[67] the leopard's inability to change its spots,[68] straining at a gnat and swallowing a camel,[69] the hen's gathering her chickens under her wings,[70] the eagles' gathering to a carcass,[71] the never dying worm of conscience,[72] the dog's returning to his vomit,[73] the sow's wallowing in the mire,[74] the wolf and the lamb,[75] lambs among wolves,[76] and wolves in sheep's clothing.[77] This last allusion undoubtedly was based on Aesopic material.

Conventional ideas about animals, transmitted through the channels which have been distinguished, were applied in a variety of ways which furnished precedents for their employment in Elizabethan prose literature. These precedents and their significance will be discussed in the next chapter.

CHAPTER THREE

Precedents for the Employment of Conventional Ideas about Animals in English Prose of the Latter Half of the Sixteenth Century

THE ALMOST UNIVERSAL EMPLOYMENT OF CONVENTIONAL IDEAS ABOUT animals, both on the Continent of Europe and in England, and the emphasis placed upon these ideas in the teachings of the humanists, established precedents for the employment of the same ideas in English prose literature of the latter half of the sixteenth century.

Beast conventions formed an important element in medieval English and Continental architecture and artistic ornamentation, heraldry, emblem writing, and other literature, and continued to be thus widely employed in the sixteenth century. Many examples could be given of medieval church pictures and carvings which represented animals performing the actions of men. The sculptors seemingly had a preference for monsters of every description, especially those which were made up of portions of incongruous animals joined together.[1]

As far as animal symbolism is concerned, popular sculpture and painting in the Middle Ages were often but the translation of popular literature. In the windows and the sculptured ornamentation of more than one church,[2] for example, appeared satirical representations of Reynard the fox, in the character of an ecclesiastic, preaching to geese and other fowls.[3]

Another series of subjects — the hare chasing the hound, the geese hanging the fox, and the mouse chasing the cat — illustrated a form of satire called in Old French and Anglo-Norman *le monde bestorne* or the tables turned. This kind of satire formed the subject of old verses, in French and English, and was pictorially represented at a rather early date.[4] A woodcut, taken from a sculptured ornament in Beverly Minster, pictures a blacksmith shoeing a gander.[5] The situation somewhat resembles the *monde bestorne*.

Animal symbolism was commonly used not only in church architecture and ornamentation but also in the signs of hostelries, inns, theaters, and other business establishments.[6] The Boar's Head, the Bear, the Mermaid, the Swan, and the Dolphin are but a few of the signs that were well known in England in the sixteenth century.

Heraldry with its colorful animal symbolism had a far-reaching influence upon the life and literature of England in the latter half of the sixteenth century. The beasts of heraldry and their symbolism not only became familiar to the Elizabethans through constant display in banners, shields, pageants, processions, architecture, and drama, but also contributed to the literature of the period and of earlier times three types of writing: the emblem book, the political poem, and the political prophecy.[7]

The story of heraldry is of considerable significance in the history of the Middle Ages and of the Elizabethan period. Its devices decorated the armor of knighthood. Its blazonry was to be seen on the battlefield, in the tournament, and at the court. Its argent and azure, its lions and leopards, formed the setting for the masques and pageants of the fourteenth and fifteenth centuries, for the banquets, and for the progresses of Queen Elizabeth. Its symbolism appears in the prophecies of the days of Henry III and in the *Faerie Queene*.

In view of the eagerness with which people in the Middle Ages seized upon whatever would serve for *exempla* and the pleasure they found in allegory, it is easy to comprehend why heraldry should draw upon the natural histories. Symbols of some kind were necessary in days when helmets prevented recognition of friend and foe; but before the days of visors and shields and knightly armor, Roman legions went into battle behind the standards of the wolf, the bear, the lion, and the eagle; and even earlier, among the Greeks, Athens had her owl, Argos her wolf, and Boeotia her bull.[8]

It is quite logical that heraldry, backed by such tradition, should draw freely upon birds and beasts for its symbols. John Ferne, an English writer of the sixteenth century, in his book written "for the instruction of all Gentlemen bearers of Armes,"[9] has his herald

(Paradinus) and a divine (Theologus) account for the use of animals in heraldry as follows:

> [Paradinus] The inuention of Armes wherein beasts be borne, is borrowed from the Hunes, the Hungarians, and Saxons, cruell, and most fierce Nations, and therefore they delighted in the bearing of beasts of the like nature in their Armes, as Lyons, Leopards, Beares, Wolfes, Hyens, and such lyke . . . and . . . I can recount . . . how that the auntient AEgyptians did use to paint out birds & beasts, to the signification of some quallitie of the minde, and therefore they used the shape of a Lyon, to signifie furie, & heate of courage: the Ant, to represent prouidence: a Lyons head, to note vigilancie: a Viper, to signifie a common woman or harlot lying in the way, to sting men with the contagion of her wantonnes and lust: the Hyen, to bewray an inconstant man: and the Wolfe, a craftie person, seditious and oppressiue, with such like.
>
> *Theolog.* The Hebrew Rabbyes do affyrme, that the Wolfe was the ensigne depainted in the estandard of the tribe of *Beniamine,* according to the prophesie of *Iacob,* Genesis cap. 49. *Beniamine* shall be as a Wolfe, going out earely in the morning to eate his pray, and at night deuideth the spoile.[10]

It should be noticed here that those beasts and birds which the folklore of the natural histories had stressed for certain traits admirable in man were selected for use in heraldry. The characteristics of each beast or bird so chosen became as conventional as did its heraldic portrait. The lion, consequently, because he was believed to combine all the noble and magnanimous qualities of a sovereign, became the most popular animal symbol in heraldry, whereas the tiger was thought to be cruel, and so never achieved importance as a symbol.[11] The lion was traditionally regarded as being the most merciful of beasts. Like the lion, king of beasts, the eagle, queen of birds, was described in the conventional manner as signifying in heraldry "true magnanimity and fortitude of mind."[12]

The study of the science of heraldry was held to be a part of the education of the well-rounded Elizabethan gentleman.[13] Works like Gerard Leigh's *Accedence of Armorie* (1562), John Bossewell's *Workes of Armorie* (1572), and John Ferne's *Blazon of Gentrie*

(1586) were written expressly to supply information on the more technical points of the system.

Leigh employs the conventional device of the dialogue, which in his work[14] takes place between a knight named Leigh and a herald named Gerard. The lessons begin with a discussion of the two metals — gold (or) and silver (argent) — and the seven colors — red (gules, "geules"), light blue (azure), black (sable), green (vert), purple (purpure), orange tawney ("tenne"), and murrey (sanguine) — used in heraldry, each section being illustrated with a shield painted in water color in the appropriate shade.[15] In the chapter on animal symbols, likewise, each example is accompanied by a paragraph or two concerning some of the natural history of the animal under discussion. For example, Leigh represents the lion as the king of beasts, of more honor than all other beasts in heraldry, of "princely porte," courageous in fight, and merciful.[16] The tiger he represents as the cruelest of beasts.[17] Of the unicorn he writes —

> This is a strong beast, as appeareth by that is spoken in Numery. God is to Jacob, as the strength of a unicorn. . . . When he is hunted he is not taken by strength, but onely by this policie. A maid is set where he haunteth, and shee openeth hir lap, to whome the Vnicorne . . . yeeldeth his head, and leaueth al his fiercenes, and resting himselfe vnder her protection, sleepeth vntill he is taken and slain. . . . His proper colour is bay. He hath in his head onlie one horne, whereof he taketh his name. It is vertuous against venime, and is most truelie called yuery. Isadore saith, the vnicorne is cruell, and mortall enimy to the Olephant.[18]

Leigh quotes Aristotle, Pliny, and Isidore among his authorities on natural history.

John Ferne, in his dedication, refers to a "late Armorist" who "gathered his stuffe from the fardels of the Parargon, and Emblemes of Alciat, the devises of Paradin, and the natural histories of Gesnerus." Whoever the "late Armorist" might have been, Ferne's reference is significant because it suggests some of the sources upon which the sixteenth-century "armorist" drew for material.[19] Ferne, like Leigh, uses the dialogue. A company of six — a herald, a knight, a divine, a lawyer, an antiquary, and a plowman — are on a journey. As they ride along, they ask questions of the herald, who, in a series of discussions, takes up the matter of coats of arms, ranks of nobility, rules of the college of heralds, marks of the true gentleman, genealogies, and other related subjects. "Foure cardinall vertues, to wit, prudence, Iustice, Fortitude, and Temperaunce," says Ferne's herald, "been the fountaynes, out of which al gentlenes, should and ought to streame."[20]

Conventional animal symbolism was employed almost as extensively in the emblem literature of the sixteenth century as in heraldry. The emblem writers drew upon both heraldry and animal fables for many of their devices and through their conceits helped to form conventions in the treatment of their symbols and to associate certain animals with certain ideas. Geffrey Whitney, in an epistle "To the Reader" in his *Choice of Emblemes* (1586), writes that "all Emblemes for the most parte, maie be reduced into these three kindes, . . . *Historicall, Naturall, & Morall.* . . . *Naturall,* as in expressing the natures of creatures," for example, "the loue of the yonge Storkes, to the oulde, or of suche like."[21]

An emblem is defined as a short piece of verse — an epigram or a sonnet — expressing some conceit, usually accompanied by a motto and a picture illustrating the conceit. The idea behind the composition of emblems was that the picture helped to impress upon the mind of the reader the moral expressed in the verse and the motto.

The early emblem books delighted the literati of their age and were patronized by popes, emperors, and kings. Their spirit became so diffused among all ranks of the people as to call for translations into six or eight languages and for imitations.[22] Early emblem books were not numerous. At the beginning of the sixteenth century, there were in Europe five outstanding emblem writers: three Italians — Andrew Alciat, Paolo Giovio, and Achilles Bocchius; a Hungarian, John Sambucus; and a German, Sebastian Brandt. Of the five, Alciat seems to have had the greatest influence in determining the course of development of the type. His work was translated, copied, and imitated throughout Europe;[23] and presumably an English version existed as early as 1551.[24]

But Englishmen apparently were interested in emblems even before the year 1509, when English translations of Brandt's great emblem book, the *Narren Schyff,* appeared, and had composed a few pieces resembling somewhat the work of Alciat. Brandt's work came to English readers in two translations: one by Henry Watson, and the other by Alexander Barclay.[25] These translations mark the beginning of a direct communication in emblem literature between England and the Continent.[26]

Between 1509, the date of publication of Barclay's *Ship of Fools,* and 1598, when Willet's *A Century of Sacred Emblems* appeared, the chief emblem books available in English were Claude Paradin's *Devises Héroïques* (1557)[27] and Whitney's *Choice of Emblemes* (1586).[28] Whitney was the first to present to the English public an emblem book complete in all its parts.[29]

In the literature of England from the twelfth century to the middle of the sixteenth century, conventional ideas about animals were employed in satire and in three other literary types closely akin to satire in the depicting of contemporary manners and conditions: the political poem, the political prophecy, and the *fabliau* or "jest." Professor Arthur Leible, who has made an excellent survey of the whole subject of conventional animal symbolism and satire, particularly in relation to Spenser's *Mother Hubberds Tale,*[30] defines satire as "a written composition that attacks with ridicule or with denunciation some vice, folly, institution, or individual"; he uses the term *animal satire* to mean "a satire that employs animals as its principal characters."[31] In this kind of satire the animals may symbolize the objects or persons to be attacked, the beasts being selected arbitrarily, without reference to their natural traits, or the beasts may be merely the speakers in a dialogue, *débat,* or assembly of beasts, talking like men, expressing the thoughts of men, with nothing of the beast about them except their names. The author of such a satire has a great deal of freedom in the manner of telling his story: "he may use a popular animal fable or legend; he may draw on folk lore; or he may invent an animal story of his own."[32]

The chief examples of animal satire written in England before the middle of the sixteenth century are to be found in the poetry, especially from the latter part of the twelfth century onward. Nigellus Wireker's *Speculum Stultorum* (late twelfth century), which is concerned with the ass Brunellus or Burnellus and his proposed exemplary monastic order, the *"Novus Ordo Burnelli,"* began a series of "fool satires" which were to appear again later in the work of Lydgate, Skelton, Barclay, and others.[33] In the fourteenth and fifteenth centuries appeared satirical fables like Chaucer's story of the cock and the fox in the *Nonnes Preestes Tale* and Henryson's *The Taill of the Dog, the Scheip, and the Wolf* and *The Tail of the Wolf and the Lamb*. The Aesopic character of these fables of Henryson is evident even in the titles. In the first half of the sixteenth century, the device of putting the main satirical comment into the mouth of a parrot was used in Skelton's *Speke, Parrot* and Lyndsay's *The Testament and Complaynt of Our Soverane Lordis Papyngo*.

Closely akin to the animal satire is the political poem, which drew its animal symbolism almost entirely from heraldry. This kind of verse, which expressed the national unrest in England at different times during the century and a half following the year 1300, reached the height of its popularity during the Wars of the Roses (1455-1485), when nearly everyone in England was enrolled under the badge of some noble and wore the insignia of his house.[34] Such heraldic badges, for example, as the bear and ragged staff of Warwick and the Dudleys, the swan of Gloucester, and the falcon of York were so well known that the men bearing them were as easily recognized by their cognizances as by their names. Heraldic badges, therefore, made intelligible symbols by which to represent the personages in a political poem.

Probably many more political poems were composed in England between 1300 and 1450 than are extant. Consideration of a few of these poems, which have survived, will show how conventional animal symbolism was used in such writings. About 1340 appeared a poem in French, called *The Vows of the Heron* ("*leus veus du hairon*"), in which Robert of Artois, in flight from France and seeking safety from Edward III, is represented as trying to arouse the King's anger against the French. Robert has a heron served up to the King and his guests, saying that the most cowardly of birds is fit food for the most cowardly of kings. Edward thereupon vows to invade France, and his guests make similar vows on the heron, which represents Philip of Valois.[35] Another poem of the same period, *An Invective Against France,* in Latin, begins with these lines:

Francia, foeminea, pharisaea, vigoris idea,
Lynxea, viperea, vulpina, lupina, Medea.

The poem points out that Edward III, represented by the boar and the leopard (*"Tertius Edwardus, aper Anglicus et leopardus"*) is the rightful sovereign of France (*"Rex tuus est verus"*) ; the leopard-like king, rightfully Parisian king (*"Rex leopardinus est juste rex Parisinus"*).[36] The boar as the symbol for Edward is used also by one of the chief poets of his reign, Lawrence Minot, in his *Songs of King Edward's Wars.*[37]

The last quarter of the fourteenth century was a time of discord and uncertainty in England. In 1389, King Richard II dismissed his regents and began to rule alone. His rule was soon threatened by the growing strength of the opposition, headed by his uncle. Such conditions were favorable for the production of political poems. In the first part of his Latin *Tripartite Chronicle,* John Gower gives an account of the years 1387-1388, in which Richard is the villain, and the heroes are the swan (Gloucester), the horse (Arundel), and the bear (Warwick).[38] In *Richard the Redeless,* a poem written some years later, most of the symbols used are drawn from heraldry and from puns on names like Bushey, Scrope, and Greene.[39] The poem contains two parables: one of the hart and the adder, employing the ancient lore from the natural histories about the deer's drawing serpents out of their holes and eating them;[40] the other of the partridge on whose nest another sits until the young birds are hatched and listen to the call of their rightful parent.[41] So the eagle (Bolingbroke), newly returned to England, Richard is told, has been fostering his nestlings, who, looking to him for leadership, tell him of King Richard's misrule.[42] The eagle has also been winning the friendship of the horse (Arundel), his colt (Fitz-alan), the swan (Gloucester), and the bear (Warwick).[43] About the year 1399 appeared two ballads, one of which laments the fates of the swan, the horse, and the bear;[44] and the other, called *On King Richard's Ministers,* refers to the swan and the heron.[45]

In 1449, the disasters abroad, the dissensions at home, the death of public favorites, and the supremacy of hated royal advisers — in short, the conditions that prevailed in England at the beginning of the Wars of the Roses — gave rise to a new series of political poems of the familiar type. In most of these new poems, one of King Henry VI's ministers, the Duke of Suffolk, popularly referred to as the "Fox" and "Jack Napes," the vulgar name for an ape, is made the villain. In so representing Suffolk, the writer, forced to depart from the usual heraldic source for his symbol, drew instead upon conventional satirical figures like the fox and the ape.[46]

One ballad of the new series expresses popular discontent at the outcome of the wars in France, lamenting that the rote (Bedford) is dead, the swan (Gloucester) gone, the white lion (Norfolk) laid to sleep through the envy of the ape (Suffolk), the talbot (Talbot) tied, the boar (Devon) far away, and the bear (Warwick) bound that was so wild, "for he hath lost his ragged staff."[47] Another ballad, on the arrest of Suffolk, uses both the fox and the ape as symbols for the Duke; the fox is accused of slaying "oure grete gandere" (Gloucester), and the author laments because the popular favorite, "the black doge withe the wide mouthe" (Talbot, Earl of Shrewsbury), is not at hand to chase the fox away.[48]

Another kind of writing, which, in England, began in the twelfth century and exerted its influence to the middle of the seventeenth, is the political prophecy, defined by Professor Rupert Taylor, in his very clear exposition of the subject, as "any expression of thought, written or spoken, in which an attempt is made to foretell coming events of a political nature."[49] Professor Taylor points out that "the most distinctive feature" of the English political prophecy is the use of animals and birds as symbols to represent men and women. His description of the type shows at a glance the close kinship between the political prophecy, the political poem, and the conventional animal satire. He points out that "an English prophecy containing this peculiar symbolism reads very much like some animal story," but with this difference: "the animals are constantly felt to represent individual men and women who are never lost sight of behind the mask, even if their identity is unknown."[50] In the *Prophecy of Merlin* in Geoffrey of Monmouth's *Historiae Regum Britanniae,* for example, it is prophesied that "the Ass of Wickedness shall succeed, swift to fall upon the workers of gold but slow against the ravening of wolves."[51]

In one of the early prophecies, *The Omen of the Dragons,* first told by Nennius, a white dragon, representing the Saxons, fights with a red dragon who represents the Britons. After William the Conqueror come two more dragons — William II of England and Robert II of Normandy — who in turn are succeeded by the "Lion of Justice," Henry I. Finally comes "the Lynx that seeth through all things," under whom the Normans lose their power.[52]

Many animal symbols in the prophecies probably were drawn from popular epithets, such as the lamb, the wolf, the ass, the fox, and the lion, that grew out of the traditional animal lore which has been considered already. It is easy to read the dominant traits of men masked behind such beasts as these. The Aesopic character of the relationship between the wolf and the lamb of Winchester in *The Prophecy of the Six Kings to follow King John*[53] shows the influence of popular animal lore. Another example is the "Lynx that seeth through all things."[54]

In troubled and unsettled reigns and in times of national crisis, the political prophecies increased in number and were used deliberately as active political propaganda. The Elizabethan dramatists ridiculed the works and their authors.[55] But the prophecies continued to be written.

The long popularity of the political prophecy employing animals to mask persons, and of the political poem employing the same method, made English readers familiar with pseudo-animal tales in which symbols representing persons were used.[56] The allegorical use of beasts in English satire, in heraldry, in emblem literature, and in political poems and prophecies was but the continuation and firmer establishment of the traditional method employed in the Bible, the animal fables, and the bestiaries.

In England, before the middle of the sixteenth century, conventional ideas about animals appeared in still another type of writing, the *fabliau* or "jest," that short, pointed tale in either verse or prose which in realistic, comic, and sometimes frankly coarse fashion satirized chiefly the knavery of monks and the moral pretensions of women. The *fabliau* flourished in France and in England during the Middle Ages, from the thirteenth century onward. In the sixteenth century the Tudor jest books, carried in the pocket or passed from hand to hand, were representative of this kind of stories.

The *Hundred Mery Talys* (1528) is the earliest example extant of a literature which was popular all through the Tudor period.[57] Similar collections of tales are the *Sackfull of Newes* (1557) and *Mery Tales, Wittie Questions and Quicke Answeres* (1567). The English black-letter *Howleglas* (Owlglass), a version of the Eulenspiegel stories, was printed by William Copland in 1528.

The stories in the Tudor jest books, like the medieval French *fabliaux*, contain few animals. In the *fabliaux* are a few allusions to the Reynard stories: the fox "Renart,"[58] the hare "Coars,"[59] and the ass "Bauduyn"[60] are referred to. Almost no other animals are mentioned, and these allusions merely constitute a bit of evidence that attests the popularity of the Reynard stories. The few conventional ideas about animals that are employed in the jest books appear in the names of persons, in epithets, or in analogies illustrating phases of human nature, and are drawn from Aesopic material and popular tradition. In Tarlton's "wit betweene a Bird and a Woodcock," the names — M. Bird and M. Woodcock — are indicative of the characters of the main persons in the story.[61] In another story, *How Tarlton fought with Black Davie,* Tarlton, "being in a taverne in the company of this damnable cockatrice [harlot], huffing Kate, called for wine"; but she told him that unless he burned it she would not drink. "No, quoth Tarlton, it shall be burnt: for thou canst burne it without fire. . . . So he, filling the cup in her hand, said it was burnt sufficiently in so fiery a place."[62] Tarlton's "jest of a red face" mentions a gentleman's "salamanders face" that "burnt like Etna for anger."[63]

In *Mery Tales, Wittie Questions and Quicke Answeres,* the tale of "the frier that brayde in his sermon" compares a foolish preacher to an ass.[64] In the same collection, the tale of "Tachas, kyng of Aegypt, and Agesilaus" makes use of the Aesopic fable of the "Mountains in Labor." Tachas, seeing Agesilaus, who has come to aid him in his wars, to be of small stature, taunts him thus: "The mountayne hath trauayled, . . . but yet hee hathe broughte forth a mouse." Agesilaus replies, "And yet the tyme wyl come, that I shall seeme to thee a Lyon."[65] In one of the *Merrie Conceited Jests of George Peele,* entitled *How the Gentleman was gulled for shauing of George,* mention is made of George's "Wife plucking of Larks, my crying Crocadile [George's daughter] turning of the spit."[66]

One of the stories about Owlglass is the tale of how he "caused an ass to read certain words out of a book at the great university of Erfurt." Owlglass, having had the ass, his pupil, demonstrate his ability to read, commends him to the professors, saying, "Behold, most learned doctors, my disciple doth now pronounce well, although yet somewhat broadly, the two vowels E and A, ... I have great hope of him that he will soon get farther." The tale ends with the remark that "they be all asses in that city unto this day."[67] Another of these stories tells "How that Owlglass hired himself unto a boor." Owlglass and the boor, going on a journey, turn back when a hare crosses their path, for the boor believes it "a most evil fortune when that a hare doth run across the way." But the boor continues his journey when a wolf crosses his path, a good omen, he thinks, and has his horse devoured. Owlglass, having turned back at sight of the wolf, will no longer serve a man who puts his trust in signs and omens.[68]

The examples given show how traditional animal lore was employed in the jest books, which were popular in England in the sixteenth century and continued to be printed in the seventeenth. A good deal also has been said to explain how Elizabethan Englishmen were confronted almost at every turn with this animal lore, appearing in one form or another, so that writers like Lyly, Greene, Lodge, Nashe, Deloney, and Sidney had ample precedent for their employment of it in their writings.

Further precedent for the employment of conventional ideas about animals in Elizabethan prose literature is to be found in the teachings of the humanists, who placed a great deal of emphasis upon the importance of studying the natural history and moral philosophy contained in ancient and medieval writings on these subjects. Humanist educators like Erasmus and Sir Thomas Elyot considered a knowledge of natural history, of beasts and birds in particular, an essential part of the study of moral philosophy. Rhetoricians like Thomas Wilson prescribed the use of beasts and birds in the expression of ideas.

The main features of the humanistic conception of moral philosophy are based upon Plutarch's revision of the Aristotelian system of ethics. The basic idea of Aristotelian ethics, that true virtue consists not in uprooting the passions but in regulating them by the reason, that virtue is the mean between the excessive and the deficient, is well known. This Aristotelian conception, the Pythagorean and Platonic theories concerning the immortality of the soul, and the Stoic belief that the law of nature was intended to govern man's moral conduct — all met in the *Morals* of Plutarch.

Ideas on moral philosophy came down from Plutarch's day to sixteenth-century England through three main channels: collections of apothegms, and similar works of an aphoristic nature; religious treatises and commentaries; and works involving allegory, such as the morality plays. The Church Fathers did not oppose altogether the idea of reason as man's guide to virtue; but they maintained that, because of the Fall, reason must give precedence to faith. They argued that although reason originally was sufficient to keep man on the path to virtue, the Fall had made it necessary for faith and divine grace to bring him back to his former condition.[69]

In Plutarch's *Morals* is a lengthy discourse entitled "Which Are the Most Crafty, Water-Animals or Those Creatures That Breed Upon the Land?" Following this discussion is the story of Ulysses, Circe, and Gryllus, in which it is argued that beasts make use of reason.[70] Before 1550, this story was elaborated by an Italian writer, Giovanni Gelli, into a satire in which eleven animals in turn demonstrate to Ulysses the advantages of the bestial state over that of man. An English translation of Gelli's work was published in 1557.[71]

Indeed, it has been remarked that the sixteenth century was "steeped in Plutarch"; that "his writings formed an almost inexhaustible storehouse for historian and philosopher alike," the age being "characterized by no diffidence or moderation in borrowing"; and that "Plutarch's aphorisms and his anecdotes meet us at every turn."[72]

This dependence of the century upon the works of Plutarch in matters of moral philosophy was the result of the humanistic program of education. In that program moral philosophy ranked second in importance only to history; and the great humanist teachers — Vittorino da Feltre and Guarino — relied upon Cicero and Plutarch to guide them.[73]

Erasmus taught that the first books the student should read should be the Gospels and Proverbs, supplemented by parts of Plutarch's *Apophthegmata* and *Moralia*. He considered important "a judicious intermingling of teaching concerning plants, animals, geographical and other natural phenomena, with classical instruction," but nowhere hinted that "observation or intercourse" could serve as a substiute for ancient authorities in any subject, although occasionally a traveler or a modern writer might supplement what had been handed down. Pliny is one of the authors, listed by Erasmus, in whose writings such a knowledge of *"res"* could be found.[74] Of the authors whose works a well-read "Master" should read, Erasmus put Pliny first.[75] Erasmus discusses the important place of reason in the scheme of things in his *De Pueris Instituendis*.[76]

Other humanist educators likewise placed great emphasis upon reason as the proper governor of man's moral conduct and upon the need of obedience to authority and the law of nature in state and church. Juan Luis Vives stressed the importance of reason in the ethical scheme no less than did Erasmus. In his *De Tradendis Disciplinis,* Vives describes the consequences of an overthrow of nature and shows how man becomes a beast when he lets himself be governed by his passions instead of his reason.[77] In Sir Thomas More's *Utopia* (1515-1516), the inhabitants of that ideal country follow the ethical system of Plutarch and Aristotle; the Utopians are said to "set great store by Plutarch's books."[78] Sir Thomas Elyot, in *The Gouernour* (1531), emphasizes the need of obedience to authority in the state and asks his readers to note examples of ideal government among insects and animals.[79] Thomas Wilson, in *The Rule of Reason* (1567), stresses a thorough course of learning as the best method of restoring to man's reason the power of judging between good and evil that it possessed before the Fall.[80] Richard Hooker, in *Of the Lawes of Ecclesiastical Politie* (completed in 1593), gives a lucid exposition of the whole humanistic attitude toward moral philosophy. His views follow closely those of Erasmus, Vives, More, and Elyot.[81] Hooker describes the importance of obedience to the law of nature.[82]

With the humanists began the systematic teaching of rhetoric in the schools.[83] Erasmus, Sir Thomas Elyot, Roger Ascham, and Thomas Wilson regarded the literatures of Greece and Rome as "the storehouses of adequate and eloquent expression, the happy hunting-ground of the right thing to discourse about, and the right way of saying it."[84] Rhetoric was one of the main subjects taught in the schools of England in the sixteenth and seventeenth centuries.[85] The rhetoricians prescribed the employment, "for oratory or description," of traditional ideas about animals drawn from the ancient works on natural history, from Pliny in particular. Erasmus held that the educated man would be careful to have readily available for oratory or description "all that varied mass of material which the curiosity of antiquity has handed down to us," to which "belongs, first, the natural history of birds, quadrupeds, wild animals, serpents, insects, fishes." This material would be "chiefly derived from ancient writers, with additions from our own observation." Next should be prized "the accounts of singular adventures handed down to us by trustworthy authorities," such as "the story of Arion and the dolphin, of the dragon who rescued his deliverer from danger, of the lion who returned kindness for kindness, and others which Pliny vouches for."[86]

Thomas Wilson, in his *Arte of Rhetorique* (1553), defines a "Similitude" as "a likenesse when two things, or more then two, are so compared and resembled together, that they both in some one propertie seeme like," and says that "oftentimes brute Beastes, and thinges that haue no life, minister great matter in this behalfe." Therefore, "those that delite to proue thinges by Similitudes, must learne to knowe the nature of diuers beastes . . . and al such as haue any vertue in them, and be applied to mans life."[87] In the same work, Wilson says that "examples gathered out of histories . . . helpe much towards perswasion" and that "brute beastes minister greate occasion of right good matter, considering many of them haue shewed vnto vs, the paterns and Images of diuers vertues."[88] He then mentions the evil of "Vnthankfulnesse" and, announcing that he "will set foorth three notable examples, the one of a Dragon, the second of a dog, and the third of a Lion (which all three in thankfulnesse . . .wonderfully exceeded)," tells the old story, attributed to Pliny, of the dragon that rescued its deliverer from danger; the story of the dog that remained loyal to its dead master Fulvius; and the Aesopic story of Androcles and the lion.[89] "The feined Fables," Wilson points out, "would not be forgotten at any hande. For not onely they delite the rude and ignorant, but also they helpe much for perswasion." As a further example, he tells the Aesopic fable of the "Scabbed Foxe," tormented by "many flies . . . feeding vppone his rawe flesh" (a version of "The Fox and the Mosquitoes") .[90]

In view of such precedents as have been described, it is easily comprehensible that the writers of English prose in the latter half of the sixteenth century should employ conventional ideas about animals in their works. The next chapter will be devoted to the consideration of these ideas in the principal non-religious prose writings of England in the period 1550-1600.

CHAPTER FOUR

Conventional Ideas about Animals in the Principal
English Non-Religious Prose Writings of the
Latter Half of the Sixteenth Century

OF THE ENGLISH NON-RELIGIOUS PROSE WRITINGS BETWEEN 1550 AND
1600 the most important as representative works of the period are
the educational treatises of Thomas Wilson and Roger Ascham;
the collections of *novelle* of William Painter, George Pettie, and
Barnabe Riche; the satirical pamphlets of Stephen Gosson, Thomas
Lodge, John Lyly, Robert Greene, Thomas Nashe, and Gabriel
Harvey; the philosophical pamphlets of Robert Greene and Thomas
Lodge; the pastoral romances of John Grange, John Lyly, Robert
Greene, Thomas Lodge, and Sir Philip Sidney; and the realistic and
picaresque tales of Thomas Deloney and Thomas Nashe. All of
these men employed conventional ideas about animals extensively
in their works.

These ideas, drawn from the Bible, from Greek and Latin classical literature, and from Aesopic material and other popular or folk
tradition, had become established as conventions in heraldry, emblem literature, English satire, and political poems and prophecies.
In Elizabethan prose, the same ideas persisted and were employed
in ways that had become conventional: in epithets, comparisons illustrating human nature and conduct, beast fables or allegories exemplifying human character and philosophical conceptions, and
proverbial sayings. Some of these ideas, it has been observed al-

ready, had been so far conventionalized as to become common words and phrases in the language itself.

The words *beast, beastly, beastliness, brute beast, brute, brutish,* and *brutishness* occur so frequently in Elizabethan prose that they may be considered favorite words;[1] and the reason is not far to seek. *Beast* or *brute,* or any of the forms derived from these nouns, as used in the educational treatises and in all the other prose writings of the period which have been mentioned, nearly always, unless used literally to designate an animal, implies the basic concept of humanistic moral philosophy: that man is the only creature capable of governing his passions through the exercise of reason and required to do so by the law of nature, which he must obey, or, not obeying, become a beast, an unreasonable creature. This conception is stressed by all the major prose writers of the Elizabethan period because their thinking and their rhetoric were influenced by the moral philosophy and rhetoric which they had been taught by humanist teachers.

Beasts, accordingly, often were represented not only as being unreasonable but also as exemplifying all kinds of sin, sensuality, grossness, and ugliness. Sir Philip Sidney's idea that beasts are incapable of perceiving beauty[2] probably stemmed from some such conception as that beasts, being unreasonable, could not perceive what is perceptible only to reasonable minds: namely κόσμος, orderly arrangement, symmetry, beauty, as distinguished from χάος the original rude unformed mass, disorder, deformity, ugliness — in short, that beauty should go with reason; ugliness, with unreason. Yet even beasts, according to the Elizabethan writers, obeyed the law of nature and set an example for men.

In the educational treatises of Thomas Wilson and Roger Ascham, not only is a knowledge of beasts considered important, but also conventional ideas about animals are employed by the authors themselves in their discussion of rhetoric and learning in general. Thomas Wilson, in his *Arte of Rhetorique* (1553), describes the disorder that prevailed "after the fall of our first Father," when nature and man's reason were overthrown, and men "like brute beastes grased vpon the ground," but points out that "after a certaine space they became through Nurture and good aduisement, . . . of beastes, men."[3]

In the same work, a number of examples are given to show how beasts, by their obedience to the law of nature, set an example for men. On the subject of "Matrimonie," for instance, Wilson writes that there is "nothing so naturall, not onely vnto mankind, but also vnto all other liuing creatures," as it is for them "to keepe their owne kind from decaie, and through increase of issue, to make their whole kinde immortal" and that "it were a foule thing that brute beastes should obey the Lawe of nature, and men . . . should fight against Nature,"[4] for "not only Stockdoues and Pigions, but also the most wilde beasts, haue a Naturall feeling of this thing [wedlock]."[5]

On the subject of maternal love, he writes that "the Hen clocketh her Chickens, feedeth them, and keepeth them from the Kite" and that likewise "Women must clocke their Children, bring them vp well, and keepe them from euill happ."[6] He mentions as further examples the tigers' fighting "for safegarde of their young whelpes" and the ass's running "through the hot fire (which is made to keepe her away) for safegarde of her issue."[7]

As an example of how one human being should love another, Wilson mentions the manner in which "beastes and birdes without reason" love one another:[8] "The Storke being not able to feede her self for age, is fed of her young ones, wherein is declared a naturall loue, and shall wee so liue that one shall not loue an other?"[9] He makes the same lesson "appeare more euident" by a contrast between storks and vipers: "Againe, in young Storkes, we may take an example of loue towards their damme," whereas "in yong Vipers there is a contrary example (for as *Plinie* saieth) they eate out their dammes wombe, and so come forth."[16]

Beasts also, Wilson points out, can teach man a lesson in how to bear grief: The cow lacking her calf; the doe, her fawn; and the hind, her calf, "seing their lacke to be without remedy, . . . cease their sorrow within short space." Birds, "perceyuing their young ones taken from their neast, chitter for a while in Trees there about, and straight after they flye abroade and make no more adoe." The "sorrowes of brute beastes are sharpe, and yet they are but short."[11]

From ancient natural history comes an example of watchfulness:

Craines in the night haue their watch, warning vs neuer to be carelesse, for if their watch faile them, they al neuer leaue till they haue killed that one Craine, teaching vs that no

traitors are worthy to liue vpon earth. The watch for his
safegard, and because he would not slepe, holdeth a stone in
his foote, the which falleth from him, when he beginneth to
waxe heauie, and so keepeth himselfe stil waking. Whereby
we may learne that all men in their vocation, should be right
ware and watchfull.[12]

Men, according to Wilson, ought to profit by the example of
beasts and obey the law of nature, for, he says, "beastes doe nothing
against Nature, but he that goeth against honestie, the same man
fighteth against Nature, which would that all men should liue
well"[13] and "that wretch that goeth against Nature, that onely hath
the shape of a man," is "worse then a beast."[14]

In his discussion of figures of speech, Wilson says that by describing an angry man as foaming at the mouth he calls to mind "a
Bore, that in fighting vseth much foming, the which is a foule and
lothly sight."[15] A second kind of figure is that in which "we goe
from the creature without reason, to that which hath reason," as,
for example, "such an vnreasonable brauler did nothing els but
barke like a dog, or like a Foxe. . . . Contrariwise we call a foxe
false, a Lion proude, and a dog flattryng."[16] Another figure Wilson
calls "a Whisht," which he says is used in speaking of any man: "we
say whisht, the Woulfe is at hand, when the same man cometh in
the meane season, of whom we spake before."[17] The figure called
"resembling of things" or "comparing or liking of looke, with looke,
shape, with shape, and one thing with an other" is exemplified in
such expressions as "He looks like a Tiger, a man would think he
would eate one, his countenance is so ougle"[18] and "He is as ramping as a Lyon."[19]

Concerning "faultes in pronunciation," Wilson says of people
that "some grunts like a Hogge";[20] some "whines like a Pigge";[21]
some "cackles like a Henne"; and some "cackles like . . . a Iacke
Dawe."[22]

On the subject of how a man can become a beast by giving himself up to vain pleasures, Roger Ascham, in his *Scholemaster* (1570),
writes that "Homer . . . doth feign that Circes by pleasant enchant-
ments did turn men into beasts, some into swine, some into asses,
some into foxes, some into wolves," and that "even so Plato . . . doth
plainly declare, that pleasure by licentious vanity . . . doth engender,
in all those that yield up themselves to her," bestial qualities:[23]

For if a man inglut himself with vanity, or welter in filthiness like a swine, all learning, all goodness, is soon forgotten. Then quickly shall he become a dull ass, to understand either learning or honesty; and yet shall he be as subtle as a fox in breeding of mischief, in bringing in misorder, with a busy head, a discoursing tongue, and a factious heart, in every private affair, in all matters of state; with this pretty property, always glad to commend the worse party, and ever ready to defend the falser opinion.[24]

In an invective against the "Englishman Italianated," Ascham says that "over-many of our travellers into Italy do not eschew the way to Circes' court" and that he could point out "some . . . that never had gone out of England, but only to serve Circes in Italy." These, "being mules and horses before they went, returned very swine and asses home again; yet very foxes with subtle and busy heads; and . . . very wolves, with cruel malicious hearts." The "Englishman Italianated" he calls "a marvellous monster," which "for wiliness in dealing with others, for malice in hurting without cause," should carry "at once in one body, the belly of a swine, the head of an ass, the brain of a fox, the womb of a wolf."[25]

Commenting upon Italian manners, Ascham says that in Venice it is counted good policy, when there are four to five brothers in one family, "one only to marry, and all the rest to welter with as little shame in open lechery, as swine do here [in England] in the common mire."[26]

Speaking of Englishmen "Italianated," of "fantastical Anabaptists and friars," and of "beastly libertines and monks" — all of them "bloody beasts, as that fat boar of the wood, or those brawling bulls of Basan, or any lurking dormouse, blind not by nature, but by malice"[27] — Ascham says that "when Aper de Silva had passed the seas, and fastened his foot again in England," not only "the two fair groves of learning [the two Universities] in England were either cut up by the root, or trodden down to the ground, and wholly went to wrack"; but also "the young spring there, and every where else, was pitifully nipt and overtrodden by very beasts"; and "the fairest standers of all were rooted up, and cast into the fire, to the great weakening even at this day of Christ's church in England both for religion and learning."[28] He blames particularly those ministers who willfully refused to acquire sufficient learning, "those blind buzzards, who in late years, of wilful maliciousness, would neither learn themselves, nor could teach others any thing at all."[29]

In a piece of literary criticism, he contrasts what he seems to consider the barbarous rudeness of that versification which did not follow Greek models with the excellence of Greek poetry. Even here he employs conventional animal imagery to point the contrast:

> Surely to follow rather the Goths in rhyming, than the Greeks in true versifying, were even to eat acorns with swine, when we may freely eat wheat bread amongst men.[30]

In his employment of animals in these passages, Ascham is following the conventions of English satire, which already have been discussed at some length.

Stressing the importance of learning languages, particularly Greek and Latin, he draws upon falconry and hawking for conventional terms to express his views, saying that "even as a hawk flieth not high with one wing [the other being clipped], even so a man reacheth not to excellency with one tongue"[31] and that "even the best translation is for mere necessity but an evil imped wing to fly withal." He points out that "such as will needs so fly, may fly at a pie, and catch a daw";[32] that is to say, those who depend upon translations may get less of the true meaning than they seek to grasp.

The Elizabethan *novelle* are English versions of Italian and French *novelle,* chiefly those of Boccaccio, Bandello, Cinthio, Straparola, and Queen Marguerite de Navarre. Some even are English renderings of the French *novelle* of François de Belleforest, which themselves are versions of the Italian stories. Although some of the conventional ideas about animals employed in the English versions appear also in the Italian and French stories, nothing would be gained by a textual comparison except the knowledge of which ideas are common to both the English versions and their originals and which ideas are peculiar to the English versions. Such a comparison would not alter the fact that these ideas were drawn from the sources already discussed and are conventional in Continental and English literature.

William Painter, in his *Palace of Pleasure* (1566), one of the principal collections of Elizabethan *novelle,* retells the Aesopic fables of Androcles and the lion ("the maruelous knowledge of a Lion, being acquainted with a man, called Androdus")[33] and the lark and the reaper.[34] In his story of "Dom Diego and Gineura" a woman is said to be "altogether like vnto AEsop's Serpent, which being deliuered from pearill and daunger of death by the shepeheard, . . . infected his whole house with his venomous hissing, and rammish Breath."[35]

From other Greek and Latin literature, including the natural histories, came Painter's tale "of the straunge and beastlie nature of Timon of Athens, enemie to mankinde,"[36] and a number of conventional references to beasts. In his story of "A Ladie falslie accused of adultrie, . . . condemned to be deuoured of Lions," for example, the generosity of lions is said to resemble the magnanimity and courage of noble men.[37] According to the story, the lady is placed in "the Parke of Lions," but because of her "vertue" (chastity) the "Lions (cruell and capitall enemies of adulterie, amonges themselues") fell to "licking and fawning vppon her, making so much of her as if they had familiarly ben nourished with her own breasts."[38]

The same lady is called "the Phenix of the fairest and moste curteous Ladies within all our Prouince";[39] in other words, like the phoenix, she is the only one of her kind in excellence. Her enduring in silence her husband's charges of adultery, which she knew to be false, "did more straungely pinche" her husband, "nerer at the harte then euer the Egle of Caucasus (whereof the Poetes haue talked so muche) did tier the mawe of the subtile thefe Prometheus."[40]

In the story of "Aristotimus the Tyrant," Aristotimus is called "more wood and sauage than the desert beast or mountaine Tigre," and his "cruelty" is compared to the tiger's.[41] In the story of "Sophonisba," Sophonisba "beemoned her self with such heauinesse, as the beastly heartes of the Hircane Tygres would haue bene made gentle . . . yf they had beheld her."[42] In a "Letter of the Emperour Traiane to the Senate of Rome," a "good Prince in a common wealth" is said to be "so rare, as the Phoenix in Arabia."[43] In "The Countesse of Celant," it is pointed out that "the eagles flight is not so high, as the Foolyshe desires, and Conceiptes of a Woman that trusteth in hir owne opinion, and treadeth out of the tract of duety, and the way of Wysedome,"[44] and that women ought not to listen to "vncomely talke" but "rather to follow the nature of the Serpent, that stoppeth his eare with his tayle, to auoide the charms and sorceries of the Enchaunter."[45]

Painter's story of "The Lady of Turin" tells of a wife who "did not forsee" that the special attentions of her husband "were the flatteries of the Crocodile, which reioyseth when he seeth one deceiued";[46] his "Duchesse of Malfi," of "Mayster Bologna," who "fantasied a thousand chimeraes in the Ayre, and formed like number of imaginations in his minde," not able "to coniecture what hee was, to whom the duchesse had vowed her loue";[47] the story of "The Lady of Boeme," of Lord Alberto and his "building castles in the Ayre, and deuising a thousand Chimeras in his braine";[48] and the story of "The Lord of Virle," of Venus, "hir Fote vpon a Tortus," signifying "the duety of a chaste Woman, . . . her feete not straying or wandering, . . . to keepe hir selfe within the limits of hir owne house,"[49] and of a woman called a "Basilisk, coloured ouer with pleasure and swetnesse," whose "sight dispersed his poyson throughout" her lover's heart.[50]

From the Bible and from popular or folk tradition came still other conventional ideas about animals in Painter's stories. In his story of "A Ladie Falslie Accused" are described those people called "admiratours and praisers of vertue," who "doe not use like indeuour for the merites of vertue" but "rather . . . imploie their onely industrie to gather some profite of vertue" and "then (followinge the nature of the dogge) they retourne to their vomite."[51] In his "King of Naples," it is told how the king, "abusing a Gentleman's wife, in the end did weare the hornes himselfe."[52] In "Two Gentlewomen of Venice," gentlemen are said to be as rare as "white Crowes" or as "Swannes of colour blacke."[53] The same story has a reference to the proverbial serpent in the grass.[54]

A passage in Painter's "Duchesse of Malfi" shows the influence of humanistic moral philosophy with its emphasis upon the governing of the passions through the exercise of reason as man's duty and his chief claim to distinction from beasts:

Ought the. wisedome of a Gentleman to stray and wandre through the assaults of an appetite rising of sensuality, and that reason gieue place to that which doeth participate with brute beasts depriued of all reason by subduinge the minde to the affections of the body? No, no, a vertuous man ought to let shine in him selfe the force of the generosity of his minde.[55]

George Pettie, in his *Petite Pallace of Pettie His Pleasure* (1576) , prefaces his collection of *novelle* with a "letter of G.P. to R.B. Concerning this Woorke," in which he exhorts R.B. to "use" the stories well, "that with the spider" he "sucke not out poyson out of them."[56] The same conventional idea about the spider's sucking poison from flowers is employed in the stories of "Cephalus and Procris" and "Pigmalions Friende, and His Image." In the former of these stories, "as the Spider out of most sweet flowers sucketh poyson," so the jealous Procris out of Cephalus' "most loving and friendly deedes towards her, picked occasions of quarrell, and conceyved causes of hate."[57] In the latter story, Pigmalion tells himself that "verely as Spiders convert to poison whatsoever they touche, so women infect with folly whom so ever they deale withall."[58] The conventional relationship between spider and fly is used in the story of "Curiatius and Horatia": Curiatius tells Horatia that "as the Spider in her webbe doth fast winde the little Flie," so Horatia's beauty "doth so fast binde" him "in the beames thereof" that he is "faine presently to yeelde" himself "a pray" to her "good pleasure."[59]

The story of "Sinorix and Camma" contains an application of the ideas, from humanistic moral philosophy, of obedience to the law of nature and profiting by the example of beasts. Sinorix tells Camma that "albeit by humane lawes" her husband only should "have interest" in her, "yet by natures lawes, which beinge more auncient ought to be of more auctority, he [whether her husband or not] ought to injoy" her "which joyeth most in her . . . & indureth most paine" for her sake; and "for proufe of natures lawes, it may please" her "to consider the quality of the shee woulfe who always choseth that woulfe for her mate who is made most leane and foule by following her."[60] Camma replies that Sinorix's "Wolves example, though it shew" his "Foxely brayne," gives "no sutch proofe" to his purpose. But she tells Sinorix that "therin truly" he observes "*decoram* very duly, in usyng the example of a Beast in so beastly a cause."[61] This last statement evidently is an allusion to the rhetoricians' emphasis upon the importance, "for oratory or description," of a knowledge of beasts and of the use of beast fables and examples.

In "Tereus and Progne," "Icilius and Virginia," "Scilla and Minos," and "Alexius," are passages that are based on the Aesopic fables of the wolf and the lamb, the wolf in sheep's clothing, the nurse and the wolf, and the cock and the pearl. In the first of these stories, old Pandion gives his daughter Philomela to Tereus: "But like a simple man hee committed the seely sheepe to the ravening Woulfe."[62] In the second story, "sutch raveninge wolves in sheepes cloathinge" (as Appius Claudius) "are rediest to devoure sutch sweete sheepe" (as Virginia), "sutch olde dogs ever bite sorest, sutch gravity for the most parte contayneth most incontinency."[63] In the third story, the statement is made that "the *Rodians* have this law, that onely the mothers have rule over the Daughters," and is followed by what Thomas Wilson, the rhetorician, calls a "Whist," expressed in the words "mum, *lupus in fabula*."[64] The *fabula* is, of course, the Aesopic fable of the wolf that overheard the nurse talking to the child. In the fourth story, Alexius tells his father that he means to continue as he is and not to change for the worse, "and with *Glaucus* to give golden harnesse for *Diomedes* his brasen, or a precious stoane for a barley corne with *AEsops* cocke."[65]

In "Tereus and Progne," the proverbial cruelty and fierceness of the tiger and pitilessness of the panther when it had caught its prey are alluded to. "Nay, there was never blouddy tiger that did so terribly teare the litle Lambe, as this tiraunt [Tereus] did furiously fare with faire *Philomela*."[66] But "what pity is to bee looked for of sutch *Panthers* [as Tereus] which passe not of piety?"[67] The whole conventional representation of the panther, however, appears in the story of "Amphiaraus and Eriphile," in which Amphiaraus upbraids Eriphile for her "daliance" with him, saying that "herein truly" she may be "fitly resembled" to "the *Panther* who with his gay colours & sweet smell allureth other beasts unto him, and beeyng within his reache hee ravenously devoureth them."[68]

In the same story, Amphiaraus compares Eriphile in her "daliance" with him to "the Cat, whiche playeth with the Mouse, whom straight shee meaneth to slay,"[69] and then charges women in general with being "naturally indued with . . . charmes to chaunge men from men to beastes, as *Cyrces* did the servauntes of *Ulisses*."[70]

Other conventional ideas about animals in Pettie's "Cephalus and Procris" are the idea of the dog's relentlessness in the pursuit of its quarry, as implied in the expression "this helhounde Jelousy"[71] and in the statement that "shee [Procris] dogged him [Cephalus], where hee was layde downe to rest";[72] the idea of the colt's unruliness, in such comparisons as "the colte the first time he is ridden snuffeth at the snaffle, and thinketh the bit most bitter unto him:

so the yoke of love seemth heavy" at first[73] and "our nature is to runne upon that which is forbidden us, . . . and a wilde coult the harder he is rained, the hotter he is";[74] the idea of a woman's being obliged to lead apes in hell if she refused matrimony, as in Procris' declaration that she "would rather, as they say, have led apes in hell . . . then have felt all the torments of hell" in her life; and the ideas of the sheep's simplicity and the fox's subtlety, as in Procris' calling herself "a simple sheepe" and Cephalus a "subtill Foxe" that could easily deceive her.[75]

"Minos and Pasiphae" contains, besides references to Pasiphae's "currishe nature"[76] and to the proverbial horns of cuckoldry, the "horned harnesse" which Pasiphae gave her husband King Minos,[77] an example of conventional irony expressed in terms of animals in the statement that "for one of meane parentage, to bee marryed with one of princely race" is "as good a match, as betweene Lions and Lambes" and "as well they will agree together, as Dogs and Cats."[78]

"Pigmalions Friende, and His Image" and "Alexius" have references to the ass's conventional stupidity and dullness and the dog's returning to his own vomit. Pigmalion says to himself that "hee whiche loveth" women "best" is sure "to be handled ye worst," for "they know he is armed with love to indure the force of their fraude, & like an Asse to beare any burthen whiche they shal lay on his back."[79] Alexius compares Aristotle to "an Asse sotted with over mutch studdy" and represents him as saying that "women are monsters in nature."[80] Reflecting upon his own experience with women, Alexius asks himself these questions: "shal I continue her company, which wil convert to my confusion? shal I with the Dog *redire ad vomitum?*"[81]

Birds as well as animals furnished a number of the conventional examples in Pettie's *novelle*. Some of these examples were drawn from falconry and hawking and were given a variety of applications. Sinorix, in "Sinorix and Camma," tells Camma that though his presumption may seem great in "practising one of so highe a calling" as her "sweet self," he trusts that, "seing in al degrees of friendship, equality is cheefly considered," she "will clere" him "of crime that way" and will not think his "flight so free to stoup at every stale, for as the haughty Hauke will not pray on carrion, so neither will courtely silkes practise country sluttes."[82] Camma says that "as a hauke the higher pitch shee flieth from the ground with the more force shee stoupeth downe upon her praye and can the more easely commaund it," so "gods vengance the longer it is deferred, the more it is to be feared."[83]

Germanicus, in "Germanicus and Agrippina," considering "natures lawes, which in the dooynges of creatures without reason are playnly set downe," tells Agrippina that she "shall see no living wight in the universall world, but that . . . apply themselves to that life whereby their kinde may bee conserved and number increased." He then uses the example of "the high flyinge Faulcon which soareth so high in the ayre that a man would think she would stoope to neither Lure nor lust, yet . . . of her owne accorde shee commeth to the call of the tassell gentle her make."[84] This passage is reminiscent of Thomas Wilson's discussion of matrimony.

On the same subject, Germanicus tells Agrippina that matrimony is "as common as the blacke crow," whereas virginity is "as rare as the blacke swan."[85] But "as the bird caught in lime, or conny in hay, or deare in toyle, the more they strive the faster they sticke," so "ye more diligently" Agrippina "laboured to get out of the *Labyrinth* of love the more doubtfully was shee intricated therein."[86] In "Icilius and Virginia," a friend reminds Icilius that "fortune . . . favoureth not the faint hearted, neither are they woorthy to win the pray" and tells him that Virginia can be won, for "there is no hauke soareth so highe but shee will stoupe to some praye," nor "any so rammishe and wilde but in time shee may bee reclaimed and made to the lure."[87]

Scilla, in "Scilla and Minos," tells herself that "if it bee lawfull to follow the example of creatures without reason," she may declare her love, for "doth not the Faulcon call to the tossell gentle, the gerfaulcon to the Gerkin, the sparehauke to the Musket?" So "of all other creatures the females are more forward that way then the males."[88] In "Pigmalions Friende, and His Image" are asked these questions: "What constancy is to bee hoped for in kytes of *Cressids* kinde: may one gather Grapes of thornes, Suger of Thistels, or constancy of women?"[89] Here, of course, the conventional baseness and flickleness of the kite are alluded to.

The same story contains a good example of the conventional Elizabethan manner of representing, in terms drawn from falconry and hawking, women's treatment of their suitors and the effects thereof. Pigmalion's soliloquy gives a complete word picture:

Now, so soone as they [women] see him [a suitor] reasonably well reclaimed to the lure of their alluring looks, they
by and by stop the lure upon him, and cause him to hover in
hope and teach him to flie a high pitche, for a pray of little
profit or pleasure. For then they cast very coy countenances
towards him, yea they will not so mutch as with a glaunce
give any signe of goodwil: but when they have made him lie
so long in the aire, that he is redy either to take a stande, or
soare away, they flinge forth a traine of treason, and cast some
flattringe hope, and faigned fawning for him to feed on, lest
his kindnes by their coldnesse should quaile, and so he retire
his desyre. But if they see him to be so sharpe set, yt he will
stoupe at every stale, or know him to be an eyesse . . . which
will never away, then they make him flye and never serve
him, they bangle him out and bob him as they list, then they
keepe themselves out of his sight to make him more sharp,
then in his presence they lend loving lookes to other[s], then
they make the matter so strange, that hee is driven to beegin
agayne, and to renew his sute afresh.[90]

Birds other than falcons and hawks are also conventionally employed. In "Icilius and Virginia," the observation is made that although "some have been surprised with love only upon a loving
looke, . . . a curteous word, . . . a single sight, . . . a vaine vision,
. . . a doubtful dreame, . . . an uncertaine report," or "some other
way," none of these things is always a sign of love; and then follows
the well-known English proverb, "as one swallow makes not som-
mer, so one particularity concludeth no generality."[91]

In "Admetus and Alcest," Atys wonders why nature has "indued
the Storke with this property to feede his damme, when shee is olde,
and men with sutch malice" as to lack this filial devotion to their
aged parents.[92] In "Minos and Pasiphae," it is said to be better for
women "to be simple then subtil, to be doves then divels."[93] Alexius,
in the story so entitled, says that no more happiness could come to
him than to have a good wife, "the onely *Phoenix* of the earth."[94]

Reptiles, fish, and other creatures are likewise conventionally
employed in Pettie's *novelle*. The proverbial snake in the grass is
used in the story of "Scilla and Minos" to show the inexperience of
Iphis, who begins fixing "his fonde fancie" upon Scilla's fine face"
but "by reason of his younge yeeres" is "ignorant that under moste
greene grasse lie most great snakes."[95] The same idea about the snake

is implied in the story of "Sinorix and Camma," in which Camma, hearing herself praised by Sinorix, thinks "no . . . serpentine malice to lie hid under these merry and sugred woordes."[96]

The cockatrice with its fatal glance appears in a description of the effect of Camma's beauty upon Sinorix, who perceives "that as the *Cocatrice* by sight only sleath, so shee [Camma] by courteous countenance" wounds and kills "his hart"; yet he cannot "refrain his eyes from beholding her."[97] The chameleon that "chaungeth him selfe into ye colour and hew of every thing hee doth viewe" serves in the story of "Tereus and Progne" to picture man's aptness "to bee transfourmed into any misfortune, and to receive any evill yt raigneth upon the face of the earth."[98]

The idea of the fish's being deceived and caught with a baited hook is used conventionally in "Scilla and Minos" to picture the inexperience of Iphis, who, fixing "his fonde fancie" upon Scilla's "fine face," is ignorant "by reason of his younge yeeres" that "under intisinge baytes" are "intanglyng hookes," and bites "so greedely at the bayte of her beutie" that he swallows "the hooke of hatefull hurte, and hurtfull heaviness to his heart."[99] The same conventional idea about the fish is used in the story of "Alexius," in which Alexius, regarding pleasure as "the very pathway to perdition" and women as "the way to wrack and ruine," asks himself whether he shall "wilfully woorke" his "owne destruction" and "greedely devoure the baite," which he knows "hath a hooke hidden in it to hurt" him.[100]

Other quite common expressions involve conventional ideas about such creatures as the moth, the worm, the flea, the wasp, the candlefly, the bumblebee, and the drone. In "Cephalus and Procris," Procris sorrowfully reflects that "there is no clothe so fine but moathes will eate it, . . . no wood so sounde but wormes will putrifie it, . . . nor no Maide so free but love will bring her into thraldome and bondage."[101] In "Sinorix and Camma," a woman, having got a bit of news that is difficult for her to keep, goes away "with a flea in her eare."[102] In "Curiatius and Horatia," Horatia gives Curiatius a "waspishe answer";[103] and in "Cephalus and Procris," Procris is watched by "her waspish parents."[104]

In "Pigmalions Friende, and His Image," it is said that "the flie playeth so long with the flame, that hee is scourched therwith" and that "men dally so longe with dainty dames" that "at length they are scorched in the flames of fancy, and the winges of their free will quight burned away."[105] Pigmalion observes that as "the Humble-bee" flies all day in the pleasant air and lights upon sweet flowers but at night lodges in "a Cowes foule sharde," so "these dainty dames, in company think skorne to yeelde love to any, but in cor-ners they care not to practise with some lothsome skullion, or horse boy."[106] In "Alexius," Alexius' father says that to make "immod-erate use" of study, to seek one's "owne carelesse securitie" and neglect his "countries commoditie," is to "live (lyke a drone by the hony) of other mens handes, and by the sweete of other mens swet."[107]

Barnabe Riche, in his *Farewell to Militarie Profession* (1581), employed conventional ideas about animals in the conventional manner. The story of "Apolonius and Silla" in this collection has an allusion to the horses of Apollo, to describe a long day, which "passed awaie so slowlie" that Silvio "had thought the statelie steedes had been tired that drawe the chariot of the sunne."[108] In the story of "Two Brethren," women who reject their suitors are called "cruell tygers" and "beares"[109] and "kites of Cressides kinde,[110] and it is said of "Mistres Dorithe" that "she cunningly armed" her husband's "hedde with hornes"[111] and that she cannot "goe abroade to any place" without being "dogged and followed by suche" as her husband "hath appointed."[112] In the story of "Phylotus and Emilia," Alberto, "seeyng his face all swolne, and the skinne scratched of," and perceiving that Phylotus has been "at a fraie," and has "good cause to complaine," wonders "that his daughter" has "so sodainly become a shrewe."[113] It is also remarked that "if it were not for monne" many young women "could bee well contented to leade apes in hell."[114]

In the story of "Sappho Duke," Valeria, considering herself "un-fortunate above all other women," says, "I have made request to him [Silvanus] . . . and yet am scornefully rejected, and an other like to catche the birdes, whilest I doe but beate the bushe."[115] Valeria's father uses a conventional expression reminiscent of Skel-ton's *Speke, Parrot:* "Have you founde your tongue now, pretie peate? then wee most have an almon for parrat."[116] Valeria is de-scribed earlier in the story as being "so farre intangled" with Sil-vanus' "sweete and pleasaunt countenaunce" that she is "constrained to yeelde to love," as "the fishe whiche by little and little sucketh upon the baite, till at the length she swalloweth doune the hooke, whereby she hangeth faste."[117]

Conventional ideas about animals abound in the satirical pamphlets of the period. Stephen Gosson, in his *School of Abuse* (1579), attacks "the whole rabble of poets, pipers, players, jugglers, jesters and dauncers," whose doings are "abuses" such as he has read of "in Rome." Such, he says, are "the caterpillers that have devoured and blasted the fruit of AEgypt"; the "dragons that are hurtfull in Affricke"; the "adders that sting with pleasure and kill with payne"; and the "basiliskes of the world that poyson, as wel with the beame of their sight, as with the breath of their mouth."[118]

In his epistle "To the Reader," Gosson compares those who will misconstrue what he writes to "curst curres" that "barke at every man but their owne friendes" and "snatch uppe bones in open streetes, and bite them with madnesse in secret corners."[119] He then proceeds to attack poets, whom he accuses of dwelling longest on "those points that profit least."[120] He says that some poets labor "with mountaines to bring forth mice"; that "Virgil sweats in describing his gnatte"; and that "Ovid bestirreth him to paint out his flea."[121] He accuses poets of forsaking "the fayre fields" to "wallowe in the myre" (an allusion to the hog) and points out by way of comparison that "the scarabe flies over many a sweet flower, and lightes in a cowsherd."[122]

To illustrate how both good and bad are to be found in the poets' works, "honie and gall . . . mixt," and how difficult it is to "sever the one from the other," he points out that "Hyena speakes like a friend, and devours like a foe"; that "the woolfe jets in weathers felles"; and that "the wholesome baite" is "the fishes bane."[123] Gosson mentions "this morall philosopher" who "toyles to draw the lions skinne upon AEsops asse."[124]

Next he attacks musicians, saying that whoever compares "our instruments with those that were used in ancient tymes" shall see "them agree like dogges and cattes." He compares "our musitions" to "Timotheus, a bird of the same broode" as Phrynis, the fiddler who "thought to amend his maisters, and marred al," for Timotheus is said to have taken "the 7 stringed harp . . . and encreased the number of the strings at his owne pleasure." Gosson implies that in like manner "our musitions" have "marred al."[125]

But these abuses, according to him, are small in comparison with those in the theaters and among players. "They that are borne" and brought up "in those islandes, where they see nothing but foxes and hares, will never be persuaded that there are huger beasts." He says that "the abuse" of the theaters is "so great, that for any chaste liver to haunt them" is "a blacke swan, and a white crow," or, in other words, a rare thing.[126] He calls it "a right comedie to marke" the behavior of the "assemblies at playes in London," to watch "their conceates, as the catte for the mouse."[127] He objects to women's going to the theaters, for "wild coultes, then they see their kind, begine to bray, and lusty bloods at the shewe of faire women give a wantone sighe or a wicked wishe."[128]

He describes the danger that lies in small abuses that go unheeded: "Small are the abuses, and slight are the faultes that nowe in Theaters escape the poets pen"; but "the fishe Remora hath a small body, and great force to staye shippes . . . : Ichneumon, a little worme, overcomes the elephant: the viper slayes the bull; the weesell the cockatrice."[129] He points out that "in those thinges that we lest mistrust the greatest daunger doeth often lurke," just as "the serpent that is hid in the grasse" is more to be feared than "the wilde beaste that openly feedes upon the mountaines."[130]

Gosson says that he does not condemn "the giftes of versifying, daunsing or singing in women, so they bee used with meane and exercised in due time"; but as "the Scythians did it without offence," so "one swallow brings not summer, nor one particular example is sufficient proofe for a generall precept."[131]

Other abuses are pointed out in fencing and bowling. "Fencing is growne to such abuse," according to Gosson, that "the schollers of this schoole" may well be compared to "them that . . . trust wolves to garde their sheepe" or "foster snakes in their owne bosoms";[132] and "common bowling allyes are privy mothes, that eate uppe the credite of many idle citizens."[133]

Addressing directly the "Lord Maior" and the magistrates of London, Gosson disclaims any intention of seeking to instruct them in how to rule but intends to warn them concerning the danger that hangs over their heads, as "the birde Trochilus with crashing of her bil awakes the crocodile, and delivereth her from her enemyes"; as "a little fishe swimmeth continually before the great whale to showe him the shelves, that he run not a grounde"; as "the elephants, when any of their kinde are fallen into the pittes that are made to catch them, thrust in stones and earth to recover them"; and as "when the lyon is caught in a trappe, AEsop's mouse, by nibbling the cordes, sets him at libertie." Gosson tells the "Lord Maior" and the magistrates that "it shall be inough" for him "with Trochilus" to have "wagged" his bill; "with the little fish" to have "gone before" them; "with the elephants" to have showed them the way to help themselves; and "with AEsop's mouse" to have "fretted the snares with a byting tooth."[134]

He expresses the wish that the abuses against which he writes were "as wel knowne" to the "Lord Maior" and the magistrates "to reformation" as they "are found out by other to their owne peril." But he points out that "the fish Sepia can trouble the water to shun the nets" and that "Torpedo hath crafte enough at the first touch to enchant the hooke, to conjure the line, to bewitch the rod, and to benoom the hands of him that angleth." He knows "not wel" whether "our players be the spawnes of such fishes," but he is "sure that how many nets soever there be laid to take them, or hooks to choke them," they have "ynke in their bowles to darken the water, and sleights in their budgettes to dry up the arme of every magistrate."[135]

According to Gosson, birds and beasts, even the most witless, show more wisdom than do people in protecting themselves from enemies: "Aristotle thinketh that in greate windes the Bees carry little stones in their mouthes to peyse their bodies, leste they bee carryed away"; the crane holds a stone in her claw to keep awake, "whereby shee is ever ready to prevent her enemyes"; geese "are foolish byrdes," but "when they flye over the mount Taurus they showe great wisdome in their own defence," for "they stop their pipes ful of gravel to avoide gaggling, and so by silence escape the eagles"; and "woodcocks, though they lack witte to save them selves," want not wit "to avoyde hurte, when they thrust their heads in a bushe and thinke their bodyes out of danger." But "wee" human beings run "most greedily to those places [theaters, etc.] where wee are soonest overthrowne."[136]

Gosson says, however, that the abuses against which he writes have in them their own destruction — "the adders death is her owne broode"[137] — for "that God . . . that stretcheth out his armes . . . to cover his children (as the hen doth her chicken with the shadow of her wings) . . . shall overthrowe them."[138]

In his *Ephemerides of Phialo* (1579), which contains an *Apologie of the Schoole of Abuse,* Gosson expresses the wish that as the bear licks her newborn cubs into shape he may be able to put his thoughts into words that will convey his meaning.[139] He says that in the *School of Abuse* he has pointed to the straw where the pad lurks[140] and that he will ignore any idle drones that may attack him because of what he has written.[141] Phialo is the "Euphues" of Gosson's *Ephemerides,* which in form resembles Lyly's work. In the dedication, Phialo is said to be too blunt for the court if judged by his coat but actually not lacking in wit any more than the fox because his coat is not comparable to the leopard's.[142]

Gosson says that libelers have barked more at him for writing the *School of Abuse* than Cerberus barked at Hercules for descending to hell and that they have tried like curs to wound him with their teeth.[143] He mentions one libeler in particular, who repeats Pliny's statement that there is ever some kind of monster to be seen in Africa and illustrates the saying by joining together different beasts. This libeler has friends among the players, who eagerly anticipate being given a new conceit to put into their plays; but they are disappointed, for the libeler produces nothing more than a dirty tale of an ass, the offspring of a Dutch mule and an English mare.[144]

The *Ephemerides* contains a fairly large number of conventional animal references of the familiar type. Flatterers are compared to apes that imitate what they see in people,[145] to vultures that stoop only where they smell prey,[146] to moths that eat holes in garments,[147] and to the polypus (octopus) and the chameleon that change themselves into many colors and shapes.[148] It is said of Socrates that he was never called beauty's bloodhound (an allusion to that dog's tenacity in the pursuit of its quarry).[149] Phialo denies that his silence in an argument is an admission of defeat, saying that like the ram he withdraws from his adversary only in order to return with greater force.[150] He says that trying to argue without sufficient grounds is like trying to make a silk purse of a sow's ear.[151] Polyphile's abuse of the word *pleasure,* taking it sometimes in one sense and sometimes in another, is compared to the hedgehog's shifting the entrance of his burrow, never staying in that quarter where the wind blows.[152] Gosson calls the libeler of his *School of Abuse* a daw (a stupid bird)[153] and, by implication, a coxcomb (a vain, foolish clown),

and pretends not to be disturbed by anything that he writes, because
it is only natural for a cock's head to produce a comb.[154]

Gosson mentions the waspishness that makes it difficult for people to bear adverse critcism,[155] but says that critics should have a
spirit of meekness, which he compares to a dove without any gall,
and should reveal without bitterness the faults of friends.[156] The
man who is always rebuking is compared to the raven that always
preys upon carrion.[157] Phialo's rival suitor is accused of triumphing
before the victory and counting his chickens before they are
hatched.[158] Philotimo's flirting with a woman in a balcony is compared to a hawk's flying at a partridge;[159] his seeing virtue and
beauty combined in Polyphile, to imagining a phoenix of Arabia;[160]
and his gazing upon Polyphile's beauty, to the chameleon's feeding
upon air.[161]

The true courtier, according to Phialo, is as rare in Italy as the
phoenix in Arabia.[162] The courtiers of Ferrara are said to have
learned that by liberality they exhaust their resources as the pelican
mortally wounds herself in nourishing her young and the adder
gives life to her brood by her own death.[163] Such courtiers or
hangers-on are compared to leeches that live by sucking the blood
of their victims.[164] Fortune is said to favor gallants in princes' courts
for a while as the sea is calm until the kingfisher's (halcyon's) eggs
are hatched.[165]

About 1580, Thomas Lodge wrote *A Reply to Stephen Gosson's
School of Abuse in Defence of Poetry Musick and Stage Plays*. Lodge
takes Gosson to task for the assertion that "Tullie in his yeres of
more iudgement despised Poetes" and, employing conventional animal references, brands Gosson as being both cowardly and lacking
in judgment. He bids Gosson notice what Cicero writes about poets
"in his *oratio pro Archia poeta*," but warns him that before "the
incounter" he should "followe the advise of the dasterdlye *Ichneumon* of AEgipt, who when shee beholdeth the *Aspis* . . . to drawe
nighe, calleth her fellowes together, bismering her selfe with claye,
against the byting and stroke of the serpent"; so Lodge bids Gosson
arm himself, call his wits together, and "want not" his weapons,
lest his "imperfect iudgement be rewardede with Midas [ass's]
eares."[166] He accuses Gosson of having been "a professed play maker,
& a paltry actor," the "windmil" of whose wit "hath bin tornd so
long wyth the wynde of folly" that it is to be feared "we shall see

the dogg returne to his vomit, and the clensed sow to her myre, and the reformed scholemayster to hys old teaching of follye."[167]

Accusing Gosson of polishing his writings "with others sentences" and misrepresenting the truth, Lodge compares him to "AEsopes craftie crowe," whose "double dealing," though he "be so destlye decked [with other birds' feathers]," is "esely desiphered";[168] to the *"Camelion"* that "can chaunge her selfe vnto all coollors saue whyte" as Gosson "can accompte of all thinges saue such as haue honesty";[169] and to a snake in the grass.[170] In answer to Gosson's attack on plays, Lodge writes that "those of iudgement can from the same flower suck honey with the bee, from whence the Spyder (. . . the ignorant) take their poison" and that "men yt haue knowledge what comedies & tragedies be, will comend the, but it is sufferable in the folish to reproue that they know not, becaus ther mouthes wil hardly be stopped."[171]

In *An Alarum against Vsurers* (1584), Lodge exposes the evil practices of usurers and those in their employ. The "Solicitour," he says, "dilygentlye intendes . . . to the compassing of some young Nouice" as "the Catte watcheth the praye of the Mouse."[172] The usurers themselves are called voracious wolves clothed "in simplicitie of Doues" (this probably is a variation of the Aesopic and Biblical wolf in sheep's clothing);[173] the "Caterpillers of a Common weale"; the "sting of the Adder";[174] the "Serpent . . . hidden in the grasse";[175] and devouring moths that consume the fine cloth, the wealth of citizens upon whom they prey.[176] "The laboursome Ant," according to Lodge, "gathereth not in excesse, but sufficient prouision for the Winter, yet without reason" but usurers "which are reasonably borne, hoorde vp more" than they "well knowe how to imploy."[177] The ichneumon is the enemy of the asp; the weasel, of the cockatrice; and usurers are "the priuie foes of all Gentrie."[178]

Of the contents of his *Alarum* Lodge writes that "what is sette downe heere, eyther as an eye witnesse I will auowe," or "informed euen by those Gentlemen, who haue swallowed the Gudgeon, and haue bene intangeled in the hooke, I haue approouedlye sette downe."[179] In similar conventional terms, he compares the victims of usurers and their agents to "the birde . . . caught in the pitfall,"[180] to the "mand Fawlcon" made to stoop to the lure,[181] to "sillie Birdes . . . lead by the call of the Fowler,"[182] and to "bride well [Bridewell] birdes."[183]

Lodge's *Catharos: Diogenes in His Singularitie* (1591) with the subtitle *A Nettle for Nice Noses* is a satire against the immorality of Athens (London). The work is in the form of a dialogue between Diogenes, who is conventionally referred to as "a dogge that biteth men but for their amendment, and not for enuy,"[184] and Philoplutos and Cosmosophos, typical Athenians (Londoners), whose names are indicative of their characters. Diogenes calls Philoplutos a fox, "pretending much grauitie, but not a graine of honestie,"[185] and compares dishonest lawyers, clergymen, landlords, merchants, and usurers to foxes and ravening wolves in sheep's clothing.[186]

Diogenes characterizes all of these types in a series of animal fables. To show how "he that ordaineth a pit for his neighbour, shall fall into it him selfe," he cites the example of *"AEsops Mouse"* in the fable about belling the cat[187] and tells auother fable of the wolf and the ass sawing wood together, the wolf underneath trying to blow sawdust into the ass's eyes but succeeding only in filling his own eyes. The story ends with the wolf's swearing that he will "ouerthrowe the porters and bearers" and in his attempt to do so causing the timber to fall upon himself.[188]

Two fables have to do with lawyers. The type of the honest lawyer is pictured in a fable of a hare and a lion. "The Hare went to *Athens* to schoole, and in processe of time became a good Lawyer"; he "repaired to the Lyon the soueraigne of beasts, and the sole patterne of bountie," and desired to "liue worshipfully" under the lion's protection. After making proof of the hare's "wisedome and cunning," the lion promoted him according to his desert.[189]

The type of the dishonest lawyer, on the other hand, is pictured in a fable of a cock, a capon, and a fox. "The Cocke like the bird of the Sunne was the commander ouer the hennes, the Capon enioyned to pennance, in that he had lost his stones, was nothing so stout." The fox caught and devoured the cock and then "cast in his minde by what meanes he might catch the Capon, wherevpon reseruing the combe of the Cocke, like a graue fellow in a garded gowne," he came to the capon and, persuading him to descend from the roost in the hope of being given the cock's comb, which would enable him to "be Lord ouer the hens," caught and devoured him. "Euen like the Fox haue our false hearted Atturnies dealt," Diogenes says: "First with faire wordes haue they got a fléece from the rich, leauing them a small title for a great summe of money;" then "these Foxes," having furnished them with their coin, "begin to gather countenance, and making poore men beléeue all by their big looks, they so rent them that they leaue them no Rent," and trouble them with so many writs that "some of them are beside their wits."[190]

In a fable of a hawk, a goshawk, and a quail, Diogenes tells how clergymen, "those that haue care of soules," must be careless of the world and of wealth and how "if danger threaten their flocke, they ought rather to suffer death, than to sée them seduced." A "Hauke called *Ormarillus* . . . met with a Goshauke, who became his confederate." They agreed to divide equally between them "whatsoeuer they tooke." Seizing upon a quail and "séeing her a little bird too abiect a morcell for their hungrie mawes," they sought "to surprise both her and her young" by giving her a choice between being devoured alone and leading them to her young, "to suffer death with them." The quail saved her brood by choosing to die alone. "After the manner of this Quaile ought our truely qualited diuines demean them selues," Diogenes points out; "of two harmes they must choose the lesse: better had they suffer with a good conscience, than their whole flock should be deuoured in error, or misled through their enuie."[191]

The Aesopic fable of the crow and the fox is told to show how grasping landlords in league with crafty lawyers fleeced poor tenants. The crow represents the tenant, who, being involved in lawsuits, "prooueth a dawe [i.e., a dupe] in the end." The fox represents the lawyer and the landlord. Diogenes entreats the Athenians to hold their own and "trust not, for trust is soonest betraide: it is better to haue one bird in the fist, than two in the field."[192]

He tells the story of "a fat Churle that had a fruitful hen which laide euery day an egge," a variation of the Aesopic fable of the goose with the golden eggs, as an example of how greedy merchants often lose all. He adds that "Merchants and Chapmen ought therefore to beware lest they get any thing wrongfully, for vniust mens goods shall be soone destroyed" and "riche lightly gotten may not last long."[193]

Usurers and their pitilessness in dealing with their victims Diogenes pictures in a fable of a "Griphon" and "his tyranny & couetousnes" in ruling "a great prouince."[194] Diogenes prefaces his fable with the description of the "Griphon" given by *Isidore* in his twenty two of Etymologies."[195] The usurer, according to Diogenes, "is com-

pared to a worme," and "he shall haue in recompence of his villanie, a worme which shal incessantly féede vpon him, and tyre vpon
his conscience" as "the Vultures that gnaw the poore liuer of *Titius,*
according to *Homers* opinio."[196]

Diogenes admonishes Philoplutos and Cosmosophos "to fly the
conversation of those which are . . . wicked," saying that "the same
also was intended in the history of the harlot *Circes,* who . . .
chaunged men into swine, Lions, Beares, and other sauage beasts."[197]
He says that Philoplutos "must haue a serpents eare to preuent the
charmes of the flatterer, and *Linx* his eie to spie out contempts."[198]

Lodge's satirical pamphlets, *Catharos* in particular, show very
well the manner in which Elizabethan writers of prose satire employed conventional ideas about animals drawn from Aesopic material, the Bible, classical story, and proverbial lore.

In the satirical pamphlets which were written between 1588,
when the Marprelate controversy began, and 1600, conventional
ideas about animals continued to be employed in the ways which
had been prescribed by the rhetoricians; but certain conventional
animal epithets, because they had become the regular terms applied
to the objects of invective, deserve special consideration. The ape,
the ass, the wolf, the sheep, the fox, the caterpillar, the moth, and
the cormorant are the principal creatures used as terms of invective
by Lyly, Greene, Nashe, and Harvey. Other creatures similarly used
by these men, though figuring less prominently, are the cony, the
vulture, the woodcock, the viper, the chameleon, the serpent, the
basilisk, the cockatrice, the crocodile, and the leech. References are
made also to the proverbial horns of cuckoldry.

Before the Marprelate controversy there was a general tendency
to represent any object of satire as an ape and to speak of the satire
itself as "whipping the ape," possibly because in the sixteenth century the words *satire* and *satyr* were confused and because satyrs
were thought to be a species of ape and sometimes were represented
with whips, scourging the objects of their disapproval.[199] During the
time of the Marprelate controversy, as contemporary references
show, several coarse dramatic sketches, now lost, were presented, in
one of which an ape, representing Martin, went through a series of
obscene and suggestive actions.[200] Lyly, in his *Pappe with an Hatchet*
(1589), alludes to one of Martin's writings, which Martin "woon-
ders at himselfe, and like an old Ape hugges the Vrchin so in his

conceipt, as though it should shew vs some new tricks ouer the chaine."[201] In the same pamphlet, Lyly represents Martin as chattering like a monkey.[202]

On the title page of *Martins Months Minde* (1589), attributed to Nashe, mention is made of "Martin the Ape, the dronke, and the madde."[203] Nashe, in his *Almond for a Parrat* (1590), implies that Martin is an ape, an imitator, of Ananias and Sapphira — in other words, a liar.[204] In *Pierce Penilesse His Svpplication to the Diuell* (1592), Nashe mentions a kind of drunkard who "is Ape drunke, and he leapes, and sings, and hollowes, and daunceth for the heavens."[205] In *Strange Newes* (1593), "vpstart Interpreters," such as Gabriel Harvey, who read into that which is written what is not intended by the author, are compared to Bidpai's apes that tried to kindle a fire with a glowworm.[206] Gabriel Harvey is called "the great Baboune"[207] and, for publishing a pamphlet entitled "*Ciceronis Consolatio ad Dolabellam*," the Ape of Tully."[208]

Again, according to *Strange Newes,* Pierce Penilesse "delivering his vnperusde papers to Powles Churchyard, the first that took them vp was the Ape *Gabriel,* who made mops and mows at them, beslauering the outside of them," but "coulde not enter into the contents, which was an ase beyonde his vnderstanding."[209] In *The Terrors of the Night* (1594), Nashe mentions "Macheuilian vaine fooles" that travel for nothing else but "to learne the vices of other countries, and disfigure the ill English faces that God hath giuen" them "with Tuscan glickes and apish trickes."[210]

The ape was used as a term of abuse because of his facetiousness and imitativeness; the ass, because of his traditional dullness and stupidity. Lyly, in his *Pappe with an Hatchet,* and Nashe, in his *Pasquills Returne to England* (1589), *First Parte of Pasquils Apologie* (1590), and *Almond for a Parrat,* call Martin and the Martinists asses.[211] The ass with his long ears is likewise used by Greene and Nashe to designate the Harveys, particularly Gabriel and Richard. Greene, in *A Quip for an Vpstart Courtier: Or, A quaint dispute between Veluet breeches and Cloth-breeches* (1592), attacks in the person of Gabriel Harvey all upstarts and parvenu aristocrats.[212] Nashe makes a similar attack in *Pierce Penilesse.*[213] Nashe's *Strange Newes* and *Have with You to Saffron-Walden: or, Gabriel Harueys Hunt is vp* (1596) are particularly abusive attacks on Gabriel Harvey,[214] who is called in *Strange Newes* "a crow troden Asse"[215] and "the Asse in the Lions skinne."[216] Greene, in *The Second Part of Conny-Catching* (1591), *A Disputation Betweene a Hee Conny-Catcher and a Shee Conny-Catcher* (1592), and *The Blacke Bookes Messenger* (1592), uses the term *ass* to designate any victim of cozeners.[217]

Ass and ape both figure prominently in the writings of Gabriel Harvey as terms of abuse which are applied to Thomas Nashe and Robert Greene. In the third and fourth letters of *Foure Letters and Certaine Sonnets* (1592), in *Pierces Supererogation, or A New Prayse of the Old Asse* (1593), and in *The Trimming of Thomas Nashe, Gentleman* (1597), the epithets "ass"[218] and "ape"[219] are made to recur so frequently that the effect is monotonous. In one lengthy passage of *Pierces Supererogation,* Nashe is called an ass on every page, almost in every sentence.[220]

Harvey writes that "our new-new writers, the Loadstones of the Presse, are wonderfully beholdinge to the Asse: in a manner the onely Autor, which they alledge: . . . or for variety, an Ape," and that "the world was euer full inough of fools, but neuer so full of Asses in print."[221] He calls Nashe "a rude Asse,"[222] a "vaine-glorious Asse,"[223] and "the only Monarch of asses,"[224] and says that "Nash, the Ape of Greene, Greene the Ape of Euphues, Euphues [Lyly], the Ape of Enuie, the three famous mammets of the presse, . . . drawe all in a yoke."[225] According to Harvey, such writers as Nashe and Greene "can tell parlous Tales of Beares and Foxes, as shrewd-lye as mother Hubbard."[226]

Not only the ass and the ape but also the wolf, because of his ravenousness and predatory habits, and the sheep, because of his innocence and simplicity, were favorite conventional animal symbols employed in the satirical pamphlets of the period. Wolves and sheep were employed as symbols especially in the Protestant tracts, of which Greene's *The Spanish Masquerado* (1589) is one example that may be mentioned in passing. In this tract, Greene, following the usage characteristic of such writings, calls Roman Catholic clergymen "rauening Wolues"[227] and the Pope a wolf "in a Sheepes skin."[228]

Similarly, in the pamphlets pertaining to the Marprelate controversy and in those pertaining to the Harvey-Nashe quarrel, the wolf and the sheep figure as symbols. Lyly, in *Pappe with an Hatchet,* and Nashe, in *A Countercuffe Giuen to Martin Iunior, Pas-*

quills Returne to England, The First Parte of Pasquils Apologie,
and *An Almond for a Parrat,* represent Martin and the Martinists
as wolves or wolves in sheep's clothing[229] and those misled by them
as sheep.[230] Nashe, in *Strange Newes,* represents Gabriel Harvey as
having "put on wolues raiment already, seduced manie simple people [sheep] vnder the habit of a sheepe in *Wolfes* print.[231]

The sly, crafty fox, another animal that was given special prom-
inence in the Elizabethan satirical pamphlets, had figured as the conventional rogue of literature and folklore from the earliest times.[232]
Nashe, in *Pasquills Returne to England* and *An Almond for a Parrat,* calls the Martinists foxes because of "theyr conspiracies, and
incontinencies."[233] In *Pierce Penilesse,* he has a fable in which a fox,
representing hypocrisy, helps a greedy bear devise means of preying
upon other animals and of driving all the bees from their honey-
combs so that he may have his fill of honey. In this fable, no doubt,
Nashe satirizes usurers and other contemporary parasites, the devil's
agents in the world.[234]

In *Christs Tears over Ierusalem* (1593), written against the
evils that would lead to the destruction of London as they had led
to that of Jerusalem, Nashe represents the usurer as being like "the
Foxe," who "vseth his witte and his teeth together" and "neuer
smyles but he seazeth" and "neuer talkes but he takes aduantage."[235]
Greene, in *The Blacke Bookes Messenger,* mentions an "olde Foxe
that . . . was subtill enough to spie a pad in the straw," and to see
that he was about to be cozened.[236] Harvey, in the third letter of his
Fovre Letters and Certaine Sonnets, alludes to the "slye practise of
the olde Foxe," Dr. Andrew Perne of Cambridge University,[237] and,
in *Pierces Supererogation,* says that Dr. Perne might have been "for
his preaching to geese, S. Frauncis, or S. Fox,"[238] and that "the Fox
[Dr. Perne] preacheth *Pax vobis,* to the Capons, and geese: and
neuer worse intended, then when the best pretended."[239]

Lyly, Greene, and Nashe, in their satirical pamphlets, designate
all kinds of dishonest professional men, usurers, cozeners, cheats, cut-
purses, and those in league with them as caterpillars, moths, and
cormorants. These epithets, drawn doubtless from the popular
speech of the day, imply the well-known destructiveness of caterpillars and moths and the voraciousness of cormorants. These terms
are used sometimes merely to represent abstractions, as in Nashe's
statement in *Pierce Penilesse* that "the richest garments are subject

to Times Moathfrets"[240] or the statement in Greene's *Euphues His Censure to Philautus* that "Prodigality, which . . . wasteth what time and diligence by long trauell hath purchased, is . . . a Moath to eate out the labours of men;[241] but the same terms, when used in invective, are epithets regularly applied to persons of the types mentioned.

Greene, in the prefatory epistle of *A Notable Discovery of Coosnage,* for example, writes of "Cunny-catchers" that the "*Chetors that . . . strike in at Hazard or Passage with their Dice of aduauntage, are nothing so daungerous as these base minded Caterpillars.*"[242] In the dedicatory epistle of *The Second Part of Conny-Catching,* he writes that his purpose is to "lay open to the world the villanie of these coosening caterpillers,"[243] whom in the dedication of *A Disputation Betweene a Hee Conny-Catcher and a Shee Conny-Catcher* he calls "the caterpillers of the Common-wealth."[244]

In his *Defence of Conny-Catching,* Greene has "Cuthbert Conycatcher" answer the "libellous inuectiues" of "R.G." in an attempt "to proue that we Conny-catchers are like little flies in the grasse, which liue on little leaues and doe no more harme," whereas "there bee in *Englande* other professions that bee great Conny-catchers and caterpillers, that make barraine the field wherein they baite."[245] Cuthbert accuses R.G. of writing against "poore Conny-catchers, that . . . winne fortie shillings from a churle that can spare it" but never mentioning "those Caterpillers that vndoo the poore, ruine whole Lordships, infect the common-wealth, and delight in . . . wrongfull extorting and purloyning of pelfe." Such, he says, "be the greatest Connycatchers of all."[246]

Nashe likewise, in *Christs Teares over Ierusalem,* refers to "Brokers" and "Usurers" as "those priuie Cankerwormes & Catterpillers."[247] In *A Wonderfull, strange and miraculous, Astrologicall Prognostication for this year . . . 1591,* which Nashe, satirizing the makers of almanacs, attributes to "Adam Foule-weather, Student in Asse-tronomy," it is predicted that "this yeere fruits shall be greatly eaten with Catterpillers as Brokers, Farmers, and Flatterers, which, feeding on the sweate of other mens browes," shall greatly "hinder the beautye of the spring" unless some northerly wind of God's vengeance" cleere the trees of such Catterpillers, with a hotte plague and the pestilence."[248] It is also predicted that "florishing bloomes of yong Gentlemens youth" shall be "greatly anoide with caterpillers, who shall intangle them in such statutes & recognances [sic] that they shall crie out against brokers, as Ieremy did against false prophets."[249]

Greene, in his "conny-catching" pamphlets and *A Quip for an Vpstart Courtier,* calls "conny-catchers" and cozeners of all kinds "moaths of the common wealth."[250] In *The Second Part of Conny-Catching,* they are "these moathes of the Common-wealth," who "apply their wìts to wrap in wealthy farmers with straunge and vncoth conceits";[251] in *The Blacke Bookes Messenger,* "these slye insinuating Mothworms, that eate men out of their substance vnséene";[252] and in *The Defence of Conny-Catching,* "moathes of the common-wealth, caterpillers worse then God rayned downe on Egypt."[253]

Greene and Nashe call greedy usurers, clergymen, and farmers cormorants. Greene, in *A Quip for an Vpstart Courtier,* calls usurers "Cormorantes" and represents a farmer as "a Cormorant of the common wealth, and a wretch that liues of the spoile of the needy,"[254] one of those "very Cormorants of the Country" who "deuoure the poore people with their monstrous exaction."[255] Nashe, in his *Anatomie of Absurditie,* represents certain covetous clergymen as "the cormorants of our age, who . . . haue alwaies their mouthes open to aske, and hauing felt the sweetnes of Abby Landes, . . . gape after Colledge liuing."[256]

Other conventional animal epithets used in the satirical pamphlets are "cony" (rabbit), for the victim of "conny-catchers" or cozeners;[257] "vulture," for a harlot or any dishonest person who lived at the expense of other people;[258] "woodcock," for Gabriel Harvey or anyone else whom the satirist wished to represent as being witless;[259] "viper," for a cozener, a usurer, or a Martinist;[260] "chameleon," for a flatterer;[261] "serpent," "basilisk," "cockatrice," or "crocodile," for a harlot;[262] and "leech" ("Horseleech"), for a quack doctor or a usurer.[263] The horns of cuckoldry are applied as a term of abuse to Martin by Lyly in *Pappe with an Hatchet.*[264]

The manner in which conventional ideas about animals were employed in the English satirical pamphlets between 1550 and 1600, the manner prescribed by the rhetoricians, has been shown. The same body of conventional ideas was employed in the same manner in the philosophical or moral pamphlets of the period, particularly those of Greene and Lodge.

The pamphlets of Greene that belong to this classification are *The Myrrour of Modestie* (1584), "wherein appeareth as in a *perfect Glasse howe the* Lorde deliuereth the innocent from all imminent perils, and plagueth the bloudthirstie hypocrites with deserued punishments";[265] *Planetomachia: Or, the first parte of the generall opposition of the seuen Planets* (1585), which is mainly a dispute between Saturn and Venus, each trying to prove that it has the greater and better influence upon men and their affairs; *The Debate Betweene Follie and Loue* (1587), in which "Follie" and "Loue" dispute the question *"of their power, dignitie, and superioritie"*;[266] *Penelopes Web* (1587), in which Penelope and her attendants — Eubola, Vygenia, and Ismena — converse about love and the qualities — obedience, chastity, and silence — necessary in a wife to make her husband happy; *Euphues His Censure to Philautus* (1587), which is mainly a philosophical combat between Achilles and Hector, "discouering in foure discourses, interlaced with diuerse delightfull Tragedies, The vertues necessary to be incident in euery gentleman";[267] *Morando: The Tritameron of Loue* (1587), a series of moral dissertations on love and classical friendship; *Perimedes the Blacke-Smith* (1588), in which the plot serves as a framework for a series of tales and the morals drawn from them; *The Royal Exchange* (1590), a collection of moral aphorisms.

The remaining pamphlets in the list, with the possible exception of the last one, are autobiographical in character: *Neuer too late, or, A Powder of Experience* (1590), the purpose of which is "to roote out the infectious follies, that *ouer-reaching conceits foster in the spring* time of . . . youth";[268] *Farewell to Folly* (1591), which is a disputation concerning different vices and passsions with stories to illustrate the philosophical discussions; *The Repentance of Robert Greene Maister of Artes* (1592), "wherein by himselfe is laid open his loose life, with the manner of his death";[269] *Greenes Vision* (1592), *"Conteyning a penitent passion for* the folly of his Pen";[270] *Groats-worth of Wit, bought with a Million of Repentaunce* (1596), which describes "the follie of youth, the falsehoode of makeshift flatterers, the miserie of the negligent, and mischiefes of deceiuing Courtezans";[271] and *Orpharion* (1599), in which Orpheus and Arion tell "diuers Tragicall and Comicall Histories," illustrating the *"branches of Vertue, ascending and descending by degrees,"* united *"in the glorious praise of women-kind."*[272]

Similar pamphlets of Lodge are *The Divel Coniured* (1596), in which a hermit discourses on the subject of virtue, and *Wits Miserie, and the Worlds Madnesse: Discouering the Deuils Incarnat of this Age* (1596), a discourse on the nature, effects, and remedies of the seven deadly sins.

These pamphlets of Greene and Lodge contain the familiar type of allusions to the lion's noble courage,[273] the fox's slyness and craftiness,[274] the ass's stupidity and dullness,[275] the ape's facetiousness and imitativeness and killing its young by hugging it,[276] the sheep's innocence and simplicity,[277] the porcupine's shooting its quills,[278] the bear's licking into shape its shapeless newborn cub,[279] the cur's baseness and cowardice,[280] the lynx's keen eyesight,[281] the cuckold's horns,[282] the shrew's ill temper,[283] the woodcock's witlessness,[284] the vulture's and the crow's appetite for carrion,[285] the peacock's pride,[286] the swan's singing at the approach of death,[287] the gudgeon's gullibility,[288] the serpent's wickedness and subtlety,[289] the chameleon's changeableness,[290] the crocodile's hypocritical weeping,[291] the sinister presence of the "pad in the straw,"[292] and the wasp's irascible temper.[293]

Deceivers are represented as "Hiena-like alluring to destruction."[294] A well-known passage, which is thought to refer to Shakespeare, represents him as "an vpstart Crow, beautified with our feathers . . . with his *Tygers heart wrapt in a Players hide.*"[295] He who conceals an evil nature under an appearance of innocence is compared to a wolf in sheep's clothing,[296] to one who carries a lamb in his shield and a tiger in his bosom,[297] and to a kite or a gripe in dove's feathers.[298] Those who persist in wicked ways are said to wallow "with the Sow in their wickednesse"[299] or to become more addicted to wickedness "as ye Salamander, the more he lyeth in the fire, the more desirous he is of the flame."[300] Likewise he who "thirsteth continuallie after wickednesse" is compared to him who is "stung with the serpent / *Dipsas*" and "burneth, but can neuer be cooled."[301] The proper deference which the inexperience of youth owes the experience of age is implied in the statement that it is "vnfite for the yoong fawne to leade the old bucke."[302]

The lion's abhorrence of adultery in the lioness is cited as an example for men to follow.[303] To attempt something in vain is "with the wolues to barke against the moone."[304] It is said that no woman is so cruel that she cannot be won, "no Tygre so fierce which cannot

be tamed,"[305] and "no Hawke so ramage which cannot be man-
ned."[306] To "buy fading pleasure with repentance" is compared to
being "tickled with the venime of *Tarantula*" and dying laughing[307]
and to riding "*Seianus* horse for his beauty" and perishing.[308] A
young lover in one story says, "*Ephestion* coulde handle *Bucephalus,*
but not ride *Bucephalus* . . . so although I haue, as a nouice, gazed
at the temple of *Venus,* yet I am not able to discourse of the Deitie
of *Cupid.*"[309] Trying to do that which is contrary to the nature of
things is compared to feeding "with the Deere against the wind"[310]
and to swimming "with the crabbe . . . against the stream."[311]

To proffer friendship when none is intended is said to be like the
cat's feigning sleep to entrap the mouse,[312] and like promising a fish
and presenting a scorpion;[313] "to trust sundry men," like seeking
for "an Eele amongst many Scorpions";[314] and to find "good precepts tempered amongst idle matter," like finding "Eeles amongst
Scorpions."[315] Loyalty is enjoined by bidding him who runs "with
the Hare holde not with the Hound."[316]

No explanation is needed for such well-known allusions to
Aesopic fables as the mountains' swelling and bringing forth a
mouse,[317] the fox and the grapes,[318] the fox's or the wolf's having his
skin pulled over his ears for "prying into the lion's den,"[319] the
cock's preferring "a barlie corne before a pretious Jewel,"[320] the
ant's providing for the time of necessity while the grasshopper passed
his days in idleness,[321] and the lion's showing gratitude to Androcles.[322]

The proverbial "Crowes foote" in the eyes is the conventional
symbol for the marks of age;[323] and the treading of the "blacke Oxe"
on the feet, for the heaviness of the cares and responsibilities of
life.[324] Returning to one's folly is compared to a dog's returning to
his vomit[325] and to a sow's returning to her wallowing in the mire.[326]
The unrighteousness of wicked men is said to increase with age as
does the crookedness of the eagle's beak[327] or the blackness of the
starfish ("the sea Star . . . most blacke being old").[328] The nature
of man is called so perverse "that hee . . . with the thirstie Serpent
Hydaspis is neuer satisfied."[329] Persons with "baze minds" are compared to "the Scarab Flye," which delighteth only to liue in dung
and mire."[330]

The infatuated lover gazing upon the beauty of his mistress is
compared to "the Leopard looking at the Panthers painted skinne"

and being "caught as a pray";[331] to the "bird Trochilus," unable to "keepe from the infectious Crockedile";[332] to "the *Camelion*" feeding upon the air;[333] to "the flie *Pyralis*" that "cannot liue out of the flame";[334] and to the candlefly, "so long dallying in the flame, that he scorcht his wings, & in time consumed his whole body."[335]

He who aspires foolishly to that which is regarded as unattainable is admonished to keep within bounds, "least in soaring with the Hobby" he "fall to the ground with the Larke."[336] But he who aspires to do "nothing but worthie" his wit and learning is encouraged to "carry spices" into his nest "with the Phenix"[337] and to "soare against ye sun with the Eagle."[338] It is also said that "what byrde gaseth against the sunne but the Eagle, waxeth blinde, and . . . such as step to dignitie, if vnfit fall."[339]

According to Greene, "some are so peremptorie in their opinions . . . that if the fox preach, tis to spie which is the fattest goose" and "that if *Greene* write his *Farewell to Follie,* tis to blind the world with follie, the more to shadow his owne follie."[340] The wise man "that seeketh to drawe the wicked from his follie" is compared to "the charmer" who "charmes in vaine if the Adder bée deafe."[341] All "wholesome warninges" are said to be odious to "such as are gracelesse," for "they with the spider sucke poison out of the most pretious flowers."[342]

The seven deadly sins are conventionally represented as follows: pride is compared to a peacock;[343] envy (jealousy), to a caterpillar that destroys content[344] and "a moath that secretly consumeth the life of man";[345] avarice (greed), to the insatiable "Serpent *Hydaspis*";[346] wrath, to a boar infuriated and foaming at the mouth;[347] gluttony, to the lions, apes, and swine into which Circe transformed Ulysses' men,[348] lechery, to "*the viper, whose venome is incurable*"[349] (harlots are called "the Basiliskes that kill with their eyes") ;[350] and sloth (idleness), to a slug,[351] to a "moath that sorest and soonest infecteth the mynde with many mischiefs,"[352] and to a helmet in which bees hive.[353]

Some miscellaneous examples of the employment of conventional ideas about animals in the philosophical or moral pamphlets are the comparisons between one's gradual discovering of a secret scheme and the gosling's beginning "to perceyue what the old goose meant by her wincking";[354] between one who uses dissimulation in order to conceal his true thoughts or feelings and "the Lapwing, that cryeth euer farthest from her nest";[355] between a woman who will not "bee persuaded by reason" and "the ramage Hawke" that "will hardlie be reclaimed";[356] between "mighty princes" who will not look at "homelie peasaunts" and eagles that will not "catch at flies";[357] between filial devotion in human beings and that in the animal world as exemplified by the young stork's feeding its aged parents;[358] between beauty, which "no sooner flourisheth but it fadeth," and "the Birde *Acanthis,* which hatched white, yet turneth blacke at the first storme";[359] and between a light woman and a falcon or hawk that "would come at euery lure."[360]

Chastity is represented as a woman treading "vpon the Tortuse," keeping her house, and not straying "abroad with euery wanton giglet,"[361] and the pains of conscience as a never-dying worm.[362] It is said that those "charmed with Loue, must seeke to loue, or els lacke remedy," as those "enuenomed with the Scorpion, must be healed by the Scorpion"[363] and as "the Tarantals sting could not be pulde out without Musicke."[364]

The conventional ideas about animals and the manner of employing these ideas are the same in the Elizabethan pastoral romances and realistic and picaresque tales as in the other prose writings of the period. The Elizabethan pastoral romances which will now be considered are John Grange's *The Golden Aphroditis* (1577); John Lyly's *Euphues: The Anatomy of Wit* (1579) and *Euphues and His England* (1580); Robert Greene's *Mamillia* (1583), *Arbasto: The Anatomie of Fortune* (1584), *Carde of Fancie* (1587), *Alcida: Greenes Metamorphosis* (1588), *Pandosto: The Triumph of Time* (1588), *Menaphon: Camillas Alurum to slumbering Euphues* (1589), *Tullies Loue* (1589), *Mourning Garment* (1590), and *Philomela* (1592); Thomas Lodge's *The Delectable Historie of Forbonius and Prisceria* (1584), *Rosalynde: Euphues golden legacie* (1590), *Euphues Shadow: The Battaile of the Sences* (1592), and *A Margarite of America* (1596); and Sir Philip Sidney's *Arcadia* (1590).

The realistic and picaresque tales are Thomas Deloney's *Iack of Newberie* (1596-1597), *Thomas of Reading* (1597-1600), and *The Gentle Craft* (1597-1600), and Thomas Nashe's *The Unfortvnate Traveller, Or, The Life of Iacke Wilton* (1594) and *Lenten Stuffe* (1599).

In these works appear frequently the noble, courageous, magnanimous lion;[365] the wily fox;[366] the imitative, facetious ape;[367] the dull, stupid ass;[368] the enraged, foaming boar;[369] the sweet breathed, deceitful, cruel panther;[370] the cruel, fierce tiger;[371] the ravenous wolf;[372] the simple, innocent sheep;[373] the timorous hare;[374] the cowardly cur;[375] the proverbial foot-treading black ox;[376] the ill-natured shrew;[377] the spotted leopard;[378]; the keen-sighted lynx;[379] the treacherous hyena;[380] the fierce, chaste unicorn;[381] the precious-skinned, spotted ermine;[382] the persistent ferret;[383] the intelligent, strong, mouse-fearing, dragon-hating elephant;[384] the cautious, water-troubling camel;[385] Sejanus' discriminating horse;[386] Alexander the Great's discriminating horse Bucephalus;[387] the noble, keen-sighted eagle;[388] the vainglorious peacock;[389] the self-sacrificing pelican;[390] the domineering, proud cock;[391] the rare phoenix;[392] the crocodile-befriending "Trochilus";[393] the filially devoted stork;[394] the despicable cuckoo;[395] the winter-brooding halcyon;[396] the rare or supposedly non-existent white crow[397] and black swan;[398] the singing dying swan;[399] the gentle, chaste, constant dove ("turtle") ;[400] the foolish goose;[401] the ominous, croaking raven;[402] the carrion crow;[403] the base, fickle, carrion-loving kite;[404] and the iron-digesting ostrich.[405]

Just as frequently in the same works appear the hypocritical, weeping crocodile;[406] the changeable, air-nourished chameleon;[407] the subtle, wicked, venomous serpent;[408] the deadly basilisk and cockatrice;[409] the fire-dwelling salamander;[410] the matricidal viper;[411] the thirst-producing serpent "Dipsas";[412] the insatiably thirsty serpent "Hidaspis";[413] the "deaf adder";[414] the poisonous spider and tarantula;[415] the venomous, stinging scorpion;[416] the industrious bee and ant;[417] the devouring moth and caterpillar;[418] the never-dying worm of conscience;[419] the slow-moving snail;[420] the venomous toad;[421] the changeable octopus ("polypus") ;[422] the home-keeping tortoise;[423] the fish deceived by a baited hook;[424] the contrary, back-ward-moving crab;[425] the benumbing fish "Torpedo";[426] the ink-emitting fish "Sepia";[427] and the affectionate, music-loving dolphin.[428]

The numerous allusions in the pastoral romances to falconry and hawking,[429] the proverbial horns of cuckoldry,[430] the snake in the grass,[431] the pad in the straw,[432] and the lapwing's crying ever farthest from its nest[433] already have been pointed out.

The conventional types of incidents involving animals are particularly significant because their occurrence in the Elizabethan pastoral romances shows the persistence of a tradition which links the Elizabethan pastoral romance with the medieval romance. One of these types is the conventional conflict in which a knight, the champion of goodnesss and righteousness, overcomes a dragon, a lion, or some other beast representing evil. The other type is the conventional situation in which a lion fawns upon a knight or a lady.

In Sidney's *Arcadia,* the knight Pyrocles, disguised as Zelmane, kills a lion that is pursuing Philoclea; and the knight Musidorus, disguised as Dorus, kills a bear that is pursuing Pamela.[434] Pyrocles' (Zelmane's) killing the lion is compared to Hercules' killing the Nemean lion.[435]

Similar incidents occur in Lodge's *Rosalynde* and *Euphues Shadow*. In *Rosalynde,* the knight Rosader kills a lion that threatens harm to the sleeping Saladyne.[436] In *Euphues Shadow,* the knight Rabinius, at Claetia's behest, kills four beasts in "Libia": a rhinoceros "pursuing a tender and yoong infant,"[437] two lions, and a monster "headed like vnto *Hidra, . . .* hauing the back partes of him like a Centaure."[438]

In Lodge's *A Margarite of America,* Margarite and Fawnia, resting beside a spring, àre surprised by a lion, "accustomed to refresh himselfe at that spring," and Fawnia is "rent in peeces (in that she had tasted too much of fleshly loue) ." Margarita expects the same fate, "but see the generositie and vertue of the beast . . . in the place of tearing her peecemeale," he lays his head gently in her lap, "licking hir milkewhite hand, and shewing al signes of humilitie, in steede of inhumanitie."[439]

All of these incidents conform to the conventional pattern: the knights — Pyrocles, Musidorus, Rosader, and Rabinius — and the young woman, Margarita, are paragons of "vertue" and, therefore, cannot be harmed by evil; the beasts are conventional representations of evil.

The Elizabethan (that is to say, Renaissance) conception of "vertue," of which much is said in the pastoral romances,[440] needs to be explained more fully. The "vertue" emphasized in the Elizabethan pastoral romances may be defined as that gentleness or ideal excellence of character which resulted from the possession of the four cardinal virtues: prudence, justice, fortitude, and temperance.

This conception, no doubt, stemmed from, or at least was in the sixteenth century almost synonymous with, what the Italians in the time of the Renaissance called *"virtù,"* or distinction expressed in individuality, personal force, and self-assertion.[441] This "vertue" or *"virtù"* implied the governing of the passions by the exercise of reason in accordance with the Aristotelian ethics of humanistic moral philosophy.

Thus Sidney's Pyrocles and Musidorus and Lodge's Rosader and Rabinius, being represented as paragons of "vertue," become types of the "complete man" of the Renaissance, who was supposed to possess "vertue" (*"virtù"*).[442]

The exploits of Pyrocles, Musidorus, Rosader, and Rabinius are reminiscent of those of Guy of Warwick, Sir Beues of Hamtoun, and other knights in the medieval romances. In both Elizabethan pastoral romance and medieval romance, the old conflict between good and evil, between virtue and vice, is conventionally represented by the conflict in which a virtuous knight overcomes evil in beast form.[443]

In the Elizabethan pastoral romances, because of the influence of humanistic moral philosophy, the same conventional conflict may justly be interpreted as a dramatization of the triumph of reason over the passions. In Lodge's *Rosalynde*, for example, Rosader may be said to represent the Elizabethan ideal of "vertue"; and the lion, the passions. It is significant that this lion, when Rosader encounters him, has not molested Saladyne, who is asleep, but appears likely to do him harm. It should be pointed out that Saladyne has recently repented and turned away from his past evil passions, and is seeking to embrace "vertue."[444] The lion's "hate to pray on dead carkasses" is, then, no doubt, an expression of the idea that base passions, though they may still beset, can no longer rule over the man who, repenting of his hitherto ill-governed passions and choosing "vertue," has become as if dead to those passions. Following his conversion, Saladyne has chosen to be governed by "vertue" (reason).

The chief mark of "vertue" in a woman, according to the Elizabethan pastoral romances, was her unassailable purity, her chastity. Lodge's Margarita is a type of the "vertuous" woman. Margarita, because of her chastity, her "vertue," is unharmed by the lion,[445] as Josian, in *The Romance of Sir Beues of Hamtoun,* for the same reason, was unharmed by two lions;[446] but Fawnia, Margarita's companion, because she lacks "vertue," is "rent in peeces."[447]

Another link between the Elizabethan pastoral romances and the medieval romances is the depicting of knightly tournaments by describing in detail, among other things, the combatants' equipment and heraldic devices, which usually are distinguished by conventional animal symbolism. Examples of this type of description are to be found in Sidney's *Arcadia*[448] and Lodge's *A Margarite of America*.[449] One such passage is Sidney's description of the "forsaken Knight" (Musidorus disguised) ready for the combat with Amphialus on "the Iland within the Lake":

> So past he [Amphialus] over into the Iland, ... where he founde the forsaken Knight, attired in his owne liverie, as blacke, as sorrowe it selfe could see it selfe in the blackest glasse: his ornaments of the same hew, but formed in the figure of Ravens, which seemed to gape for carrion: onely his raynes were snakes, which finely wrapping themselves one within the other, their heads came together to the cheekes and bosses of the bit, where they might seeme to bite at the horse, and the horse (as he champte the bit) to bite at them; and that the white foame was ingendred by the poysonous furie of the combatt. His *Impresa* was a *Catoblepta* which so long lies dead, as the Moone (whereto it hath so naturall a sympathie) wants her light. The worde signified that *The Moone wanted not the light, but the poore beast wanted the Moones light*. He had in his headpiece, a whippe, to witnesse a self-punishing repentaunce."[450]

A similar example is Lodge's description of Arsadachus and his chariot at the beginning of a tournament:

> *Arsadachus* in his triumphant chariot drawen by foure white vnicornes entred the tiltyard, vnder his seate the image of fortune, which he seemed to spurne, with this posie, *Quid haec?* on his right hand enuy, whom he frowned on by hir this posie, *Nec haec;* on his left hand the portraiture of *Cupid,* by whome was written this posie, *Si hic;* ouer his head the picture of *Margarita* with this mot, *Sola haec.*[451]

The unicorns of this passage symbolize in the conventional manner not only Arsadachus' strength and fierceness in battle but also Margarita's chastity.

In some of the pastoral romances and other prose writings of the Elizabethan period are allusions to "blind Bayard" or "bold Bayard," which express the idea of forwardness or rash boldness.[452] These allusions, no doubt, are based on medieval romance material, for Bayard, the horse of Renaud de Montauban (Rinaldo di Montalbano), one of the most famous personages in the French and Italian Charlemagne romances of the twelfth and thirteenth centuries, had passed into popular legend and had become proverbial.

In Nashe's *Lenten Stuffe,* a realistic tale about Great Yarmouth and its herring fisheries, are two fables which, like the previously described incidents of the pastoral romances, deserve special consideration because of their possible significance beyond the stories themselves. The two fables together constitute Nashe's "praise of the Red Herring."[453]

In one of these fables, Nashe tells how the herring became "King of all fishes." According to the story, a falcon, which had escaped from confinement on its passage from Ireland to England, not finding its ordinary prey, struck at a fish, and thereby came within reach of a "sharke or Tuberon," which swallowed her, bells and all. "The newes of this murderous act, carried by the Kings fisher to the eares of the land foules," caused all the birds to marshal their forces and make war upon the fishes. "An old goshawke for general was appointed, for Marshall of the field, a Sparhawke"; and "of the rest euery one" was appointed "to that place by nature hee was most apt for"; the peacocks were heralds; the cocks, trumpeters; the kestrels, standard bearers; the cranes, pikemen; and the woodcocks, demilances. These birds went to "the water foules" and "besought Ducke and Drake, Swanne and Goose, Halciones & Seapies, Cormorants & Sea-guls, of their oary assistance."[454]

Information having been carried to the fishes by "the puffin, that is halfe fish halfe flesh (a Iohn indifferent, and an *Ambodexter* betwixt either)," they prepared for the danger and met in council to choose a king. Since the larger members of "the fraternity of fishes," the "greater giants of Russia & Island, as the whale, the sea horse, the Norse, the wasserman, the Dolphin, the Grampoys," ridiculed the idea of danger, the council decided to choose the king from among the smaller and weaker fishes. After much deliberation, the fishes elected as their king the herring, "whom they might depose when they list, if he should begin to tyranize, and such a one as of himselfe were able to make a sound partie if all fayled." All the fishes saluted the herring with *"Viue le roy,* God saue the King, . . . saue only the Playse and the Butte, that made wry mouthes at him, and for their mocking haue wry mouthes euer since." The herring "euer since weares a coronet on his head, in token that hee is as he is."[455]

The narration of the war between birds and fishes and its outcome Nashe leaves to "some *Alfonsus, Poggius,* or *AEsope* to vnwrap," and proceeds to his second fable, in which he tells how the herring's color was changed, "camelionized," by smoking, from white to red, and what consequences ensued.[456]

In this second fable, a herring fisherman, having sold smoked red herrings throughout England, "spirted ouer seas to Rome with a Pedlers packe of the" and sold all but three. The "Popes caterer" asked what it was he had to sell and learned that it was "the king of fishes."[457] Twice the peddler, seeing the caterer's eagerness to buy a herring, raised the price above what the caterer thought the Pope would be willing to pay, and ate the unsold fish. The Pope, however, determined to have a herring, sent back his caterer, who succeeded in buying the last herring, which was half spoiled.[458]

The herring, when cooked, caused a stink which offended the Pope's nostrils and threatened to drive everyone out of the papal palace:[459]

> Negromantick sorcery, . . . some euill spirit of an heretique it is, which thus molesteth his Apostoliqueship. The friars and munkes caterwawled, from the abbots and priors to the nouices, wherefore *tanquam in circo,* wee will trownse him in a circle, and make him tell what Lanterneman or groome of Hecates close stoole hee is, that thus nefariously and proditoriously prophanes & penetrates our holy fathers nostrils. What needes there any more ambages? the ringoll or ringed circle was compast and chalkt out, and the king of fishes, by the name of the king of fishes, coniured to appeare in the center of it; but . . . hee was a king absolute, and would not be at euery mans cal, & if frier *Pendela* and his fellowes had any thing to say to him, in his admiral court of the sea let them seek him, and neither in Hull, Hell, nor Halifax.[460]

The clergymen, "seeing that by theyr charmes and spels they could spell nothing of him, fell to a more charitable suppose," that "it might bee the distressed soule of some king that was drowned, who, being long in Purgatorie, and not releeued by the praiers of the church," had leave, "in that disguised forme, to haue egresse and regresse to Rome, to craue theyr beneuolence . . . to helpe him onward to his iourney to *Limbo patrum* or *Elisium.*" They supposed that in order to make them believe that he had sustained these tortures in purgatory "hee thought to represent to all theyr sences the image and *Idea* of his combustion and broyling there and the horrible stinch of his sins accompanying," both "vnder his frying and broyling on the coles in the Popes kitchin, & the intollerable smel or stink" that he sent forth.

"*Vna voce*," therefore, "in this plene to Pope *Vigilius* they ran," and desired that "this king of fishes might first haue Christian buriall, next, that hee might haue masses sung for him, and last, that for a saint hee would canonize him." All of these things the Pope granted in order "to bee ridde of the filthy redolence" of the king of fishes.[461]

Nashe adds the following passage to his story:

> I had well nie forgot a speciall poynt of my Romish history, & that is how Madam *Celina Cornificia,* one of the curiousest curtizans of Rome, when the fame of the king of fishes was canon-rored in her eares, shee sent all hir iewells to the iewish lumbarde to pawne, to buy and encaptiue him to her trenchour, but her purueyour came a day after the faire, & as he came, so hee farde, for not a scrap of him but the cobs of the two Herrings the Fisherman had eaten remained of him, and those Cobbes, rather than hee woulde go home wyth a sleeuelesse answer, he bought at the rate of fourescore ducats.[462]

Nashe, referring, no doubt, to these fables, comments scornfully upon those readers who, "out of some discourses of mine, which . . . I knew not what to make of my selfe," have fished out "such a deepe politique state meaning as if I had al the secrets of court or commonwealth at my fingers endes." To such readers, according to Nashe, "Talke I of a beare, . . . it is such a man that emblazons him in his armes, or of a woolfe, a fox, or a camelion, any lording whom they do not affect it is meant by."[463]

In spite of Nashe's statements, however, the animal symbolism in these two fables appears to have the same kind of significance as the animal symbolism in the political poems of the fourteenth and fifteenth centuries. It seems at least possible that the "praise of the Red Herring" might have been intended as an allegory of the coming of the Tudors to the English throne and of subsequent momentous happenings during the period of their rule.

According to such an interpretation, the falcon's being swallowed up by the shark in the sea between Ireland and England would be taken to symbolize Henry Tudor's coming, upon invitation, from Ireland in 1485 and his being accepted by the English. Henry Tudor, who became King Henry VII of England, was related by blood to the royal house of Lancaster and had made certain pledges to win the support of some of the house of York; as king, therefore, he came nearer than anyone else to being acceptable to both houses after the long and bloody Wars of the Roses. The war between the birds and the fishes in the first fable and the herring's changing its color from white to red in the second, which may be regarded almost as a continuation of the first, seem to suggest, however vaguely, the Wars of the Roses, in which, if either side can be said to have been victorious, the red rose of Lancaster won the ascendancy over the white rose of York.

In the second fable, which may be considered the second part of his "praise of the Red Herring," what Nashe calls his "Romish history" possibly may be interpreted as an allegory of Henry VIII's troublous dealings with the Pope, which led to Henry's break with Rome and his marriage with Catherine of Aragon. The Pope's difficulty in purchasing the herring, the impossibility of doing anything with the cooked king of fishes, and the "intollerable smel or stink" that assailed the papal nostrils certainly suggest the actual difficulties that Henry VIII's independent actions must have caused the Pope as recorded in history. "Madam *Celina Cornificia*" and her purchase of the king of fishes likewise seem to suggest Catherine of Aragon and her marriage with Henry VIII.

If such an interpretation of Nashe's "praise of the Red Herring" be not too farfetched, the logical conclusion to be drawn is that the "Red Herring" symbolizes the Tudors, whose rule, from the accession of Henry VII to the English throne, Nashe celebrates, praising in particular Henry VIII's independence in his dealings with Rome. The "praise of the Red Herring" becomes, then, an expression of nationalism, of English patriotic pride, and Nashe's nearest approach to open praise of Queen Elizabeth, a Tudor, the daughter of Henry VIII.

The extensive and varied employment in Elizabethan non-religious prose literature of conventional ideas about animals is evidence that these ideas constitute, as will be pointed out in the next chapter, a major aspect of the literary expression characteristic of the English Renaissance.

CHAPTER FIVE

Conventional Ideas about Animals as a Major Aspect of the Literary Expression Characteristic of the English Renaissance

THE CONVENTIONAL IDEAS ABOUT ANIMALS IN EUROPEAN LITERATURE, Continental and English, were drawn from that ocean of animal lore which came into being as the result of the gradual accumulation and retention in language, both spoken and written, of the impressions gained by men through contemplation from time immemorial of their fellow creatures of the animal world. The conventionalization of these ideas about animals was the natural consequence of the long-continued habit of associating the same ideas with the same creatures.

Almost the whole body of conventional ideas about animals contained in ancient literature and popular tradition, Greek, Latin, and Oriental, came down through the Middle Ages and into the Renaissance with little, if any, modification. Medieval and Renaissance writers on natural history and writers in general followed ancient authorities, particularly Aristotle and Pliny, without questioning the accuracy of these men's information. Hence a great many erroneous and fantastic ideas were perpetuated.

In the second half of the sixteenth century, Lyly, Greene, Lodge, Nashe, Sidney, and other writers of English prose were following in their works conventions which had become well established earlier than the sixteenth century. Whether these Elizabethan writers drew upon native British animal lore, upon the natural histories, or upon other classical sources for their animal imagery, they made this material conform to the same conventional patterns. These writers showed little regard for scientific accuracy but used in the traditional manner whatever traditional ideas about animals would serve the purposes of illustration or description in accordance with the precepts laid down by the humanist teachers and the rhetoricians.

The conventionality pertaining to the animal imagery in Elizabethan non-religious prose writings is threefold: the ideas about animals had themselves become conventional; it was conventional to employ these ideas in literature; and the ways in which they were employed were conventional. The lion and the fox, for example, with certain well-known ideas crystallized around them, were almost invariably used to symbolize certain qualities of human character, either in similes, metaphors, and proverbial maxims or in fables and other forms of allegory. In relation to the Elizabethan prose writers' employment of animal conventions, the importance of the precedents established by the almost universal use of such conventions and by the influence of the humanist educators and the rhetoricians can hardly be overemphasized.

Conventional animal symbolism is present as a distinguishing feature in nearly every kind of prose writing of the period 1550-1600. If all the conventional ideas about animals were taken out of the Elizabethan prose writings, the concreteness, the picturesqueness, the color, the quaintness, the variety, and the charm of the literary expression in these works would be almost entirely gone. Although Elizabethan writers like Grange, Lyly, Greene, and Lodge, who wrote in that peculiarly ornate style called euphuism, often made excessive use of conventional ideas about animals, multiplying similes, metaphors, and proverbial sayings, these men gave to their literary style its distinctive character chiefly by their use of this kind of imagery. Though excessively used, these animal illustrations were nevertheless apt vehicles for the expression of ideas.

The flourishing of these animal conventions in the English non-religious prose of the period bespeaks a continued humanistic interest in preserving ancient, especially Greek and Roman, knowledge (or what passed for knowledge) of zoological species, whether real or imaginary, through the study of the natural histories of Aristotle and Pliny or other works that included material from these authorities. The humanist educators' and rhetoricians' emphasis upon the importance of acquiring from these ancient authorities a knowledge of beasts, birds, and other creatures leaves no doubt as to why English Renaissance authors went to the natural histories for material which would serve the purposes of literary expression. Even the supplementing of this material with ideas about native British creatures is a following of the prescriptions of the humanist educators and the rhetoricians.

The non-religious prose literature of the English Renaissance, then, shows in its animal conventions the continuity of the study of natural history in relation to language and literature from ancient to modern times and the preservation of conventional ideas about animals that have remained in use since the Renaissance.

Many of the common words and expressions that are still used in spoken and written English on both sides of the Atlantic Ocean show the persistence in the living language of the same conventional animal symbolism that was employed in Elizabethan times and earlier. Fox, ass, ape, lion, tiger, leopard, chimera, eagle, swan, goose, halcyon, crocodile, serpent, bee, wasp, ant, wolf in sheep's clothing, crow's foot in the eyes, and snake in the grass, to list only a few of many such examples that could be mentioned, are still given the same figurative meanings that English-speaking people of the sixteenth century and earlier gave them.

To study the conventions of animal symbolism in Elizabethan prose literature is to study, in one of its phases, the English Renaissance, and to be able to comprehend and interpret the significance of this period as a time of transition in language and literature from the medieval to the modern age.

Appendix

[A LIST OF THE ANIMALS, BIRDS, REPTILES, AND OTHER CREATURES USED
conventionally in Elizabethan non-religious prose and the ideas pertaining to them. The asterisks indicate British creatures accompanied by some conventional ideas that are as likely to be of native
as of classical or Biblical origin.]

ADDER (deaf adder or death adder) : its stopping its ears against the
  voice of the charmer, Topsell, *Historie of Serpents*, pp. 57-58;
  Painter, *The Palace of Pleasure* (Jacobs), I, 219; *ibid.*, III, 48;
  Works of Lodge (Hunterian Club), II, ii, 61; *Works of Greene*
  (Grosart), III, 27; *ibid.*, VIII, 155; *ibid.*, IX, 95, 273, 310-11;
  ibid., X 70; *ibid.*, XI, 169; *ibid.*, XII, 174.
AMPHISBAENA: *see* Serpent.
*ANT: its industriousness and providence, *Works of Aristotle* (Smith
  and Ross), IV, 622; *Pliny: Natural History* (Rackham), III,
  499; Lyly, *Euphues* (Arber), pp. 153, 157; Lyly, *Euphues and
  His England* (Arber), p. 235; *Works of Lodge* (Hunterian
  Club), I, iii, 50; *ibid.*, II, iii, 10; *ibid.*, III, iv, 17; *ibid.*, IV, i, 114;
  Works of Greene (Grosart), XII, 146-48; *Works of Nashe* (Mc-
  Kerrow), II, 285; *Works of Deloney* (Mann), pp. 27-29, 38.
APE: its facetiousness and imitativeness, Topsell, *Historie of Foure-
  Footed Beastes*, pp. 2-7; Gosson, *The Ephemerides of Phialo*
  (Huntington Library facsimile), pp. 41 *verso*, 47 *recto;* Grange,
  The Golden Aphroditis, pp. A iv *verso*, L ii *recto*, N *recto;* Lyly,
  Euphues and His England (Arber), pp. 280, 458; *Works of Lyly*
  (Bond), III, 412; *Works of Lodge* (Hunterian Club), II, ii, 31;
  ibid., IV, i, 8, 16, 90; *Works of Greene* (Grosart), III, 83, 88;
  ibid., IX, 163, 333; *ibid.*, XII, 144; *Works of Nashe* (McKer-
  row), I, 224, 242, 290, 306, 385; *ibid.*, II, 40, 142, 269, 277, 301;
  ibid., III, 313, 352; *Works of Harvey* (Grosart), I, 234; *ibid.*, II,
  82, 222-24; *Works of Sidney* (Feuillerat), I, 87; *ibid.*, III, 45;
  Works of Deloney (Mann), p. 208; — its killing its young by
  hugging, *Pliny: Natural History* (Rackham), III, 151; Topsell,
  Historie of Foure-Footed Beastes, pp. 2-7; Lyly, *Euphues and His*

England (Arber), p. 215; *Works of Lyly* (Bond), III, 412; *Works of Lodge* (Hunterian Club), II, iii, 44; *ibid.*, IV, i, 14; *Works of Greene* (Grosart), VIII, 26; *ibid.*, X, 238; *Works of Harvey* (Grosart), II, 7; — its lasciviousness (leading apes in hell), Topsell, *Historie of Foure-Footed Beastes,* pp. 2-7; *A Petite Pallace of Pettie His Pleasure* (Hartman), p. 207; Riche, *Farewell to Militarie Profession (Eight Novels,* etc.), p. 79; Lyly, *Euphues* (Arber), pp. 75, 87; Lyly, *Euphues and His England* (Arber), p. 282; *Works of Lodge* (Hunterian Club), II, iii, 57, 59; *Works of Greene* (Grosart), IX, 167.

ASP: its hostility to the ichneumon (mongoose), *Works of Aristotle* (Smith and Ross), IV, 612; *Pliny: Natural History* (Rackham), III, 65; Topsell, *Historie of Serpents,* p. 448; *Works of Lodge* (Hunterian Club), I, ii, 9-10; *ibid.*, I, iii, 23; — its incurable bite, *Pliny: Natural History* (Rackham), III, 63; Lyly, *Euphues and His England* (Arber), pp. 381, 401; *Works of Lodge* (Hunterian Club), I, iii, 49; *ibid.*, II, iii, 51; *ibid.*, III, iv, 49; *Works of Greene* (Grosart), VII, 202; *ibid.*, IX, 47; — its vengeance upon the killer of its mate, *Pliny: Natural History* (Rackham), III, 63; *Works of Nashe* (McKerrow), III, 121.

*ASS: Balaam's ass, *Works of Greene* (Grosart), II, 122; *ibid.*, IV, 63; — the ass's stupidity and dullness, Topsell, *Historie of Foure-Footed Beastes,* p. 20; *Works of Ascham* (Giles), III, 153-54, 156; *A Petite Pallace of Pettie His Pleasure* (Hartman), p. 263; Gosson, *The School of Abuse,* p. 11; Gosson, *The Ephemerides of Phialo* (Huntington Library facsimile), pp. 1 *verso*-2 *recto;* Grange, *The Golden Aphroditis,* p. M ii *verso;* Lyly, *Euphues* (Arber), pp. 145, 203; Lyly, *Euphues and His England* (Arber), p. 239; *Works of Lyly* (Bond), III, 400-402; *Works of Lodge* (Hunterian Club), I, ii, 9-10; *ibid.*, I, v, 8; *ibid.*, II, ii, 19; *ibid.*, II, iii, 32, 53, 103; *ibid.*, IV, i, 10; *Works of Greene* (Grosart), II, 92, 106-107, 122, 156, 186; *ibid.*, III, 58, 83; *ibid.*, IV, 63; *ibid.*, VI, 70; *ibid.*, VII, 8; *ibid.*, VIII, 186, 192, 204, 220; *ibid.*, IX, 163, 200, 221, 230, 232-33, 243; *ibid.*, X, 99, 223; *ibid.*, XI, 7, 27, 211, 238, 288, 292; *ibid.*, XII, 42, 68; *Works of Nashe* (McKerrow), I, 90, 102, 134, 161, 196, 199, 207, 240, 242, 282, 288, 290, 314, 328-29, 333; *ibid.*, II, 216, 220, 229, 233, 259, 297, 299; *ibid.*, III, 38, 54, 85, 112, 128, 130, 193, 341-42, 351, 368; *Works of Harvey* (Grosart), I, 233-34; *ibid.*, II, 23, 34, 37, 39-43, 52, 59, 69, 73, 79, 82, 90-91, 113-14, 222, 236-38, 245-65, 292, 294, 322, 331; *ibid.*, III, 10-11, 14, 29, 32-33, 35, 61-62; *Works of Sidney* (Feuillerat), II, 83; *Works of Deloney* (Mann), pp. 14, 17, 28, 61, 126, 217.

BASILISK (cockatrice): its fatal glance and breath, *Pliny: Natural History* (Rackham), III, 57, 59; Topsell, *Historie of Serpents*, pp. 119-25; Painter, *The Palace of Pleasure* (Jacobs), III, 171; *A Petite Pallace of Pettie His Pleasure* (Hartman), p. 15; Gosson, *The School of Abuse*, p. 23; Grange, *The Golden Aphroditis*, p. H iii *recto;* Lyly, *Euphues and His England* (Arber), pp. 363, 409; *Works of Lodge* (Hunterian Club), I, v, 68; *ibid.*, II, iii, 43; *Works of Greene* (Grosart), II, 74, 228, 233, 262; *ibid.*, III, 194, 239, 251; *ibid.*, IV, 37, 65; *ibid.*, VI, 45; *ibid.*, VII, 123; *ibid.*, VIII, 26, 71, 134; *ibid.*, IX, 27-28, 60, 189, 200; *ibid.*, X, 235; *ibid.*, XI, 152; *ibid.*, XII, 174; *Works of Nashe* (McKerrow), I, 25, 77, 236; *ibid.*, II, 140; *ibid.*, III, 63; *Works of Harvey* (Grosart), II, 57, 59; *ibid.*, III, 37; *Works of Deloney* (Mann), p. 24; — its hostility to the weasel, *Pliny: Natural History* (Rackham), III, 59; Gosson, *The School of Abuse*, p. 28; *Works of Lodge* (Hunterian Club), I, iii, 23.

BEAR: its licking its newborn cubs into shape, *Works of Aristotle* (Smith and Ross), IV, 580; *Pliny: Natural History* (Rackham), III, 91; Topsell, *Historie of Foure-Footed Beastes*, p. 37; Gosson, *The Ephemerides of Phialo* (Huntington Library facsimile), p. 1; *Works of Lyly* (Bond), III, 413; *Works of Greene* (Grosart), XII, 101; *Works of Nashe* (McKerrow), III, 153.

*BEE: its carrying a pebble as ballast in a high wind, *Works of Aristotle* (Smith and Ross), IV, 622; *Pliny: Natural History* (Rackham), III, 447; Gosson, *The School of Abuse*, p. 33; — its hiving in a helmet (symbolical of idleness or peace), Lyly, *Euphues and His England* (Arber), p. 472; *Works of Greene* (Grosart), XII, 28; — its industriousness and social instincts, *Works of Aristotle* (Smith and Ross), IV, 622; *Pliny: Natural History* (Rackham), III, 439; Gosson, *The Ephemerides of Phialo* (Huntington Library facsimile), p. 68 *verso;* Lily, *Euphues and His England* (Arber), pp. 252, 261-66; *Works of Lodge* (Hunterian Club), II, iii, 8, 10; *Works of Greene* (Grosart), V, 208; *ibid.*, VIII, 65; *ibid.*, IX, 86; *ibid.*, X, 105; *Works of Nashe* (McKerrow), I, 221, 354; *ibid.*, II, 28; *Works of Sidney* (Feuillerat), I, 94; *ibid.*, II, 20; *Works of Deloney* (Mann), pp. 29, 38, 204; — its portending the gift of eloquence by alighting on a person's mouth, *Pliny: Natural History* (Rackham), III, 467; Grange, *The Golden Aphroditis*, p. H iii *recto;* *Works of Greene* (Grosart), VII, 138; — its possessing a sting as well as honey, Lyly, *Euphues* (Arber), p. 79; Lyly, *Euphues and His England* (Arber), p. 472; *Works of Lodge* (Hunterian Club), II, iii, 54; *Works of Greene* (Grosart), III, 184; *ibid.*, VIII, 219; *ibid.*, IX,

59, 221; *ibid.,* XI, 118, 173; *ibid.,* XII, 158, 219; *Works of Nashe* (McKerrow), II, 185; — its spontaneous generation in the carcass of a bullock, *Pliny: Natural History* (Rackham), III, 475; *Works of Harvey* (Grosart), II, 233; — its stinging but once and dying,. *Works of Aristotle* (Smith and Ross), IV, 622; *Pliny: Natural History* (Rackham), III, 469; Grange, *The Golden Aphroditis,* p. K iv *recto; Works of Lodge* (Hunterian Club), IV, i, 80; — its sucking honey from the same flower whence the spider sucked poison, Painter, *The Palace of Pleasure* (Jacobs), II, 301; *A Petite Pallace of Pettie His Pleasure* (Hartman), pp. 6, 203, 241; Grange, *The Golden Aphroditis,* pp. N iii *verso*-N iv *recto;* Lyly, *Euphues* (Arber), pp. 35, 100, 107, 360; *Works of Lodge* (Hunterian Club), I, ii, 35; *Works of Greene* (Grosart), XII, 180; *Works of Nashe* (McKerrow), I, 30; *Works of Deloney* (Mann), p. 19; — the drone's indolence, Topsell, *Historie of Serpents,* pp. 78-82; Gosson, *The Ephemerides of Phialo* (Huntington Library facsimile), pp. 2, 37 *verso; Works of Lodge* (Hunterian Club), II, iii, 36; *Works of Greene* (Grosart), IX, 133; *ibid.,* X, 71; *Works of Nashe* (McKerrow), I, 159, 352.

*BEETLE (scarab) : its preferring dung to the fairest flower, *A Petite Pallace of Pettie His Pleasure* (Hartman), p. 240; Gosson, *The School of Abuse,* p. 9; *Works of Greene* (Grosart), IV, 132-33; *ibid.,* V, 16; *ibid.,* VIII, 26; *ibid.,* X, 246; *ibid.,* XI, 87; *Works of Nashe* (McKerrow), I, 262; — its spontaneous generation in the carcass of an ass, *Pliny: Natural History* (Rackham), III, 475.

*BOAR: its foaming ferocity, Topsell, *Historie of Foure-Footed Beastes,* p. 697; *Wilson's Arte of Rhetorique* (Mair), p. 171; *Works of Lodge* (Hunterian Club), IV, i, 83.

BULL: its losing its strength when tied to a fig tree, Topsell, *Historie of Foure-Footed Beastes,* p. 63; Lyly, *Euphues* (Arber), p. 78; *Works of Lodge* (Hunterian Club), III, iv, 54; *Works of Deloney* (Mann), p. 82.

*BUMBLEBEE (humblebee) : *see* Beetle.

*BUTTERFLY: its insignificance and idleness, Gosson, *The Ephemerides of Phialo* (Huntington Library facsimile), p. 65 *verso; Works of Deloney* (Mann), pp. 27-28, 248.

*BUZZARD: its baseness and witlessness, *Works of Ascham* (Giles), III, 201; *Works of Lodge* (Hunterian Club), IV, i, 108-109; *Works of Greene* (Grosart), VIII, 195; *Works of Nashe* (McKerrow), I, 9, 24; *Works of Harvey* (Grosart), II, 277.

*CALF: its stupidity, Lyly, *Euphues* (Arber), p. 203; *Wilson's Arte* *of Rhetorique* (Mair), p. 163; *Works of Greene* (Grosart), II, 225; *Works of Nashe* (McKerrow), III, 54.

CAMEL: its troubling the water by trampling in it before drinking, *Works of Aristotle* (Smith and Ross), IV, 580; *Pliny: Natural History* (Rackham), III, 51; Topsell, *Historie of Foure-Footed Beastes,* pp. 92-99; Lyly, *Euphues and His England* (Arber), pp. 378, 380; *Works of Nashe* (McKerrow), II, 226; *Works of Harvey* (Grosart), III, 34.

*CANDLEFLY: its insignificance and its flying about the fire until its wings were singed, *Works of Aristotle* (Smith and Ross), IV, 605; *Pliny: Natural History* (Rackham), III, 473; *A Petite Pallace of Pettie His Pleasure* (Hartman), p. 237; Lyly, *Euphues* (Arber), p. 66; *Works of Greene* (Grosart), II, 30, 95, 97-98, 259; *ibid.,* V, 50; *ibid.,* VII, 171; *ibid.,* VIII, 68, 71, 223; *ibid.,* IX, 31; *ibid.,* X, 244; *ibid.,* XI, 139; *ibid.,* XII, 28; *Works of Nashe* (McKerrow), I, 260, 376; *ibid.,* II, 221.

*CAT AND MOUSE: the cat's watching for the mouse and playing with it before devouring it, *A Petite Pallace of Pettie His Pleasure* (Hartman), p. 93; Gosson, *The School of Abuse,* p. 25; Grange, *The Golden Aphroditis,* p. H ii *verso;* Lyly, *Euphues and His England* (Arber), p. 420; *Works of Lodge* (Hunterian Club), I, iii, 15; *ibid.,* II, iii, 35; *Works of Greene* (Grosart), II, 93, 292; *ibid.,* IV, 109, 130; *ibid.,* V, 84-85; *ibid.,* VIII, 48; *ibid.,* IX, 81, 167; *ibid.,* X, 207; *Works of Deloney* (Mann), p. 230.

*CATERPILLAR (canker): its greediness and destructiveness, Topsell, *Historie of Serpents,* pp. 102-11; *A Petite Pallace of Pettie His Pleasure* (Hartman), p. 23; Lyly, *Euphues* (Arber), p. 39; Lyly, *Euphues and His England* (Arber), p. 315; *Works of Lyly* (Bond), III, 394; *Works of Lodge* (Hunterian Club), I, iii, 5, 24, 37; *ibid.,* I, v, 34; *ibid.,* II, i, 37; *ibid.,* IV, i, 34, 69; *Works of Greene* (Grosart), II, 129, 132; *ibid.,* IV, 22, 120; *ibid.,* V, 231; *ibid.,* VII, 12, 122; *ibid.,* VIII, 16, 47, 71; *ibid.,* IX, 29, 171, 218, 263, 343; *ibid.,* X, 9, 29, 72, 89, 97, 125, 201, 267-68; *ibid.,* XI, 47, 50-52, 59-60, 76, 78; *ibid.,* XII, 254; *Works of Nashe* (McKerrow), I, 213; *ibid.,* II, 97, 106, 284-85; *ibid.,* III, 382, 391; *Works of Deloney* (Mann), p. 28.

CATOBLEPAS (catoblepta): a heavy-headed beast whose eyes were fatal to all who beheld them, *Pliny: Natural History* (Rackham), III, 57; *Works of Sidney* (Feuillerat), I, 455.

CHAMELEON: its changeableness, *Works of Aristotle* (Smith and Ross), IV, 503; *Pliny: Natural History* (Rackham), III, 87; Topsell, *Historie of Serpents,* p. 114; *A Petite Pallace of Pettie His Pleasure* (Hartman), p. 40; Gosson, *The Ephemerides of Phialo*

(Huntington Library facsimile), p. 40 *recto; Works of Lodge*
Hunterian Club), I, ii, 25; *ibid.,* I, v, 54; *ibid.,* IV, i, 10; *Works
of Greene* (Grosart), II, 24, 120, 156, 225, 261, 263; *ibid.,* III,
148, 179, 184; *ibid.,* IV, 202; *ibid.,* VII, 107, 196; *ibid.,* VIII, 22;
ibid., IX, 56-57, 63, 79; *ibid.,* XI, 76; *ibid.,* XII, 28; *Works of
Nashe* (McKerrow), I, 6, 75, 221-26; *ibid.,* III, 204; — its feeding
upon air, *Pliny: Natural History* (Rackham), III, 87; Topsell,
Historie of Serpents, p. 114; Gosson, *The Ephemerides of Phialo*
(Huntington Library facsimile), p. 53 *recto;* Lyly, *Euphues*
(Arber), p. 45; *Works of Lodge* (Hunterian Club), IV, i, 10;
Works of Greene (Grosart), III, 127; *ibid.,* VI, 57; *ibid.,* VIII,
180; *ibid.,* XII, 28, 70, 133; *Works of Nashe* (McKerrow), I, 36;
Works of Sidney (Feuillerat), II, 27.

*CHICKEN: chickens' being counted before being hatched, Gosson,
The Ephemerides of Phialo (Huntington Library facsimile), p.
19 *recto;* — the hen's gathering her chickens under her wings,
Wilson's Arte of Rhetorique (Mair), pp. 125, 191; Gosson, *The
School of Abuse,* p. 40; Gosson, *The Ephemerides of Phialo*
(Huntington Library facsimile), p. 44 *verso; Works of Nashe*
(McKerrow), II, 42-43, 57.

CHIMERA: a monster of the imagination, Topsell, *Historie of Foure-
Footed Beastes,* p. 458; Painter, *The Palace of Pleasure* (Jacobs),
III, 17, 212; Gosson, *The Ephemerides of Phialo* (Huntington
Library facsimile), p. 45 *recto; Works of Lyly* (Bond), III, 402;
Works of Greene (Grosart), V, 76-77; *ibid.,* VIII, 17; *Works of
Nashe* (McKerrow), II, 181; *ibid.,* III, 217.

*CHOUGH: its baseness and sourness of disposition, *Works of Greene*
(Grosart), XI, 250, 285; *Works of Nashe* (McKerrow), I, 163;
ibid., II, 107; *ibid.,* III, 211.

*COCK: its vain pride and domineering, *Pliny: Natural History*
(Rackham), III, 323; Gosson, *The Ephemerides of Phialo* (Huntington Library facsimile), p. 2 *verso;* Lyly, *Euphues* (Arber),
p. 106; Lyly, *Euphues and His England* (Arber), pp. 331, 366,
397, 473; *Works of Lodge* (Hunterian Club), I, v, 8; *ibid.,* II, ii,
27-28; *ibid.,* II, iii, 8, 43, 64; *Works of Greene* (Grosart), II, 285,
295; *ibid.,* III, 222; *ibid.,* IV, 133; *ibid.,* IX, 233; *Works of Nashe*
(McKerrow), I, 44, 170, 257; *ibid.,* II, 85; *ibid.,* III, 149; *Works
of Sidney* (Feuillerat), III, 22; *Works of Deloney* (Mann), pp.
28, 155, 162, 170; — its preferring a barleycorn to a pearl, *A
Petite Pallace of Pettie His Pleasure* (Hartman), p. 257; *Works
of Lodge* (Hunterian Club), I, v, 80; *Works of Greene* (Grosart), IV, 132; *ibid.,* VI, 179; *ibid.,* VII, 35; *Works of Nashe*
(McKerrow), I, 31; *ibid.,* III, 329-30.

*CONY (rabbit): its simplicity (victim of cozeners), *Works of Greene* (Grosart), X, 8-9, 17-18; *ibid.*, XI, 53.

*CORMORANT: its voraciousness, *Works of Lodge* (Hunterian Club), IV, i, 73; *Works of Greene* (Grosart), XI, 253, 283, 285; *Works of Nashe* (McKerrow), I, 36, 160, 164-65, 204; *ibid.*, II, 106; *ibid.*, III, 178.

*CRAB: its swimming ever against the stream and crawling sideways (or backward), *Works of Lyly* (Bond), III, 404; *Works of Greene* (Grosart), II, 28, 30, 178, 199, 264; *ibid.*, III, 78, 98, 192-93, 204; *ibid.*, IV, 15, 17, 86; *ibid.*, V, 41, 51-52, 97, 99, 115, 164; *ibid.*, VII, 78, 203; *ibid.*, IX, 32, 60-61, 66, 221; *ibid.*, XII, 75; *Works of Nashe* (McKerrow), I, 91, 307; *ibid.*, II, 128, 275; *Works of Deloney* (Mann), pp. 163, 234-35, 260-61.

CRANE: its carrying stones for ballast or for silence on long flights, *Works of Aristotle* (Smith and Ross), IV, 597; *Pliny: Natural History* (Rackham), III, 331; Lyly, *Euphues and His England* (Arber), p. 416; — its warring with the Pygmies, *Works of Aristotle* (Smith and Ross), IV, 597; *Pliny: Natural History* (Rackham), III, 329; *Works of Sidney* (Feuillerat), I, 404; — its watchfulness maintained by holding a stone with one foot to keep awake, *Pliny: Natural History* (Rackham), III, 329; 331; *Wilson's Arte of Rhetorique* (Mair), p. 191; Gosson, *The School of Abuse*, pp. 33-34; Lyly, *Euphues and His England* (Arber), p. 216.

CROCODILE: its deceitfulness (feigned tears), Topsell, *Historie of Serpents*, pp. 126-41; Painter, *The Palace of Pleasure* (Jacobs), I, 245; Gosson, *The School of Abuse*, p. 15; Grange, *The Golden Aphroditis*, pp. C ii *verso*, N *verso*; Lyly, *Euphues* (Arber), p. 75; Lyly, *Euphues and His England* (Arber), pp. 364, 379; *Works of Lodge* (Hunterian Club), I, ii, 33; *ibid.*, II, iii, 15, 35; *ibid.*, III, iii, 71; *ibid.*, IV, i, 29, 52; *Works of Greene* (Grosart), II, 228, 257, 259-60; *ibid.*, V, 71, 94, 155; *ibid.*, VIII, 104, 138, 142; *ibid.*, IX, 47, 191, 199, 297; *ibid.*, X, 199, 235; *ibid.*, XI, 35; *Works of Nashe* (McKerrow), I, 184, 224; *ibid.*, II, 307; *ibid.*, III, 96; *Works of Harvey* (Grosart), I, 287; *Works of Sidney* (Feuillerat), II, 186; *Works of Deloney* (Mann), p. 232; — its friendship with the bird trochilus, *Works of Aristotle* (Smith and Ross), IV, 612; *Pliny: Natural History* (Rackham), III, 65; Topsell, *Historie of Foure-Footed Beastes*, pp. 448-51; Topsell, *Historie of Serpents*, pp. 126-41; Gosson, *The School of Abuse*, p. 45; Lyly, *Euphues* (Arber), p. 44; Lyly, *Euphues and His England* (Arber), p. 379; *Works of Greene* (Grosart), V, 60; *ibid.*, VII, 72; *Works of Harvey* (Grosart), III, 21-22.

*CROW: its blackness and appetite for carrion, *A Petite Pallace of Pettie His Pleasure* (Hartman), p. 69; *Works of Lodge* (Hunterian Club), II, iii, 10; *ibid.*, III, iv, 17; *ibid.*, IV, i, 27; *Works of Greene* (Grosart), II, 86, 131; *ibid.*, III, 153; *ibid.*, XII, 144; *Works of Nashe* (McKerrow), III, 320; *Works of Sidney* (Feuillerat), I, 82; *Works of Deloney* (Mann), p. 182; — its parading vainly in other birds' feathers, *Works of Lodge* (Hunterian Club), I, ii, 1; *Works of Greene* (Grosart), XII, 144; — the crow's foot in the eye (symbolical of the marks of age), *Works of Greene* (Grosart), XII, 158; — the white crow's rareness or supposed non-existence, Painter, *The Palace of Pleasure* (Jacobs), III, 154; Gosson, *The School of Abuse,* pp. 19-20; Lyly, *Euphues and His England* (Arber), p. 366; *Works of Harvey* (Grosart), I, 288.

*CUCKOO: its despicable nature shown by its imposing on other birds (depositing its eggs in other birds' nests), *Works of Aristotle* (Smith and Ross), IV, 563-64, 618; *Pliny: Natural History* (Rackham), III, 309, 311; *Works of Lodge* (Hunterian Club), III, iv, 61; *Works of Harvey* (Grosart), III, 10-11; — the cuckold's chorister, *Works of Greene* (Grosart), XI, 54, 143, 213, 219.

*CUR: *see* Dog.

*DEER: its antlers (horns) as a symbol of cuckoldry, Painter, *The Palace of Pleasure* (Jacobs), II, 36-37; *A Petite Pallace of Pettie His Pleasure* (Hartman), pp. 219, 225; Riche, *Farewell to Militarie Profession (Eight Novels,* etc.), p. 128; Lyly, *Euphues and His England* (Arber), p. 284; *Works of Lyly* (Bond), III, 404; *Works of Lodge* (Hunterian Club), IV, i, 6, 17, 92; *Works of Greene* (Grosart), II, 114, 229; *ibid.*, IV, 89, 133; *ibid.*, VI, 78; *ibid.*, X, 257, 260; *ibid.*, XI, 143, 155, 219; *ibid.*, XII, 229; *Works of Nashe* (McKerrow), I, 162; *ibid.*, II, 246, 263, *ibid.*, III, 348, 387, 390-91, 394-95; *Works of Deloney* (Mann), pp. 7, 32, 50; — the buck more skillful than the fawn in choosing food, *Works of Greene* (Grosart), II, 112-13, 278; *ibid.*, VIII, 44, 59; *ibid.*, IX, 185; — the deer's feeding against the wind, *Works of Lodge* (Hunterian Club), I, v, 59-60; *Works of Greene* (Grosart), III, 195; *ibid.*, V, 62, 115; *ibid.*, VII, 73; *ibid.*, VIII, 81; — the deer's standing at gaze and being shot with an arrow, *Pliny: Natural History* (Rackham), III, 81, 83; Topsell, *Historie of Foure-Footed Beastes,* pp. 126-31; Lyly, *Euphues* (Arber), pp. 78-79; *Works of Greene* (Grosart), II, 129, 188, 274; *ibid.*, IV, 82; *ibid.*, V, 72; *ibid.*, IX, 29; — the hart's (or stag's) eating dittany to extract arrows from the flesh, *Pliny: Natural History* (Rackham), III, 71; Topsell, *Historie of Foure-Footed Beastes,* pp. 126-

31; Grange, *The Golden Aphroditis,* p. F iii *recto;* Lyly, *Euphues* (Arber) , p. 61; *Works of Greene* (Grosart) , IV, 58; — the hart's (or stag's) renewing its youth by eating serpents, *Pliny: Natural History* (Rackham) , III, 85; *Works of Deloney* (Mann) , p. 266; — the stag's burning serpents with its breath, *Pliny: Natural History* (Rackham) , III, 609; Lyly, *Euphues and His England* (Arber) , p. 462; — the wounded deer's (or hart's) shedding tears, Lyly, *Euphues* (Arber) , p. 120; *Works of Greene* (Grosart) , VII, 113; *Works of Sidney* (Feuillerat) , I, 61.

*DIDAPPER: its diving and emerging as if playing hide and seek with a pursuer, *Works of Lyly* (Bond) , III, 395; *Works of Nashe* (McKerrow) , I, 256-57; *ibid.,* III, 195.

DIPSAS: its fatal thirst-producing bite, Topsell, *Historie of Serpents,* pp. 147-51; Lyly, *Euphues and His England* (Arber) , p. 347; *Works of Greene* (Grosart) , III, 36-37; *ibid.,* VIII, 140; *ibid.,* XI, 217.

*DOG: its affectionate fawning, *Works of Aristotle* (Smith and Ross) , IV, 488; *Wilson's Arte of Rhetorique* (Mair) , p. 173; Lyly, *Euphues* (Arber) , p. 109; Lyly, *Euphues and His England* (Arber) , p. 392; *Works of Greene* (Grosart) , III, 99, 236; *ibid.,* V, 103; *ibid.,* VIII, 189, *ibid.,* IX, 259; *Works of Nashe* (McKerrow) , I, 224; *ibid.,* II, 260, 297; *ibid.,* III, 106, 196, 369; — its antipathy for the cat, Gosson, *The School of Abuse,* p. 17; *Works of Greene* (Grosart) , VIII, 190; — its enviousness and tenacity in the pursuit of its quarry, *A Petite Pallace of Pettie His Pleasure* (Hartman) , pp. 186, 200-207; Riche, *Farewell to Militarie Profession (Eight Novels,* etc.) , p. 145; Gosson, *The School of Abuse,* p. 25; Gosson, *The Ephemerides of Phialo* (Huntington Library facsimile) , pp. 6 *recto,* 56 *recto;* Grange, *The Golden Aphroditis,* p. C ii *verso; Works of Lyly* (Bond) , III, 405, 407, 412; *Works of Lodge* (Hunterian Club) , II, ii, 4, 19, 61; *ibid.,* IV, i, 39, 44; *Works of Greene* (Grosart) , III, 78; *ibid.,* IV, 63; *ibid.,* V, 250; *ibid.,* X, 199, 207, 214; *Works of Nashe* (McKerrow) , I, 185; *ibid.,* II, 109, 113, 237, 298, 321; *ibid.,* III, 191, 315, 351, 354; — its returning to its own vomit, Painter, *The Palace of Pleasure* (Jacobs) , I, 199; *A Petite Pallace of Pettie His Pleasure* (Hartman) , p. 270; Lyly, *Euphues and His England* (Arber) , pp. 319, 329; *Works of Lodge* (Hunterian Club) , I, ii, 32; *Works of Greene* (Grosart) , II, 121; *ibid.,* VIII, 94, 138, *ibid.,* X, 140; *ibid.,* XI, 34; *ibid.,* XII, 163, 176; 251; *Works of Nashe* (McKerrow) , I, 74-75; *Works of Harvey* (Grosart) , II, 168; — the cur's cowardly, contemptible nature, *A Petite Pallace of Pettie His Pleasure* (Hartman) , p. 216; Gosson, *The School of Abuse,*

p. 7; Gosson, *The Ephemerides of Phialo* (Huntington Library facsimile), pp. 1 *recto*, 13 *recto*; Lyly, *Euphues* (Arber), p. 55; *Works of Lodge* (Hunterian Club), III, iv, 52; *ibid.*, IV, i, 70; *Works of Greene* (Grosart), II, 15, 31, 92, 154, 264; *ibid.*, III, 79, 102, 181, 222, 236; *ibid.*, IV, 17, 39-40, 57, 61-62, 122, 229; *ibid.*, V, 83; *ibid.*, X, 97; *ibid.*, XI, 223, 253; *Works of Nashe* (McKerrow), I, 60, 175, 191; *ibid.*, II. 240, 290; *ibid.*, III, 106, 119; *Works of Harvey* (Grosart), III, 62; *Works of Sidney* (Feuillerat), II, 115, 119; *ibid.*, III, 64; *Works of Deloney* (Mann), pp. 24, 121, 127; — the dog in the manger, Lyly, *Euphues* (Arber), p. 191; *Works of Deloney* (Mann), p. 25; — the greyhound's swiftness, *Works of Ascham* (Giles), III, 103; *Works of Sidney* (Feuillerat), I, 415-16, 517; — the mastiff's sturdiness and fierceness, *Works of Nashe* (McKerrow), II, 240, 291; *Works of Sidney* (Feuillerat), I, 312, 459, 517; *ibid.*, II, 119-20; — the old dog's bite the sorest, *A Petite Pallace of Pettie His Pleasure* (Hartman), p. 124; *Works of Nashe* (McKerrow), I, 321; the puppy's impudence, Gosson, *The Ephemerides of Phialo* (Huntington Library facsimile), p. 18 *verso*; *Works of Lyly* (Bond), III, 404; *Works of Greene* (Grosart), X, 241; *Works of Deloney* (Mann), p. 179.

DOLPHIN: its gentleness and affection for mankind, *Works of Aristotle* (Smith and Ross), IV, 631; *Pliny: Natural History* (Rackham), III, 177; Gosson, *The Ephemerides of Phialo* (Huntington Library facsimile), p. 86 *verso*; Lyly, *Euphues* (Arber), p. 93; *Works of Lodge* (Hunterian Club), I, ii, 26; *Works of Greene* (Grosart), IV, 81, 85; *ibid.*, XII, 68-69; — harbinger of storms, Grange, *The Golden Aphroditis*, p. A iv *verso*; *Works of Lodge* (Hunterian Club), II, iii, 62-63; *Works of Greene* (Grosart), IV, 74; *Works of Nashe* (McKerrow), I, 59; — its love of music, *Pliny: Natural History* (Rackham), III, 179; Gosson, *The Ephemerides of Phialo* (Huntington Library facsimile), p. 86; *verso*; Lyly, *Euphues* (Arber), pp. 66, 78-79; *Works of Lodge* (Hunterian Club), I, ii, 26; *ibid.*, II, iii, 25; *Works of Greene* (Grosart), VI, 36-37; *ibid.*, VIII, 210; *ibid.*, XII, 68-69.

DOVE (turtle): its gentleness and constancy. *Works of Aristotle* (Smith and Ross), IV, 612-13; *Pliny: Natural History* (Rackham), III, 359; *Wilson's Arte of Rhetorique* (Mair), p. 48; *A Petite Pallace of Pettie His Pleasure* (Hartman), p. 226; Gosson, *The Ephemerides of Phialo* (Huntington Library facsimile), p. 13 *recto*; Grange, *The Golden Aphroditis*, pp. K ii *verso*, L iv *verso*; Lyly, *Euphues* (Arber), p. 153; Lyly, *Euphues and His England* (Arber), pp. 273, 312, 323, 333, 335, 454; *Works of*

sart), IV, 68-69, 280; *ibid.,* V, 277; *ibid.,* VI, 184; *ibid.,* VII, 37, 72, 155; *ibid.,* IX, 30; *Works of Nashe* (McKerrow), III, 85; — its shaking dust into the stag's (or other birds') eyes, *Pliny: Natural History* (Rackham), III, 303; Lyly, *Euphues and His England* (Arber), p. 462; *Works of Nashe* (McKerrow), II, 219; the eagle a symbol of war, *Works of Greene* (Grosart), V, 61-62, 72; *ibid.,* VII, 72; *ibid.,* IX, 130, 256; — the eagle's feathers' consuming other birds' feathers, *Pliny: Natural History* (Rackham), III, 303; Grange, *The Golden Aphroditis,* p. L ii *recto;* Lyly, *Euphues* (Arber), p. 58; Lyly, *Euphues and His England* (Arber), p. 214; — the eagles' gathering to a carcass, *Works of Greene* (Grosart), VIII, 108; *ibid.,* IX, 209, *ibid.,* X, 250-51; *Works of Sidney* (Feuillerat), I, 264; — the Eagle of Caucasus' tearing Prometheus' liver, Painter, *The Palace of Pleasure* (Jacobs), I, 205; — the ossifrage's inferiority to other eagles, *Pliny: Natural History* (Rackham), III, 299; *Works of Greene* (Grosart), III, 198; *ibid.,* IV, 61; *ibid.,* IX, 33.

*EEL: its slipperiness, Lyly, *Euphues* (Arber), p. 97; Lyly, *Euphues and His England* (Arber), pp. 381, 414; *Works of Greene* (Grosart), VII, 62; *ibid.,* VIII, 219; *ibid.,* XII, 235-36; *Works of Nashe* (McKerrow), I, 98.

ELEPHANT: its aversion to the mouse, *Pliny: Natural History* (Rackham), III, 23; *Works of Lodge* (Hunterian Club), II, iii, 35; *Works of Greene* (Grosart), V, 61; *ibid.,* VII, 72, 201; *ibid.,* IX, 96, 104; — its engendering serpents with its breath, *Pliny: Natural History* (Rackham), III, 609; Lyly, *Euphues and His England* (Arber), p. 462; — its gentleness toward weaker beings, *Pliny: Natural History* (Rackham), III, 19; Gosson, *The Ephemerides of Phialo* (Huntington Library facsimile), p. 68 *verso;* — its great size and strength, *Pliny: Natural History* (Rackham), III, 19; Gosson, *The School of Abuse,* p. 28; Lyly, *Euphues* (Arber), p. 135; Lyly, *Euphues and His England* (Arber), p. 347; *Works of Lodge* (Hunterian Club), IV, i, 10, 20; *Works of Greene* (Grosart), II, 144-45, 156, 177; *ibid.,* XI, 47, 51, 132; *Works of Nashe* (McKerrow), I, 282; *ibid.,* III, 220; *Works of Sidney* (Feuillerat), I, 300; *Works of Deloney* (Mann), p. 40; — its helping a lost human being find his way, *Pliny: Natural History* (Rackham), III, 9; Gosson, *The Ephemerides of Phialo* (Huntington Library facsimile), p. 68 *verso; Works of Deloney* (Mann), p. 81; — its helping its fellows out of pitfalls, *Pliny: Natural History* (Rackham), III, 19; Gosson, *The School of Abuse,* p. 46; — its hostility to the serpent (dragon), *Pliny: Natural History* (Rackham), III, 27, 29; Lyly, *Euphues and His*

England (Arber), p. 372; *Works of Greene* (Grosart), II, 74; *Works of Nashe* (McKerrow), I, 121; *Works of Deloney* (Mann), p. 81; — its intelligence, *Pliny: Natural History* (Rackham), III, 3; Gosson, *The Ephemerides of Phialo* (Huntington Library facsimile), p. 68 *verso; Works of Lodge* (Hunterian Club), III, iv, 73; *Works of Nashe* (McKerrow), II, 285.

*ERMINE: its precious spotted skin, Lyly, *Euphues and His England* (Arber), p. 282; *Works of Lodge* (Hunterian Club), II, iii, 15, 63; *ibid.*, III, iv, 56; *Works of Greene* (Grosart), II, 263.

*FALCON (or hawk): its stooping to the lure and always being reclaimed to the fist and mewed even though sometimes inclined to be haggard, Lyly, *Euphues* (Arber), pp. 35, 41, 127; Lyly, *Euphues and His England* (Arber), p. 372; *A Petite Pallace of Pettie His Pleasure* (Hartman), pp. 21, 24, 64, 113, 172, 239; Grange, *The Golden Aphroditis,* pp. H *recto,* J iii *recto;* Gosson, *The School of Abuse,* p. 43; *Works of Lodge* (Hunterian Club), I, iii, 17; *ibid.*, I, v, 73, 112, 118; *ibid.*, II, iii, 62; *ibid.*, III, iv, 27, 69; *Works of Greene* (Grosart), II, 21, 25, 38, 93, 102-103, 112-13, 122, 129, 153, 169, 190, 198; *ibid.*, III, 39-40, 209, 215; *ibid.*, IV, 43, 56, 91, 103, 120, 141, 286; *ibid.*, V, 56-57; *ibid.*, VI, 68, 163, 176, 180, 192; *ibid.*, VII, 34, 37, 68, 116, 162, 167; *ibid.*, VIII, 25, 96, 134, 143-44, 222; *ibid.*, IX, 33, 41, 64, 132, 185, 200, 206, 302; *ibid.*, X, 19, 239; *ibid.*, XI, 7, 14, 44, 138; *ibid.*, XII, 36-37, 237, 242, 265; *Works of Nashe* (McKerrow), I, 126; *ibid.*, II, 169; *Works of Sidney* (Feuillerat), I, 435; *ibid.*, II, 45; *Works of Deloney* (Mann), p. 160.

*FERRET: its persistence, *Pliny: Natural History* (Rackham), III, 153; Gosson, *The School of Abuse,* p. 25; *Works of Lodge* (Hunterian Club), II, iv, 30; *Works of Greene* (Grosart), X, 9, 18, 210; *ibid.*, XI, 53; *Works of Nashe* (McKerrow), I, 63; *ibid.*, III, 78; *Works of Sidney* (Feuillerat), I, 237; *Works of Deloney* (Mann), p. 174.

*FISH: its being deceived and caught with a baited hook, Riche, *Farewell to Militarie Profession* (*Eight Novels,* etc.), pp. 34-35; Gosson, *The Ephemerides of Phialo* (Huntington Library facsimile), p. 3; Lyly, *Euphues* (Arber), pp. 35, 63; Lyly, *Euphues and His England* (Arber), pp. 353, 392, 469; *Works of Lodge* (Hunterian Club), I, v, 72, 111; *Works of Greene* (Grosart), II, 27, 38, 93, 108, 113-14, 129, 255-56; *ibid.*, III, 66, 208-209; *ibid.*, IV, 67, 120; *ibid.*, VIII, 47, 73; *ibid.*, IX, 29, 65-66; *ibid.*, XI, 7; *Works of Nashe* (McKerrow), I, 112, 361; *ibid.*, II, 124, 299; *Works of Sidney* (Feuillerat), I, 244, 279, 300; *Works of Deloney* (Mann), p. 152; — the minnow's swimming in schools and nibbling at the bait, Lyly, *Euphues* (Arber), p. 97; Grange, *The Golden Aphroditis,* p. P iii *recto; Works of Greene* (Grosart), II, 31; *ibid.,* XI, 139; *Works of Nashe* (McKerrow), I, 112.

*FLEA: its insignificance and provocativeness, *Wilson's Arte of Rhetorique* (Mair), p. 126; Lyly, *Euphues* (Arber), p. 85; *Works of Lodge* (Hunterian Club), I, v, 97; *ibid.,* IV, i, 26; *Works of Greene* (Grosart), II, 29, 53; *ibid.,* III, 15, 81, 141; *ibid.,* IV, 110, 276; *ibid.,* V, 79, 216; *ibid.,* VIII, 106; *ibid.,* XI, 71, 173, 265-66; *Works of Nashe* (McKerrow), I, 195; *ibid.,* III, 38, 206; *Works of Deloney* (Mann), p. 200.

*FLY: *see* Candlefly.

*FOX: its craftiness, slyness, *Works of Aristotle* (Smith and Ross), IV, 488; *Pliny: Natural History* (Rackham), III, 75; Topsell, *Historie of Foure-Footed Beastes,* p. 221; *Wilson's Arte of Rhetorique* (Mair), p. 173; *Works of Ascham* (Giles), III, 153-54, 156; *A Petite Pallace of Pettie His Pleasure* (Hartman), pp. 18, 97, 207; Gosson, *The School of Abuse,* pp. 19, 38; Gosson, *The Ephemerides of Phialo* (Huntington Library facsimile), p. 2; Grange, *The Golden Aphroditis,* p. G iv *recto;* Lyly, *Euphues* (Arber), pp. 35, 41, 75, 87; Lyly, *Euphues and His England* (Arber), pp. 260-61, 319, 322, 327, 337, 364, 475; *Works of Lodge* (Hunterian Club), II, ii, 6, 21, 23, 27-28; *ibid.,* III, iv, 30, 70; *ibid.,* IV, i, 8; *Works of Greene* (Grosart), II, 27, 63, 108, 111, 118-19, 132, 163, 263; *ibid.,* III, 16, 198, 208-209; *ibid.,* IV, 108-109, 130, 242; *ibid.,* V, 49, 84-85; *ibid.,* VI, 119; *ibid.,* VIII, 44, 58; *ibid.,* IX, 33, 43, 65, 228; *ibid.,* X, 89, 205, 219; *ibid.,* XI, 13, 52, 63; *ibid.,* XII, 120-21, 227; *Works of Nashe* (McKerrow), I, 93, 95, 174-75, 208, 220-26, 260, 292, 295; *ibid.,* II, 94, 99, 259-60; *ibid.,* III, 122, 214, 316, 362; *Works of Harvey* (Grosart), I, 179, 205, 288; *ibid.,* II, 23, 54, 168, 294, 297, 302, 306, 311-14; *Works of Deloney* (Mann), p. 29; — the fox and the grapes, Lyly *Euphues and His England* (Arber), p. 313; *Works of Lodge* (Hunterian Club), I, v, 105; *Works of Greene* (Grosart), II, 52; *ibid.,* V, 233; — the fox cubs' learning by the old fox's example, *Works of Greene* (Grosart), IV, 17-18; *ibid.,* VIII, 44; — the fox's having his skin pulled over his ears for presumptuously prying into the lion's den, *Works of Greene* (Grosart), VII, 22.

*GNAT: its insignificance, *Wilson's Arte of Rhetorique* (Mair), p. 8; Gosson, *The School of Abuse,* pp. 9-10; Grange, *The Golden Aphroditis,* p. N iii *recto; Works of Lodge* (Hunterian Club), I, ii, 3; *Works of Greene* (Grosart), II, 156, 177; *ibid.,* XI, 47, 51;

Works of Nashe (McKerrow), I, 173, 376; *ibid.*, III, 220; *Works of Harvey* (Grosart), I, 223.

GOAT: its always having fever (ague), *Pliny: Natural History* (Rackham), III, 141; Lyly, *Euphues and His England* (Arber), p. 422; *Works of Deloney* (Mann), p. 75; — its breathing through the ears, *Pliny: Natural History* (Rackham), III, 141; *Works of Nashe* (McKerrow), II, 231; its lecherousness, *Pliny: Natural History* (Rackham), III, 141; Topsell, *Historie of Foure-Footed Beastes,* pp. 230-31; Grange, *The Golden Aphroditis,* pp. K recto, M ii verso; *Works of Greene* (Grosart), III, 165; *Works of Nashe* (McKerrow), I, 207-208.

*GOOSE: its drinking as deep as the gander, Lyly, *Euphues and His England* (Arber), p. 275; — its filling its throat with gravel for silence when flying over Mount Taurus, Gosson, *The School of Abuse,* pp. 33-34; — its foolishness, *Wilson's Arte of Rhetorique* (Mair), p. 136; Gosson, *The School of Abuse,* p. 33; Lyly, *Euphues* (Arber), p. 109; *Works of Nashe* (McKerrow), I, 281; *ibid.*, II, 28; *ibid.*, III, 333; — the old goose's ability to see the gosling wink, *Works of Greene* (Grosart), II, 108; *ibid.*, VIII, 52-53; — the gosling's beginning to perceive the meaning of the old goose's winking, *Works of Greene* (Grosart), V, 70; — the uselessness of shoeing the gander, *Works of Nashe* (McKerrow), II, 230.

*GREYHOUND: *see* Dog.

GRIFFIN ("griffon," "griphon," "gryphon"): its bearing the "Smaragdus" (emerald) to its nest as a defense against serpents, *Works of Lodge* (Hunterian Club), II, ii, 38-39; *ibid.*, II, iii, 13; — its covetousness, *Works of Lodge* (Hunterian Club), II, ii, 38-39; *Works of Greene* (Grosart), III, 224; *ibid.*, V, 55, 60; *ibid.*, VII, 67, 71.

*GUDGEON: its gullibility, Gosson, *The Ephemerides of Phialo* (Huntington Library facsimile), p. 37 verso; Lyly, *Euphues* (Arber), pp. 68, 97; *Works of Lodge* (Hunterian Club), I, iii, 14; *ibid.*, IV, i, 10; *Works of Greene* (Grosart), XI, 28; *Works of Nashe* (McKerrow), III, 213.

HALCYON (kingfisher): its breeding during the "halcyon days" of midwinter and hatching its brood in a nest on the calm sea, *Works of Aristotle* (Smith and Ross), IV, 542, 616; *Pliny: Natural History* (Rackham), III, 349, 351; Gosson, *The Ephemerides of Phialo* (Huntington Library facsimile), p. 36 verso; Lyly, *Euphues and His England* (Arber), p. 215; *Works of Lodge* (Hunterian Club), I, v, 4; *Works of Greene* (Grosart), II, 30; *ibid.*, III, 205; *ibid.*, VIII, 58; *ibid.*, XI, 156; *Works of*

Nashe (McKerrow), III, 182; — its whiteness when young becoming black with age, *Works of Lodge* (Hunterian Club), I, v, 11; *Works of Greene* (Grosart), VIII, 78-79; *ibid.,* XII, 206.

*HARE: its prolificness, *Pliny: Natural History* (Rackham), III, 151, 153; Gosson, *The Ephemerides of Phialo* (Huntington Library facsimile), p. 27 *verso;* Lyly, *Euphues* (Arber), p. 76; — the hare and the hound (injunction against running with the hare and holding with the hound), Lyly, *Euphues* (Arber), p. 107; *Works of Greene* (Grosart), V, 170; — the hare not to be caught with a tabor, Lyly, *Euphues* (Arber), p. 44; Lyly, *Euphues and His England* (Arber), p. 327; *Works of Lodge* (Hunterian Club), II, iii, 25; *Works of Greene* (Grosart), III, 208-209; *ibid.,* IX, 167; *ibid.,* XI, 252; — the hare's timidity, *Works of Aristotle* (Smith and Ross), IV, 488; Gosson, *The School of Abuse,* p. 19; Lyly, *Euphues and His England* (Arber) p. 273; *Works of Lodge* (Hunterian Club), II, ii, 23; *Works of Greene* (Grosart), II, 62, 87, 131; *ibid.,* IV, 105; *ibid.,* IX, 43; *Works of Nashe* (McKerrow), I, 271; *ibid.,* II, 219; — the leverets' learning by the example of the old hare, *Works of Greene* (Grosart), IV, 17-18.

HART: *see* Deer.

HEDGEHOG: its carrying apples impaled on its spines to store for winter food, *Pliny: Natural History* (Rackham), III, 95; Topsell, *Historie of Foure-Footed Beastes,* p. 278; *Works of Nashe* (McKerrow), II, 113; — its shifting the outlook of its den according to the shifting of the wind, *Works of Aristotle* (Smith and Ross), IV, 612; *Pliny: Natural History* (Rackham), III, 95; Topsell, *Historie of Foure-Footed Beastes,* p. 278; Gosson, *The Ephemerides of Phialo* (Huntington Library facsimile), p. 65 *verso;* Lyly, *Euphues and His England* (Arber), p. 326.

*HOBBY: its high soaring, *Works of Lodge* (Hunterian Club), I, v, 5, 11, 119; *Works of Greene* (Grosart), VI, 66-67; *ibid.,* VIII, 180-81; *ibid.,* XII, 37, 271.

*HORNET: its irascible disposition, Lyly, *Euphues and His England* (Arber), p. 381; *Works of Greene* (Gosart), XI, 220; *Works of Nashe* (McKerrow), I, 122; *ibid.,* III, 368.

*HORSE: its responsiveness to bridle and spur, Lyly, *Euphues and His England* (Arber), p. 473; *Works of Lodge* (Hunterian Club), I, iii, 43; *ibid.,* I, v, 20; *ibid.,* II, iii, 11; *Works of Greene* (Grosart), II, 53, 77, 87; *ibid.,* III, 15; *ibid.,* IV, 54; *ibid.,* V, 64, 68; *ibid.,* VI, 49-50, 56, 111, 257; *ibid.,* VII, 52, 193; *ibid.,* XI, 150, 183; *ibid.,* XII, 235; *Works of Nashe* (McKerrow), II, 92; — Sejanus' horse's refusing to be mounted by anyone but its master, *Pliny: Natural History* (Rackham), III, 109; *Works of Greene* (Grosart), III, 86, 184; *ibid.,* V, 58; *ibid.,* VII, 69; *ibid.,* IX, 259; — the colt's unruliness, Lyly, *Euphues* (Arber), p. 115; Lyly, *Euphues and His England* (Arber), pp. 244, 383, 385, 412; *A Petite Pallace of Pettie His Pleasure* (Hartman), pp. 187, 204; Gosson, *The School of Abuse,* pp. 34, 48-49; Gosson, *The Ephemerides of Phialo* (Huntington Library facsimile), pp. 5 *verso,* 42 *verso; Works of Lodge* (Hunterian Club), I, iii, 43; *ibid.,* I, v, 18; *ibid.,* III, iv, 56; *Works of Greene* (Grosart), II, 128; *ibid.,* VI, 113; *ibid.,* X, 240-41; *Works of Nashe* (McKerrow), I, 78, 281; — the galled horse's kicking, Grange, *The Golden Aphroditis,* p. A iii *verso; Works of Greene* (Grosart), II, 52; — the horse Bayard's blindness and boldness, *Works of Greene* (Grosart), II, 6; *ibid.,* VI, 264; *ibid.,* VII, 102; *ibid.,* IX, 182, 221; *ibid.,* XI, 223; *ibid.,* XII, 5, 212; *Works of Nashe* (McKerrow), III, 220; *Works of Harvey* (Grosart), I, 67, 161; *ibid.,* II, 82, 237; 311; *Works of Deloney* (Mann), p. 183; — the horse Bucephalus' refusing to be mounted by anyone but Alexander the Great, *Pliny: Natural History* (Rackham), III, 109; Topsell, *Historie of Foure-Footed Beastes,* p. 312; *Works of Greene* (Grosart), IX, 289; *Works of Deloney* (Mann), p. 50; — the horses that draw the chariot of the sun, Riche, *Farewell to Militarie Profession (Eight Novels,* etc.), p. 79; Grange, *The Golden Aphroditis,* pp. G iii *verso-* G iv *recto,* J iv *verso; Works of Lodge* (Hunterian Club), I, v, 126; *ibid.,* III, iv, 27; *Works of Sidney* (Feuillerat), I, 165; — the jade's tiredness, Lyly, *Euphues and His England* (Arber), p. 405; *Works of Greene* (Grosart), VIII, 102; *ibid.,* IX, 232; *ibid.,* XI, 59; *Works of Nashe* (McKerrow), I, 195; *ibid.,* II, 181; *ibid.,* III, 344.

*HOUSEDOVE: see Dove.

HYDASPIS (hidaspis): its insatiable thirst and fatal thirst-producing bite, *Works of Greene* (Grosart), III, 70; *ibid.,* V, 16, 203; *ibid.,* VI, 175-76; *ibid.,* VII, 48, 59, 237; *ibid.,* VIII, 104, 204; *ibid.,* IX, 42, 178, 199; *ibid.,* XII, 251.

HYDRA ("hidra"): its multiple heads a symbol of multiform and persistent evil, *Works of Lodge* (Hunterian Club), II, iii, 41-42; *ibid.,* IV, i, 58; *Works of Nashe* (McKerrow), I, 59; *ibid.,* III, 189.

HYENA ("hiena"): its causing the hunter approaching on its right-hand side to fall senseless, Topsell, *Historie of Foure-Footed Beastes,* pp. 435-36; Lyly, *Euphues and His England* (Arber), pp. 287-88; — its changing its sex (becoming male and female in alternate years): *Pliny: Natural History* (Rackham), III, 77;

Topsell, *Historie of Foure-Footed Beastes,* pp. 435-36; *Works of Nashe* (McKerrow), II, 284; — its learning men's names and, imitating man's voice, calling victims out to be devoured, Topsell, *Historie of Foure-Footed Beastes,* pp. 435-36; Gosson, *The School of Abuse,* p. 10; Lyly, *Euphues* (Arber), p. 110; *Works of Lodge* (Hunterian Club), I, v, 15; *Works of Greene* (Grosart), II, 263; *ibid.,* III, 204-205; *ibid.,* V, 53; *ibid.,* VII, 63; *ibid.,* VIII, 138; *ibid.,* IX, 200; *ibid.,* X, 199; *ibid.,* XII, 114; *Works of Nashe* (McKerrow), II, 284.

ICHNEUMON (mongoose) : *see* Asp.

*JACKDAW (daw) : its simple-mindedness, Gosson, *The Ephemerides of Phialo* (Huntington Library facsimile), p. 1 *verso; Works of Lyly* (Bond), III, 412; *Works of Lodge* (Hunterian Club), II, ii, 29; *Works of Greene* (Grosart), XI, 74.

*JAY: its stealing and jangling, *Works of Green* (Grosart), IV, 62-63; *Works of Nashe* (McKerrow), II, 285.

*KESTREL ("kistrel") : its baseness, *Works of Greene* (Grosart), II, 155; *ibid.,* VI, 102; *Works of Nashe* (McKerrow), III, 62.

*KITE: its deceitfulness and appetite for carrion, *A Petite Pallace of Pettie His Pleasure* (Hartman), p. 231; Riche, *Farewell to Militarie Profession (Eight Novels,* etc.), p. 139; Grange, *The Golden Aphroditis,* pp. E ii *verso,* K ii *recto; Works of Lodge* (Hunterian Club), I, v, 72; *Works of Greene* (Grosart), II, 16, 230-31; *ibid.,* IV, 43-44, 61, 132, 314; *Works of Sidney* (Feuillerat), I, 79, 470-71.

*LAMB: *see* Sheep.

LAMIA (woman-serpent) : its Siren-like, fatal allurements, Topsell, *Historie of Foure-Footed Beastes,* pp. 452-55; *Works of Greene* (Grosart), II, 205-206; *ibid.,* XI, 217-18; *ibid.,* XII, 128; *Works of Nashe* (McKerrow), I, 236.

*LAPWING: its crying ever farthest from its nest, Lyly, *Euphues and His England* (Arber), pp. 214, 416; *Works of Greene* (Grosart), III, 78; *ibid.,* V, 192-93; *ibid.,* VII, 131-32; *ibid.,* IX, 102; *ibid.,* X, 77; *ibid.,* XI, 137; *Works of Nashe* (McKerrow), III, 58.

*LARK: its early rising and appetite for leeks, Lyly, *Euphues and His England* (Arber), p. 229; *Works of Greene* (Grosart), VI, 76; *ibid.,* VIII, 124.

*LEECH (horseleech) : its bloodthirstiness, *Pliny: Natural History* (Rackham), III, 503; *Works of Greene* (Grosart), VIII, 107, 138, 140; *ibid.,* IX, 191; *ibid.,* XI, 243; *Works of Nashe* (McKerrow), I, 351, 365; *ibid.,* II, 93; *ibid.,* III, 349.

LEOPARD: its unalterable spots, Gosson, *The School of Abuse,* p. 44; Gosson, *The Ephemerides of Phialo* (Huntington Library fac-

(Grosart), IX, 97; *Works of Nashe* (McKerrow), I, 287, 309, 321, 349; *ibid.,* III, 29, 224.

LYNX ("Lynceus") : its keen eyesight, Topsell, *Historie of Foure-Footed Beastes,* p. 489; Grange, *The Golden Aphroditis,* p. D iii *recto; Works of Lodge* (Hunterian Club), II, ii, 61; *ibid.,* IV, i, 108-109; *Works of Greene* (Grosart), VIII, 82; *Works of Nashe* (McKerrow), I, 226; *ibid.,* III, 218; *Works of Sidney* (Feuillerat), II, 201.

*MAGPIE (pie) : its scolding and merry chattering, *Works of Greene* (Grosart), IV, 62-63; *Works of Deloney* (Mann), pp. 4, 125, 216.

*MASTIFF: *see* Dog.

*MAY COCK ("meacock," "mecocke") : its effeminacy, Lyly, *Euphues* (Arber), p. 109; *Works of Lodge* (Hunterian Club), I, iii, 22; *Works of Greene* (Grosart), IV, 47; *ibid.,* VII, 128; *ibid.,* VIII, 195; *ibid.,* IX, 132-33, 173; *Works of Nashe* (McKerrow), I, 304; *ibid.,* II, 123.

*MINNOW: *see* Fish.

*MOLE: (moldwarp) : its acute sense of hearing, *Pliny: Natural History* (Rackham), III, 415; Lyly, *Euphues* (Arber), p. 153; *Works of Greene* (Grosart), II, 62; *ibid.,* IV, 105; *ibid.,* IX, 43; — its being deprived of sight, *Works of Lodge* (Hunterian Club), III, iv, 25; *Works of Greene* (Grosart), II, 62, 131; *ibid.,* IV, 105; *ibid.,* IX, 43; — its digging underground, Lyly, *Euphues* (Arber), p. 145; Lyly, *Euphues and His England* (Arber), p. 475; *Works of Lyly* (Bond), III, 413; *Works of Lodge* (Hunterian Club), IV, i, 37, 50; *Works of Greene* (Grosart), VI, 57; *Works of Deloney* (Mann), p. 28.

*MOTH: its consuming the finest cloth, Lyly, *Euphues* (Arber), pp. 109; 111; Gosson, *The School of Abuse,* p. 35; Gosson, *The Ephemerides of Phialo* (Huntington Library facsimile), p. 48 *recto; Works of Lodge* (Hunterian Club), I, iii, 43; *ibid.,* II, iii, 67; *ibid.,* III, iii, 12; *ibid.,* IV, i, 8; *Works of Greene* (Grosart), VI, 266; *ibid.,* VII, 11-12, 122, 301; *ibid.,* IX, 26-27; *ibid.,* X, 18, 90; *ibid.,* XI, 50, 243; *ibid.,* XII, 254; *Works of Nashe* (McKerrow), I, 216; *ibid.,* II, 138.

*MOUSE: its being a wily mouse that could breed in the cat's ear, Lyly, *Euphues* (Arber), p. 63; Lyly, *Euphues and His England* (Arber), p. 233; — the mouse's insignificance and timidity, Gosson, *The School of Abuse,* p. 11; *Works of Lodge* (Hunterian Club), IV, i, 10; *Works of Greene* (Grosart), II, 144-45; *ibid.,* V, 147; *ibid.,* VIII, 181; *ibid.,* XII, 7; *Works of Nashe* (McKerrow), I, 323; *ibid.,* III, 85, 179, 312, 329; *Works of Sidney* (Feuillerat), II, 84; — its nibbling at the bait until caught, *A*

Petite Pallace of Pettie His Pleasure (Hartman), p. 56; Grange, *The Golden Aphroditis*, p. J iii *recto; Works of Greene* (Grosart), II, 114; *ibid.,* XII, 15.

OCTOPUS ("polypus") : its changing its color to match its surroundings, *Works of Aristotle* (Smith and Ross), IV, 621-22; *Pliny: Natural History* (Rackham), III, 219, 221; Gosson, *The Ephemerides of Phialo* (Huntington Library facsimile), p. 40 *recto;* Lyly, *Euphues* (Arber), p. 73; Lyly, *Euphues and His England* (Arber), p. 320; *Works of Lodge* (Hunterian Club), I, v, 12, 108; *Works of Greene* (Grosart), II, 17, 61, 77, 222, 257, 261; *ibid.,* III, 79, 179, 184; *ibid.,* VIII, 55, 195; *ibid.,* IX, 75, 82, 85.

OSSIFRAGE: *see* Eagle.

OSTRICH: its digesting objects (iron among other things) swallowed indiscriminately, *Pliny: Natural History* (Rackham), III, 293; Lyly, *Euphues* (Arber), p. 124; *Works of Lyly* (Bond), III, 399; *Works of Nashe* (McKerrow), I, 359; *ibid.,* II, 273; *Works of Harvey* (Grosart), II, 236; — its fair feathers and rank flesh, Lyly, *Euphues* (Arber), pp. 54, 208; Lyly, *Euphues and His England* (Arber), pp. 443, 466; — its spurring itself with its wings in running, *Pliny: Natural History* (Rackham), III, 293; Lyly, *Euphues and His England* (Arber), p. 341; *Works of Lodge* (Hunterian Club), II, iii, 9; *Works of Nashe* (McKerrow), II, 272-73.

*OWL: its association with the goddess Minerva *("Mineruaes Owle"), Works of Greene* (Grosart), III, 77; *ibid.,* IV, 232; *ibid.,* VI, 264; —its funereal, ominous character and nocturnal habits, *Pliny: Natural History* (Rackham), III, 315; Gosson, *The Ephemerides of Phialo* (Huntington Library facsimile), p. 28 *verso; Works of Lodge* (Hunterian Club), I, ii, 10, 28; *ibid.,* II, i, 41; *Works of Nashe* (McKerrow), I, 289, 385-86; *ibid.,* II, 38, 58, 273-74; *Works of Sidney* (Feuillerat), I, 241, 475; *Works of Deloney* (Mann), pp. 53, 258; — its non-existence in Crete, *Pliny: Natural History* (Rackham), III, 341; Lyly, *Euphues* (Arber), p. 113.

OX: the black ox's treading on one's foot, Lyly, *Euphues* (Arber), p. 55; *Works of Lodge* (Hunterian Club), I, v, 36; *ibid.,* II, iii, 12; *Works of Greene* (Grosart), V, 152; *ibid.,* IX, 135, 180; *ibid.,* XII, 158, 271.

PANTHER: its attracting with its sweet breath (or body scent) and beautiful skin, other animals in order to catch and devour them, *Works of Aristotle* (Smith and Ross), IV, 612; *Pliny: Natural History* (Rackham), III, 49; Topsell, *Historie of Foure-Footed Beastes,* pp. 580-82; *A Petite Pallace of Pettie His Pleasure* (Hartman), pp. 51, 93; Lyly, *Euphues* (Arber), p. 54; *Works of Lodge* (Hunterian Club), I, v, 69; *Works of Greene* (Grosart), II, 20, 44-45, 51, 60, 207, 232, 255, 279; *ibid.*, III, 239; *ibid.*, VI, 174; *ibid.*, VIII, 67, 138, 142; *ibid.*, IX, 74, 129, 138, 190, 207; *ibid.*, XII, 23, 203, 206; *Works of Nashe* (McKerrow), I, 21; *ibid.*, II, 52, 117, 284.

PARROT (popinjay): its imitating human speech, *Works of Ascham* (Giles), III, 116; Riche, *Farewell to Militarie Profession (Eight Novels,* etc.), p. 63; *Works of Greene* (Grosart), III, 50; *ibid.*, IX, 243-44; *ibid.*, X, 238; *Works of Nashe* (McKerrow), III, 116, 344; *Works of Harvey* (Grosart), I, 229; II, 8.

PEACOCK: its jealousy and self-conceit, *Works of Aristotle* (Smith and Ross), IV, 488; *Pliny: Natural History* (Rackham), III, 321; Grange, *The Golden Aphroditis,* p. S iv *recto;* Lyly, *Euphues and His England* (Arber), pp. 312, 443; *Works of Lodge* (Hunterian Club), II, iii, 27, 75; *ibid.*, IV, i, 26, 30-31; *Works of Greene* (Grosart), II, 232-33; *ibid.*, III, 75; *ibid.*, IV, 152; *ibid.*, V, 229; *ibid.*, VIII, 22, 194; *ibid.*, IX, 25, 50, 163-64; *ibid.*, X, 234; *ibid.*, XI, 215, 266, 292; *Works of Nashe* (McKerrow), I, 175, 242; *ibid.*, II, 112; *Works of Harvey* (Grosart), I, 229; *ibid.*, II, 7-8, 82; *Works of Sidney* (Feuillerat), I, 98, 238; *Works of Deloney* (Mann), pp. 29, 238; — its shame at the time of molting its tail feathers (whence probably the Elizabethan idea of its being ashamed of its ugly feet), *Pliny: Natural History* (Rackham), III, 321; *Works of Lodge* (Hunterian Club), II, iii, 75; *ibid.*, IV, i, 30-31; *Works of Greene* (Grosart), II, 232-33; *ibid.*, V, 229; *ibid.*, VIII, 22, 194; *ibid.*, IX, 25, 50; *ibid.*, X, 90; *ibid.*, XI, 215; *Works of Nashe* (McKerrow), II, 112; *Works of Deloney* (Mann), p. 29.

PELICAN: its shedding the blood of its own breast to nourish its brood, Gosson; *The Ephemerides of Phialo* (Huntinton Library facsimile), p. 32 *verso;* Lyly, *Euphues* (Arber), p. 124; Lyly, *Euphues and His England* (Arber), pp. 341, 462; *Works of Lodge* (Hunterian Club), II, iv, 10; *Works of Greene* (Grosart), III, 114; *ibid.*, XI, 226; *Works of Nashe* (McKerrow), II, 57-58; *ibid.*, III, 124; *Works of Deloney* (Mann), p. 19.

PHOENIX: its rareness (uniqueness), *Pliny: Natural History* (Rackham), III, 293, 295; Painter, *The Palace of Pleasure* (Jacobs), I, 203; *ibid.*, II, 288; *A Petite Pallace of Pettie His Pleasure* (Hartman), p. 261; Gosson, *The School of Abuse,* p. 42; Gosson, *The Ephemerides of Phialo* (Huntington Library facsimile), pp. 26 *recto,* 64 *verso;* Lyly, *Euphues and His England* (Arber), pp. 312, 390, 432; *Works of Lodge* (Hunterian Club), I, v, 63;

Works of Greene (Grosart), II, 43, 49; *ibid.,* IV, 36; *ibid.,* VIII, 182; *ibid., IX,* 128, 207; *ibid.,* XII, 24, 252; *Works of Nashe* (McKerrow), I, 5, 182-83; *Works of Sidney* (Feuillerat), III, 32; — its self-immolation and resurrection, *Pliny: Natural History* (Rackham), III, 293, 295; *Works of Lodge* (Hunterian Club), I, v, 10; *ibid.,* II, iv, 9; *Works of Greene* (Grosart), VII, 192; *ibid.,* XI, 156; *ibid.,* XII, 271; *Works of Nashe* (McKerrow), I, 23; *ibid.,* II, 50, 243; *ibid.,* III, 331; *Works of Sidney* (Feuillerat), I, 286.

PORCUPINE ("porpentine," "porcuntine") : its shooting its quills, *Works of Aristotle* (Smith and Ross), IV, 623; *Pliny: Natural History* (Rackham), III, 87, 89; Topsell, *Historie of Foure-Footed Beastes,* p. 588; *Works of Greene* (Grosart), IV, 51, 82; *ibid.,* V, 97; *ibid.,* IX, 275; *ibid.,* XII, 23; *Works of Nashe* (McKerrow), I, 259.

*RAM: *see* Sheep.

*RAVEN: its ominous character and appetite for carrion, *Pliny: Natural History* (Rackham), III, 313; Gosson, *The Ephemerides of Phialo* (Huntington Library facsimile), pp. 13 *verso-*14 *recto;* *Works of Greene* (Grosart), IV, 132; *ibid.,* VII, 60; *ibid.,* X, 50; *ibid.,* XI, 52; *Works of Nashe* (McKerrow), I, 346; *Works of Sidney* (Feuillerat), I, 455; *Works of Deloney* (Mann), p. 258.

REMORA (suckfish) : its stopping ships under full sail by attaching itself to the hulls, *Pliny: Natural History* (Rackham), III, 215, 217; Gosson, *The School of Abuse,* p. 28.

SALAMANDER: its quenching fire by chilliness of bodily contact (hence its ability to live in fire), *Pliny: Natural History* (Rackham), III, 411; Topsell, *Historie of Serpents,* pp. 217-21; Lyly, *Euphues* (Arber), p. 73; Lyly, *Euphues and His England* (Arber), p. 298; *Works of Greene* (Grosart), II, 61; *ibid.,* III, 142, 192-93; *ibid.,* IV, 54; *ibid.,* V, 203; *ibid.,* VI, 57, 234; *ibid.,* VII, 205, 229-30; *ibid.,* VIII, 22, 50, 174, 180; *ibid.,* IX, 31, 75, 149-50; 180; *ibid.,* XI, 119; *ibid.,* XII, 240; *Works of Nashe* (McKerrow), II, 46-47; *ibid.,* III, 223; *Works of Deloney* (Mann), p. 4.

SCORPION: its being the remedy for its own sting, *Pliny: Natural History* (Rackham), III, 485, 487; Topsell, *Historie of Serpents,* pp. 222-31; Lyly, *Euphues* (Arber), pp. 68-69, 107; Lyly, *Euphues and His England* (Arber), pp. 356, 411; *Works of Lodge* (Hunterian Club), I, v, 120; *Works of Greene* (Grosart), II, 59; *ibid.,* IV, 51; *ibid.,* VIII, 210; *ibid.,* IX, 74; *ibid.,* XI, 141; *ibid.,* XII, 9.

*SEA GULL: its gullibility, *Works of Nashe* (McKerrow), III, 34, 212-13.

SEA MOUSE ("Musculus," *"Talpa Marina"*) : its swimming in front
of the whale and pointing out dangerous shallows, *Pliny: Natural History* (Rackham), III, 289; Gosson, *The School of Abuse,*
pp. 45-46; *Works of Greene* (Grosart), IV, 125-26; *Works of Deloney* (Mann), pp. 95-96.

SEPIA (cuttlefish) : its discharging a dark fluid in the water in order
to conceal itself and elude capture, *Works of Aristotle* (Smith
and Ross), IV, 621-22; *Pliny: Natural History* (Rackham), III,
219, 221; Gosson, *The School of Abuse,* p. 46; *Works of Nashe*
(McKerrow), I, 87; *Works of Sidney* (Feuillerat), I, 107.

SERPENT (snake) : its evilness and subtlety (venomousness), *Works
of Aristotle* (Smith and Ross), IV, 488; *Pliny: Natural History*
(Rackham), III, 63; Topsell, *Historie of Serpents,* pp. 52-53;
Painter, *The Palace of Pleasure* (Jacobs), I, 199, 219; *ibid.,* II,
414; *A Petite Pallace of Pettie His Pleasure* (Hartman), p. 15;
Grange, *The Golden Aphroditis,* p. H iv *verso;* Lyly, *Euphues*
(Arber), pp. 99, 116, 196; Lyly, *Euphues and His England* (Arber), pp. 224, 368, 372, 376; *Works of Lodge* (Hunterian Club),
I, v, 63; *ibid.,* II, ii, 8, 32, 48; *ibid.,* II, iii, 13, 63, 67; *ibid.,* III,
iii, 15, 71; *ibid.,* IV, i, 7-9, 22, 24-25, 36, 47; *Works of Greene*
(Grosart), II, 119, 175, 187, 192, 222-23, 257, 261, 279-80, 284;
ibid., III, 19, 26, 209, 220, 240; *ibid.,* VIII, 143, 149; *ibid.,* IX,
189-90; *ibid.,* X, 235; *ibid.,* XI, 146; *ibid.,* XII, 111, 202-203, 220;
Works of Nashe (McKerrow), I, 34, 93, 110, 116, 224, 235-36;
348; *ibid.,* II, 96, 136, 141, 221, 284, 293; *ibid.,* III, 195, 353, 365;
Works of Harvey (Grosart), III, 70; *Works of Sidney* (Feuillerat), I, 210, 266; *ibid.,* II, 11, 96, 181; *Works of Deloney* (Mann),
pp. 29, 77; — its generation from the spinal marrow of a human
being, *Pliny: Natural History* (Rackham), III, 411, 413; *Works
of Nashe* (McKerrow), II, 138; — its hostility to the elephant,
Pliny: Natural History (Rackham), III, 27, 29; Topsell, *Historie of Foure-Footed Beastes,* pp. 190-209; *Works of Greene*
(Grosart), IX, 190; *Works of Deloney* (Mann), p. 81; — its in-
gratitude and treacherousness (the fable of the man who warmed
the serpent in his bosom), Painter, *The Palace of Pleasure*
(Jacobs), III, 250; Gosson, *The School of Abuse,* p. 37; *Works
of Lodge* (Hunterian Club), II, ii, 8; *ibid.,* II, iii, 36; *ibid.,* III,
iv, 41; *Works of Greene* (Grosart), IV, 159; *ibid.,* X, 268; *Works
of Nashe* (McKerrow), II, 120; *ibid.,* III, 106; *Works of Sidney*
(Feuillerat), II, 179; *Works of Deloney* (Mann), p. 225; — the
serpent "Amphisbaena" with a head at each end, *Pliny: Natural
History* (Rackham), III, 63; Topsell, *Historie of Serpents,* pp.
151-53; Lyly, *Euphues and His England* (Arber), p. 286; *Works*

of Greene (Grosart), III, 208; — the serpent's (snake's) aversion to the odor of burned hart's (or stag's) horn, *Pliny: Natural History* (Rackham), III, 85; Topsell, *Historie of Foure-Footed Beastes,* pp. 126-31; *Works of Greene* (Grosart), IV, 115-16; — the snake in the grass, Painter, *The Palace of Pleasure* (Jacobs), II, 247; *ibid.,* III, 141; *A Petite Pallace of Pettie His Pleasure* (Hartman), p. 148; Gosson, *The School of Abuse,* p. 27; Lyly, *Euphues* (Arber), pp. 53-54; Lyly, *Euphues and His England* (Arber), p. 384; *Works of Lodge* (Hunterian Club), I, ii, 32; *ibid.,* I, iii, 31; *ibid.,* III, iv, 34; *Works of Greene* (Grosart), II, 110, 182, 257; *ibid.,* V, 143; *ibid.,* VI, 84, 251; *ibid.,* VII, 203-204; *Works of Nashe* (McKerrow), I, 345; *Works of Deloney* (Mann), p. 79.

*SHEEP: its gentle simplicity and innocence, *Wilson's Arte of Rhetorique* (Mair), p. 166; *A Petite Pallace of Pettie His Pleasure* (Hartman), pp. 48, 119, 124, 207, 211; Gosson, *The Ephemerides of Phialo* (Huntington Library facsimile), p. 88 *recto;* Lyly, *Euphues* (Arber), pp. 35, 78, 177; Lyly, *Euphues and His England* (Arber), pp. 273, 320, 322, 363-64, 435, 453, 461-62, 472; *Works of Lodge* (Hunterian Club), I, ii, 7; *ibid.,* II, ii, 15, 17-18, 23-25; *ibid.,* II, iii, 12, 32, 44; *ibid.,* III, iv, 61; *Works of Greene* (Grosart), II, 20, 27, 62, 65, 93, 154-55, 163, 167, 188, 235, 255; *ibid.,* III, 11, 17, 42, 62, 198; *ibid.,* IV, 130; *ibid.,* V, 43, 249, 278; *ibid.,* VI, 75, 119; *ibid.,* IX, 65, 76, 96; *ibid.,* X, 8, 13; *ibid.,* XI, 239, 241; *ibid.,* XII, 120-21, 174; *Works of Nashe* (McKerrow), I, 37, 62, 93, 125, 134, 198, 220, 333; *ibid.,* II, 18, 31, 75, 103, 214, 240, 302; *ibid.,* III, 188; *Works of Harvey* (Grosart), I, 199, 236, 277; *ibid.,* II, 38; *Works of Sidney* (Feuillerat), I, 7, 104, 107; *ibid.,* II, 119, 137; *Works of Deloney* (Mann), pp. 7, 61, 85, 90, 217; — the fighting ram's going back from its adversary to return with greater force, Gosson, *The Ephemerides of Phialo* (Huntington Library facsimile), p. 62 *recto;* *Works of Lodge* (Hunterian Club), III, iii, 68; *Works of Nashe* (McKerrow), II, 292; *Works of Sidney* (Feuillcrat), I, 131; — the sheep's eye (amorous glance), Grange, *The Golden Aphroditis,* p. D *recto; Works of Lodge* (Hunterian Club), II, iii, 73; *Works of Greene* (Grosart), VIII, 197; *Works of Nashe* (McKerrow), III, 54; *Works of Sidney* (Feuillerat), I, 157; *Works of Deloney* (Mann), p. 155.

*SHREW: its ill temper, *Pliny: Natural History* (Rackham), III, 157; *Wilson's Arte of Rhetorique* (Mair), p. 49; Riche, *Farewell to Militarie Profession* (*Eight Novels,* etc.), p. 213; Lyly, *Euphues and His England* (Arber), p. 471; *Works of Lodge* (Hunterian Club), II, ii, 14; *ibid.,* II, iii, 44, 55; *Works of Greene* (Grosart),

II, 107; *ibid.*, III, 62, 101; *ibid.*, IX, 37-38, 240; *ibid.*, X, 59; *ibid.*, XI, 214; *ibid.*, XII, 17, 221; *Works of Nashe* (McKerrow), I, 321; *ibid.*, III, 29, 200, 390; *Works of Sidney* (Feuillerat), I, 309; *Works of Deloney* (Mann), pp. 19, 152, 217, 253.

*SLUG: its sluggishness, *Works of Lodge* (Hunterian Club), IV, i, 112; *Works of Greene* (Grosart), II, 28; *ibid.*, IV, 198.

*SNAIL: its slowness and timidity, Lyly, *Euphues and His England* (Arber), p. 419; *Works of Lodge* (Hunterian Club), I, v, 123; *Works of Greene* (Grosart), II, 28; *ibid.*, VI, 63, 180; *ibid.*, VIII, 181; *ibid.*, IX, 66, 91; *ibid.*, X, 244; *Works of Nashe* (McKerrow), I, 131; *ibid.*, II, 221.

*SPARROW: its lecherousness, Painter, *The Palace of Pleasure* (Jacobs), III, 382; Grange, *The Golden Aphroditis*, p. K ii *verso; Works of Lodge* (Hunterian Club), IV, i, 52; *Works of Nashe* (McKerrow), II, 225.

SPHINX: its inscrutability, *Pliny: Natural History* (Rackham), III, 53; Topsell, *Historie of Foure-Footed Beastes*, pp. 17-18; *Works of Greene* (Grosart), II, 81; *ibid.*, III, 140; *ibid.*, VI, 7; *ibid.*, IX, 57.

*SPIDER: its spinning its web to entrap the fly, Lyly, *Euphues* (Arber), pp. 78, 91; *A Petite Pallace of Pettie His Pleasure* (Hartman), p. 168; *Works of Greene* (Grosart), XI, 51; *Works of Nashe* (McKerrow), I, 93; — its sucking poison from the flower whence the bee sucked honey, *see* Bee.

STAG: *see* Deer.

*STARFISH ("sea Star") : its blackness, especially when old, *Works of Greene* (Grosart), II, 176; *ibid.*, III, 12.

STORK: its being fed in old age by its grateful young, *Works of Aristotle* (Smith and Ross), IV, 615; *Pliny: Natural History* (Rackham), III, 333; *Wilson's Arte of Rhetorique* (Mair), pp. 26, 125; *A Petite Pallace of Pettie His Pleasure* (Hartman), p. 139; Gosson, *The School of Abuse*, p. 29; *Works of Greene* (Grosart), IV, 165; *ibid.*, VII, 269; *ibid.*, IX, 145-46, 239-40.

*SWALLOW: one swallow's not making summer, *Wilson's Arte of Rhetorique* (Mair), p. 54; *A Petite Pallace of Pettie His Pleasure* (Hartman), p. 104; Gosson, *The School of Abuse*, p. 13; Lyly, *Euphues* (Arber), p. 91; *Works of Lyly* (Bond), III, 403; *Works of Lodge* (Hunterian Club), II, iii, 100; *Works of Greene* (Grosart), VIII, 77-78; *ibid.*, IX, 191; *Works of Deloney* (Mann), p. 11.

*SWAN: its singing at the approach of death (swan song), *Works of Aristotle* (Smith and Ross), IV, 615; *Pliny: Natural History* (Rackham), III, 333; Gosson, *The School of Abuse*, p. 42;

Grange, *The Golden Aphroditis,* p. H ii *verso; Works of Lodge* (Hunterian Club), I, v, 10; *Works of Greene* (Grosart), IV, 244; *ibid.,* XII, 101; *Works of Sidney* (Feuillerat), II, 166; — the black swan's rareness or supposed non-existence, *A Petite Pallace of Pettie His Pleasure* (Hartman), p. 69; Lyly, *Euphues and His England* (Arber), p. 229; *Works of Greene* (Grosart), VIII, 27; *ibid.,* IX, 147-48; — the cygnets' obedience to the old swan, *Works of Greene* (Grosart), II, 167; *ibid.,* III, 62.

*swine: its brutishness, *Pliny: Natural History* (Rackham), III, 145; *Works of Ascham* (Giles), III, 153, 156; 250; Gosson, *The Ephemerides of Phialo* (Huntington Library facsimile), p. 2 *verso;* Lyly, *Euphues* (Arber), p. 61; *Works of Lodge* (Hunterian Club), II, ii, 53-54; *Works of Greene* (Grosart), IX, 163, 333; *Works of Nashe* (McKerrow), I, 207, 352; *ibid.,* II, 99-100, 113, *ibid.,* III, 89, 373; *Works of Sidney* (Feuillerat), I, 153; — its wallowing in the mire, *Works of Ascham* (Giles), III, 153-54, 164; Gosson, *The School of Abuse,* p. 9; *Works of Lodge* (Hunterian Club), I, ii, 32; *Works of Greene* (Grosart), III, 14; *ibid.,* XII, 163; *Works of Nashe* (McKerrow), I, 205; *ibid.,* II, 100, 293; *ibid.,* III, 344; — no silk purse to be made of a sow's ear, Gosson, *The Ephemerides of Phialo* (Huntington Library facsimile), pp. 62 *recto*-62 *verso.*

tarantula: its bite remedied by music, *Works of Lodge* (Hunterian Club), I, v, 129; *Works of Greene* (Grosart), VIII, 103-104; *ibid.,* IX, 42; *ibid.,* XI, 175; *ibid.,* XII, 9; *Works of Sidney* (Feuillerat), I, 58; — its venom the cause of death by laughter, *Works of Greene* (Grosart), V, 57; *ibid.,* VI, 45; *ibid.,* VII, 69; *ibid.,* IX, 185, 207.

tiger: its fierceness and cruelty, Topsell, *Historie of Foure-Footed Beastes,* p. 708; *Wilson's Arte of Rhetorique* (Mair), p. 207; Painter, *The Palace of Pleasure* (Jacobs), II, 211, 239; Riche, *Farewell to Militarie Profession* (*Eight Novels,* etc.), p. 142; *A Petite Pallace of Pettie His Pleasure* (Hartman), pp. 23, 48, 54, 119; Grange, *The Golden Aphroditis,* p. A iii *verso;* Lyly, *Euphues and His England* (Arber), pp. 273, 474; *Works of Lodge* (Hunterian Club), I, ii, 46; *ibid.,* I, iii, 81; *ibid.,* II, iii, 35, 40; *ibid.,* II, iv, 60; *Works of Greene* (Grosart), II, 28, 62, 154, 167, 188, 235, 261, 279; *ibid.,* III, 205, 233; *ibid.,* V, 43, 57; *ibid.,* VI, 180; *ibid.,* VII, 68; *ibid.,* VIII, 142; *ibid.,* IX, 52, 96; *ibid.,* X, 252; *ibid.,* XII, 144; *Works of Nashe* (McKerrow), I, 16; *Works of Sidney* (Feuillerat), I, 300, 388; *ibid.,* II, 12, 27, 182; *Works of Deloney* (Mann), p. 90.

*toad ("paddock," "pad"): its having a fair stone in its head, Topsell, *Historie of Serpents,* pp. 187-89; Lyly, *Euphues* (Arber), p. 53; Lyly, *Euphues and His England* (Arber), p. 327; *Works of Lodge* (Hunterian Club), II, iii, 103; *Works of Greene* (Grosart), III, 209; — its venomousness, *Pliny: Natural History* (Rackham), III, 555, 609; Topsell, *Historie of Serpents,* pp. 187-89; Lyly, *Euphues* (Arber), pp. 44, 53; Lyly, *Euphues and His England* (Arber), p. 327; *Works of Lyly* (Bond), III, 395; *Works of Lodge* (Hunterian Club), IV, i, 23; *Works of Greene* (Grosart), III, 209; *Works of Harvey* (Grosart), II, 77; *Works of Sidney* (Feuillerat), I, 196; — the sinister presence of the pad in the straw, Gosson, *The Ephemerides of Phialo* (Huntington Library facsimile), p. 3 *recto; Works of Lodge* (Hunterian Club), I, v, 19; *ibid.,* II, iii, 90; *Works of Greene* (Grosart), II, 110, 184, 210; *ibid.,* V, 84-85; *ibid.,* VI, 71, 161, 252-53; *ibid.,* IX, 94; *ibid.,* XI, 13; *Works of Nashe* (McKerrow), I, 123; *Works of Deloney* (Mann), p. 162.

TORPEDO: its transmitting a benumbing shock, *Works of Aristotle* (Smith and Ross), IV, 620; *Pliny: Natural History* (Rackham), III, 259, 261; Gosson, *The School of Abuse,* p. 46; Lyly, *Euphues and His England* (Arber), p. 269; *Works of Lodge* (Hunterian Club), II, iii, 36; *Works of Greene* (Grosart), II, 175, 228; *ibid.,* IV, 20-21; *Works of Harvey* (Grosart), III, 41; *Works of Sidney* (Feuillerat), I, 415.

TORTOISE: its not leaving its own shell a symbol of the chaste woman's duty not to stray wantonly from home, Painter, *The Palace of Pleasure* (Jacobs), III, 160; Grange, *The Golden Aphroditis,* p. K iii *verso;* Lyly, *Euphues and His England* (Arber), p. 326; *Works of Greene* (Grosart), II, 65; *ibid.,* VI, 63; *ibid.,* VIII, 40; *ibid.,* X, 244; *ibid.,* XII, 241.

TROCHILUS: *see* Crocodile.

UNICORN: its fierceness, chastity, and strength, *Pliny: Natural History* (Rackham), III, 57; Topsell, *Historie of Foure-Footed Beastes,* pp. 32, 712, 719, 721; Lyly, *Euphues* (Arber), pp. 71, 127; *Works of Lodge* (Hunterian Club), III, iv, 46; *Works of Greene* (Grosart), II, 49, 208; *ibid.,* IV, 125.

VIPER: its matricidal birth by eating through the mother's belly, *Pliny: Natural History* (Rackham), III, 401; Topsell, *Historie of Serpents,* pp. 290-306; *Wilson's Arte of Rhetorique* (Mair), p. 125; *A Petite Pallace of Pettie His Pleasure* (Hartman), pp. 29, 52; Gosson, *The School of Abuse,* p. 36; Gosson, *The Ephemerides of Phialo* (Huntington Library facsimile), p. 32 *verso;* Lyly, *Euphues* (Arber), p. 129; Lyly, *Euphues and His England* (Arber), pp. 215, 417; *Works of Lodge* (Hunterian Club), II, ii, 61; *ibid.,* II, iii, 33, 62; *Works of Greene* (Grosart), X, 9, 29, 33, 39, 72-73, 97, 144; *ibid.,* XI, 53; *ibid.,* XII, 134; *Works of Nashe* (McKerrow), I, 93; *Works of Harvey* (Grosart), II, 20; *ibid.,* III, 10-11; *Works of Sidney* (Feuillerat), I, 289; *ibid.,* III, 4.

VULTURE: its keen sense of smell, *Pliny: Natural History* (Rackham), III, 413, 415; Gosson, *The Ephemerides of Phialo* (Huntington Library facsimile), p. 42 *recto;* Lyly, *Euphues* (Arber), p. 153; — its predatory habits, *Works of Greene* (Grosart), V, 49, 143; *ibid.,* VII, 60; *ibid.,* IX, 178, 302; *ibid.,* X, 44, 70, 96, 268; *ibid.,* XI, 52; *Works of Nashe* (McKerrow), I, 20; — its tearing Prometheus' and Titius' livers, Lyly, *Euphues and His England* (Arber), p. 341; *Works of Lodge* (Hunterian Club), II, ii, 33, 61; *ibid.,* VI, i, 36; *Works of Greene* (Grosart), VII, 122; *Works of Nashe* (McKerrow), I, 377.

*WASP: its irascible disposition, *A Petite Pallace of Pettie His Pleasure* (Hartman), pp. 168, 190; Gosson, *The School of Abuse,* p. 28; Gosson, *The Ephemerides of Phialo* (Huntington Library facsimile), p. 11 *verso; Works of Lodge* (Hunterian Club), II, iii, 46; *Works of Greene* (Grosart), III, 157; *ibid.,* IV, 102, 109; *ibid.,* IX, 240; *ibid.,* XII, 68, 79; — its spontaneous generation in the carcass of a horse, *Pliny: Natural History* (Rackham), III, 475; *Works of Nashe* (McKerrow), I, 174.

*WOLF: its ravenousness, *Works of Ascham* (Giles), III, 153; *A Petite Pallace of Pettie His Pleasure* (Hartman), pp. 48, 124, 207; Gosson, *The School of Abuse,* pp. 10, 37; Gosson, *The Ephemerides of Phialo* (Huntington Library facsimile), pp. 15 *verso,* 36 *recto,* 88 *recto;* Grange, *The Golden Aphroditis,* p. L ii *recto;* Lyly, *Euphues* (Arber), p. 78; Lyly, *Euphues and His England* (Arber), pp. 256, 316, 435, 462, 475; *Works of Lodge* (Hunterian Club), I, iii, 49; *ibid.,* II, ii, 9, 12, 15, 17-19, 23; *ibid.,* II, iii, 10, 12, 14; *Works of Greene* (Grosart), II, 20, 65, 119, 132, 163, 257; *ibid.,* III, 11; *ibid.,* V, 75, 248-49; *ibid.,* VII, 75; *ibid.,* IX, 76; *ibid.,* XI, 239, 244; *Works of Nashe* (McKerrow), I, 62, 93, 184-85, 333; *ibid.,* II, 18, 214, 240, 284; *ibid.,* III, 376; *Works of Harvey* (Grosart), I, 199, 236; *ibid.,* II, 38, 168; *Works of Sidney* (Feuillerat), I, 7, 388; *ibid.,* II, 134, 137, 191; *ibid.,* III, 62; *Works of Deloney* (Mann), p. 82; — its vainly barking at the moon, Lyly, *Euphues and His England* (Arber), p. 386; *Works of Lodge* (Hunterian Club), I, v, 119; *ibid.,* II, ii, 13; *Works of Greene* (Grosart), III, 224; *ibid.,* V, 55; *ibid.,* VI, 85, 145; *ibid.,* VII, 67, 121, 160; *ibid.,* IX, 32; — *"lupus in fabula," Wilson's Arte of Rhetorique* (Mair), p. 199; *A Petite Pallace of Pettie*

His Pleasure (Hartman), p. 165; *Works of Lodge* (Hunterian Club), I, v, 91; *Works of Harvey* (Grosart), III, 43; — the dangerous predicament of holding a wolf by the ears, *Works of Greene* (Grosart), V, 49; *Works of Sidney* (Feuillerat), II, 12; — the proverbial effort to keep the wolf from the door, *Works of Greene* (Grosart), VIII, 219; *Works of Deloney* (Mann), p. 112; — the she-wolf's choosing for her mate the wolf that made himself most foul in following her, *A Petite Pallace of Pettie His Pleasure* (Hartman), pp. 16-17; *Works of Greene* (Grosart), IV, 132.

*woodcock: its simple-mindedness and lack of wit, Gosson, *The School of Abuse*, pp. 33-34; Gosson, *The Ephemerides of Phialo* (Huntington Library facsimile), p. 89 *recto; Works of Lodge* (Hunterian Club), II, ii, 20; *ibid.*, IV, i, 45; *Works of Greene* (Grosart), VIII, 219; *ibid.*, X, 212; *ibid.*, XII, 118, 128; *Works of Nashe* (McKerrow), I, 83, 167; *ibid.*, III, 17, 373.

*worm: its lowliness and destructiveness, Gosson, *The School of Abuse*, pp. 25, 36; Gosson, *The Ephemerides of Phialo* (Huntington Library facsimile), p. 45 *verso; Works of Lodge* (Hunterian Club), II, ii, 33; *ibid.*, II, iii, 13, 67; *ibid.*, III, iii, 12; *ibid.*, III, iv, 34; *ibid.*, IV, i, 14, 36; *Works of Greene* (Grosart), IX, 19, 178; *ibid.*, X, 9, 30, 97; *ibid.*, XI, 29, 128; *Works of Nashe* (McKerrow), II, 90, 92, 117, 128, 138-39; *Works of Sidney* (Feuillerat), I, 145, 156, 429; *ibid.*, II, 12, 177.

Bibliography

ADAMS, M. (ed.). *The "Utopia" and the "History of Edward V,"* by Sir Thomas More. London: Walter Scott, 1890.

AVELING, S. T. *Heraldry: Ancient and Modern* (Including Boutell's Heraldry). London: Frederick Warne & Co., 1891.

BATMAN, S. *Batman vppon Bartholome, his Booke De Proprietatibus Rerum.* London: Thomas East, 1582.

BIBLE, The (A. V.) New York: Saalfield Publishing Co., n.d.

BOND, R. W. (ed.). *The Complete Works of John Lyly.* Oxford: Clarendon Press, 1902. 3 vols.

BROOKE, C. F. T. (ed.). *Shakespeare's Plutarch* (Shakespeare Classics, edited by Israel Gollancz). London: Chatto & Windus, 1909. 2 vols.

CAXTON, W. (trans.). *The History of Reynard the Fox* (edited by Edward Arber). London: English Scholar's Library of Old and Modern Works, No. 1, 1878.

CHAMBERS, E. K. *The Mediaeval Stage.* Oxford: Clarendon Press, 1903. 2 vols.

Complete Works of Thomas Lodge, The (Hunterian Club). Glasgow: Robert Anderson, 1883. 4 vols.

ELYOT, Sir T. *The Gouernour* (Everyman's Library ed.). London: J. M. Dent & Sons, Ltd., 1937.

Emblemas de Andres Alciato, Las. Valencia: Francisco Mestre, 1684.

FERNE, J. *The Blazon of Gentrie.* London: John Windet, 1586.

FEUILLERAT, A. (ed.). *The Complete Works of Sir Philip Sidney* (Cambridge English Classics). Cambridge: University Press, 1922. 3 vols.

FURNIVALL, F. J. (ed.). *Political, Religious, and Love Poems* (Early English Text Society). London: N. Trübner & Co., 1866.

GILES, J. A. (ed.). *Galfredi Monumetensis Historia Britonum* (Publications of the Caxton Society). Londini: D. Nutt, 1844.

―――― (ed.). *The Whole Works of Roger Ascham.* London: John Russell Smith, 1864. 3 vols.

GOODWIN, W. W. (ed.). *Plutarch's Morals* (Translated from the Greek by Several Hands). Boston: Little, Brown, & Co., 1878. 5 vols.

GOSSON, S. *The Ephemerides of Phialo* (Photostat Facsimile, Reproduced from the Copy in the Henry E. Huntington Library), n.d.

———. *The School of Abuse, Containing a Pleasant Invective Against Poets, Pipers, Players, Jesters, &c.* London: Shakespeare Society, 1841.

GRANGE, J. *The Golden Aphroditis.* New York: Scholars' Facsimiles and Reprints, n.d.

GREEN, H. (ed.). *Whitney's "Choice of Emblemes"* (Facsimile reprint). London: Lovell Reeve & Co., 1866.

GROSART, A. B. (ed.). *The Complete Works of Thomas Nashe* (Huth Library). London: Hazell, Watson, & Viney, 1883-1884. 4 vols.

——— (ed.). *The Life and Complete Works in Prose and Verse of Robert Greene, M.A.* (Huth Library). London: Hazell, Watson, & Viney, 1881-1886. 15 vols.

——— (ed.). *The Works of Gabriel Harvey, D.C.L.* (Huth Library). London: Hazell, Watson, & Viney, 1884-1885. 3 vols.

Hadriani Iunii Medici Emblemata ad D. Arnoldum Cobelium. Antverpiae: Ex officina Christophori Plantini. M.D. LXV.

HARTMAN, H. (ed.). *A Petite Pallace of Pettie His Pleasure.* New York: Oxford University Press, 1938.

HAZLITT, W. C. (ed.). *Shakespeare Jest-Books* (Reprints of the early and very rare Jest-books supposed to have been used by Shakespeare). London: Willis & Sotheran, 1864. 3 vols.

HENDERSON, P. (ed.). *The Complete Poems of John Skelton, Laureate.* London: J. M. Dent & Sons, Ltd., 1931.

HERCHER, R. (ed.). *AEliani De Natura Animalium, Varia Historia, Epistolae et Fragmenta; Porphyrii Philosophi De Abstinentia et De Antro Nympharum; Philonis Byzantii De Septem Orbis Spectaculis.* Parisiis: Editore Ambrosio Firmin Didot, 1858.

JACOBS, J. (ed.). *The Fables of AEsop.* London: Macmillan & Co., Ltd., 1917.

JOHNSON, F. R. "Two Renaissance Textbooks of Rhetoric: Aphthonius' *Progymnasmata* and Rainolde's *A booke called the Foundacion of Rhetorike*," *Huntington Library Quarterly,* VI (1942-1943), 427-44.

KEBLE, J. (ed.). *The Works of That Learned and Judicious Divine, Mr. Richard Hooker.* New York: D. Appleton & Co., 1844. 2 vols.

KÖLBING, E. (ed.). *The Romance of Sir Beues of Hamtoun* (Early English Text Society). London: Kegan Paul, Trench, Trübner, & Co., 1885-1886, 1894.

LEIBLE, A. B. *Conventions of Animal Symbolism and Satire in Spenser's Mother Hubberds Tale* (Dissertation). Chicago: University of Chicago Press, 1928.

————. The Philosophical Background of *King Lear* (Unpublished paper), n.d.

LEIGH, G. *The Accedence of Armorie.* London: Richard Tottell, 1591.

LYLY, J. *Euphues: The Anatomy of Wit* (English Reprints, edited by Edward Arber). Westminster: A Constable & Co., 1895.

————. *Euphues and His England* (English Reprints, edited by Edward Arber). Westminster: A. Constable & Co., 1895.

MAIR, A. W. (trans.) *Oppian, Colluthus, Tryphiodorus* (Loeb Classical Library ed.). New York: G. P. Putnam's Sons, 1928.

MAIR, G. H. (ed.). *Wilson's Arte of Rhetorique 1560.* Oxford: Clarendon Press, 1909.

MACKENZIE, K. R. H. (trans.). *Master Tyll Owlglass His Marvellous Adventures and Rare Conceits.* London: George Routledge & Sons, Ltd., n.d.

McKERROW, R. B. (ed.). *The Works of Thomas Nashe.* London: A. H. Bullen, 1904. 4 vols.

MANN, F. O. (ed.). *The Works of Thomas Deloney.* Oxford: Clarendon Press, 1912.

MOMMSEN, T. (ed.). *C. Iulii Solini Collectanea Rerum Memorabilium.* Berolini: Weidmannos, MDCCCXCV.

MONTAIGLON, A. de, et G. Raynaud (eds.). *Recueil Général et Complet des Fabliaux des XIIIe et XIVe Siècles* (Imprimés ou inédits, publiés d'après les Manuscrits). Paris: Librairie des Bibliophiles, 1872, 1877-1878, 1880, 1883, 1890. 6 vols.

NORTH, T. (trans.). *The Morall Philosophie of Doni* (Photostat Facsimile, Reproduced from the Copy in the Henry E. Huntington Library). London: Henry Denham, 1570.

PAINTER, W. *The Palace of Pleasure* (Edited by Joseph Jacobs). London: David Nutt, 1890. 3 vols.

PALMER, H. R. *List of English Editions and Translations of Greek and Latin Classics Printed Before 1641* (Bibliographical Society). London: Blades, East, & Blades, 1911.

PARADIN, C. *Princeliike Deviisen.* Leyden: Plantijnsche Druckerije van Françoys van Ravelenghien, 1635.

RACKHAM, H. (trans.). *Pliny: Natural History* (Loeb Classical Library ed.). Cambridge, Mass.: Harvard University Press, 1938-1940. 10 vols.

RICHE, B. "Riche his Farewell to Militarie Profession," *Eight Novels Employed by English Dramatic Poets of the Reign of Queen Elizabeth.* London: Shakespeare Society, 1846.

ROBIN, P. A. *Animal Lore in English Literature.* London: John Murray, 1932.

SKEAT, W. W. (ed.). *Vision of William Concerning Piers the Plowman Together with Richard the Redeless.* Oxford: Clarendon Press, 1886. 2 vols.

SMITH, J. A., and W. D. Ross (eds.). *The Works of Aristotle* (Translated into English). Oxford: Clarendon Press, 1910. 11 vols.

TAYLOR, A. "The Proverb 'The Black Ox Has not Trod on His Foot' in Renaissance Literature," *Philological Quarterly,* XX (October, 1941), 266-78.

TAYLOR, R. *The Political Prophecy in England* (Columbia University Studies in English and Comparative Literature, No. 37). New York: Columbia University Press, 1911.

THOMS, W. J. (ed.). *Early English Prose Romances.* New York: E. P. Dutton & Co., 1908.

THORNDIKE, L. *A History of Magic and Experimental Science.* New York: Macmillan Co., 1923. 6 vols.

TOPSELL, E. *The Historie of Foure-Footed Beastes.* London: William Jaggard, 1607.

———. *The Historie of Serpents, or, The second Booke of liuing Creatures.* London: William Jaggard, 1608.

TUCKER, S. M. *Verse Satire in England Before the Renaissance* (Columbia University Studies in English and Comparative Literature, No. 20). New York: Columbia University Press, 1908.

WARNER, C. D. (ed.). *Library of the World's Best Literature, Ancient and Modern.* New York: J. A. Hill & Co., 1902. 46 vols.

WATSON, F. *The English Grammar Schools to 1660: their Curriculum and Practice.* Cambridge: University Press, 1908.

——— (trans.). *Vives: On Education* (A Translation of the *De Tradendis Disciplinis* of Juan Luis Vives). Cambridge: University Press, 1913.

WELSFORD, E. *The Court Masque.* Cambridge: University Press, 1927.

WESTCOTT, B. F., and F. J. A. Hort (eds.). *The New Testament in the Original Greek.* London: Macmillan & Co., Ltd., 1901.

WOODWARD, W. H. *Desiderius Erasmus concerning the Aim and Method of Education.* Cambridge: University Press, 1904.

——— (ed.). *Vittorino da Feltre and Other Humanist Educators.* Cambridge: University Press, 1897.

WRIGHT, T. (ed.). *Alexandri Neckam De Naturis Rerum Libri Duo* (Rolls Series). London: Longman, Green, Longman, Roberts, & Green, 1863.

———. *A History of Caricature and Grotesque in Literature and Art.* London: Chatto & Windus, 1875.

——— (ed.). *Political Poems and Songs Relating to English His-*

tory, Composed During the Period from the Accession of Edward III to That of Richard III (Rolls Series). London: Longman, Green, Longman, & Roberts, 1859-1861. 2 vols.

────── and J. O. Halliwell (eds.). *Reliquiae Antiquae* (Scraps from Ancient Manuscripts, illustrating chiefly Early English Literature and the English Language). London: John Russell Smith, 1845. 2 vols.

ZUPITZA, J. (ed.). *The Romance of Guy of Warwick* (Early English Text Society Publications, Extra Series, No. 25). London: N. Trübner & Co., 1875. 2 vols.

Notes

CHAPTER ONE:

1. Percy Ansell Robin, *Animal Lore in English Literature*, p. 13.
2. *Ibid.*, p. 6.
3. J. A. Smith and W. D. Ross (eds.), *The Works of Aristotle, Translated into English*, IV, 488-631.
4. A. W. Mair (trans.), *Oppian, Colluthus, Tryphiodorus* (Loeb Classical Library ed.), pp. xxv-xxvii. Mair points out that, according to Cuvier, in the introduction to his *Histoire Naturelle des Poissons*, "Alexandre [le Grand] donna à Aristote, pour recueiller les matériaux de son histoire des animaux, des sommes qui montèrent à neuf cents talens, à quoi Pline [viii. 44] ajoute que le roi mit plusieurs milliers d'hommes à la disposition du philosophe, pour chasser, pêcher et observer tout ce qu'il désirait connaître."
5. Besides his *Historia Animalium*, Aristotle wrote *De Partibus Animalium, De Animalium Motione, De Animalium Incessu,* and *De Animalium Generatione.*
6. Mair, *op cit.*, p. xxv.
7. H. Rackham (trans.), *Pliny: Natural History* (Loeb Classical Library ed.), III, 1-609.
8. Mair, *op. cit.*, pp. xxix-xxx. Mair states that Juba II, king of Mauritania, after the death of his father in 46 B.C., was brought a prisoner to Rome, where he remained till his restoration by Octavian in 30 B.C., and that he wrote on Assyria, Arabia, and Africa — his work on the latter supplying information on the elephant, the lion, and the crocotta.
9. *Ibid.*, pp. 1-501.
10. Theodor Mommsen (ed.), C. *Julii Solini Collectanea Rerum Memorabilium*, pp. 1-193.
11. R. Hercher (ed.), *AEliani De Natura Animalium, Varia Historia, Epistolae et Fragmenta; Porphyrii Philosophi De Abstinentia et De Antro Nympharum; Philonis Byzantii De Septem Orbis Spectaculis*, pp. 1-538.
12. Lynn Thorndike, *A History of Magic and Experimental Science*, I, 497.

13. *Ibid.*, I, 624.
14. John de Trevisa's English translation of *De Proprietatibus Rerum* (completed in 1398) was printed by Wynkyn de Worde. Stephan Batman, a London physician, published an abridged reprint of the work in a folio of 1582, *Batman vppon Bartholome*, a copy of which is in the rare book collection of the Harper Library at the University of Chicago.
15. Thomas Wright (ed.), *Alexandri Neckam De Naturis Rerum Libri Duo* (Rolls Series), pp. 1-354.
16. Robin, *op. cit.*, p. 12.
17. Robin, *op. cit.*, p. 13.
18. Thorndike, *op. cit.*, VI, 271.
19. A folio volume containing these two works is in the rare book collection of the Harper Library at the University of Chicago.
20. *The Historie of Foure-Footed Beastes*, p. 489. A marginal note accompanying the discussion of the lynx is as follows: "A story of a Linxe by D[r]. [John] Cay, taken in England by the sight of this beast in the Tower." Naturalists in the sixteenth century quite commonly sent each other specimens, drawings, or written descriptions of strange animals which they had run across.
21. *Ibid.*, pp. 2-7.
22. *Ibid.*, pp. 12-15.
23. *Ibid.*, pp. 17-18.
24. *The Historie of Foure-Footed Beastes*, p. 32.
25. *Ibid.*, p.714.
26. *Ibid.*, pp. 32, 721.
27. *Ibid.*, p. 712.
28. *The Historie of Foure-Footed Beastes*, p. 37.
29. *Ibid.*, pp. 92-99.
30. *Ibid.*, p. 126.
31. *Ibid.*, pp. 456-72.
32. *Ibid.*, p. 708.
33. *Ibid.*, pp. 580-82.
34. *Ibid.*, p. 221.
35. *Ibid.*, pp. 20-26.
36. *Ibid.*, p. 697.
37. *The Historie of Serpents*, pp. 52-53, 57-58, 147-53, 290-306.
38. *Ibid.*, pp. 126-41.
39. *Ibid.*, pp. 119-25.
40. *Ibid.*, pp. 186-89.
41. *Ibid.*, pp. 64-67.
42. *Ibid.*, pp. 102-11.

43. For the list of these beasts, birds, reptiles, and other creatures, and the traditional ideas pertaining to them, see the Appendix.

CHAPTER TWO:

1. Stephen Gosson, *The School of Abuse, Containing a Pleasant Invective Against Poets, Pipers, Players, Jesters, &c.,* pp. 33-34; Stephen Gosson, *The Ephemerides of Phialo* (Huntington Library facsimile), p. 89 *recto; The Complete Works of Thomas Lodge* (Hunterian Club ed.), ii, 20; *Ibid.,* IV, i, 45; Alexander B. Gosart (ed.), *The Life and Complete Works in Prose and Verse of Robert Greene,* M.A. (Huth Library), VIII, 219; *ibid.,* X, 212; *ibid.,* XII, 118, 128; Ronald B. McKerrow (ed.). *The Works of Thomas Nashe,* I, 83; 167; *ibid.,* III, 17, 373.

2. John Lyly, *Euphues and His England* (English Reprints, edited by Edward Arber), pp. 214, 416; *Works of Greene* (Grosart), III, 78; *ibid.,* V, 192-93; *ibid.,* VII, 131-32; *ibid.,* IX, 102; *ibid.,* X, 77; *ibid.,* XI, 137; *Works of Nashe* (McKerrow), III, 58.

3. John Lyly, *Euphues: The Anatomy of Wit* (English Reprints, edited by Edward Arber), pp. 53-54; Herbert Hartman (ed.), *A Petite Pallace of Pettie His Pleasure,* p. 148; Stephen Gosson, *The School of Abuse,* p. 27; *Works of Lodge* (Hunterian Club), I, ii, 32; *ibid.,* I, iii, 31; *ibid.,* III, iv, 34; *Works of Greene* (Grosart), II, 110, 182, 257; *ibid.,* VI, 84; *Works of Nashe* (McKerrow), I, 345.

4. Stephen Gosson, *The Ephemerides of Phialo* (Huntington Library facsimile), p. 3 *recto; Works of Lodge* (Hunterian Club)), I, v, 19; *ibid.,* II, iii, 90; *Works of Greene* (Grosart), II, 110, 184, 210; *ibid.,* V, 84-85; *ibid.,* VI, 71, 161, 252-53; *ibid.,* IX, 94; *ibid.,* XI, 13; *Works of Nashe* (McKerrow), I, 123; Francis Oscar Mann (ed.), *The Works of Thomas Deloney,* p. 162.

5. See Appendix (the asterisked entries).

6. John Lyly, *Euphues and His England* (Arber), p. 284; R. Warwick Bond (ed.), *The Complete Works of John Lyly,* III, 404; *A Petite Pallace of Pettie His Pleasure* (Hartman), pp. 219, 225; *Works of Lodge* (Hunterian Club), IV, i, 6, 17, 92; *Works of Greene* (Grosart), II, 114, 229; *ibid.,* IV, 89, 133; *ibid.,* VI, 78; *ibid.,* X, 257, 260; *ibid.,* XI, 143, 155, 219; *ibid.,* XII, 229; *Works of Nashe* (McKerrow), I, 162; *ibid.,* II, 246, 263; *ibid.,* III, 348, 387, 390-91, 394-95; *Works of Deloney* (Mann), pp. 7, 32, 50; Barnabe Riche, "Riche His Farewell to Militarie Pro-

fession," *Eight Novels Employed by English Dramatic Poets of the Reign of Queen Elizabeth,* p. 128.

7. John Allen Giles (ed.), *The Whole Works of Roger Ascham,* III, 164; Stephen Gosson, *The School of Abuse,* p. 9; *Works of Nashe* (McKerrow), I, 205, 207, 352; *ibid.,* II, 63, 100, 113; *ibid.,* III, 373.

8. George Herbert Mair (ed.), Wilson's *Arte of Rhetorique 1560,* p. 171; *Works of Lodge* (Hunterian Club), IV, i, 83.

9. John Lyly, *Euphues* (Arber), pp. 35, 41, 127; John Lyly, *Euphues and His England* (Arber), p. 372; *A Petite Pallace of Pettie His Pleasure* (Hartman), pp. 21, 24, 64, 113, 172, 239; John Grange, *The Golden Aphroditis* (facsimile), p. H *recto,* p. J iii *recto;* Stephen Gosson, *The School of Abuse,* p. 43; Albert Feuillerat (ed.), *The Complete Works of Sir Philip Sidney,* I, 435; *ibid.,* II, 45; *Works of Lodge* (Hunterian Club), I, iii, 17; *ibid.,* I, v, 73, 112, 118; *ibid.,* II, iii, 62; *ibid.,* III, iv, 27, 69; *Works of Greene* (Grosart), II, 21, 25, 38, 93, 102-103, 112-13, 122, 129, 153, 169, 190, 198; *ibid.,* III, 39-40, 209, 215; *ibid.,* IV, 43, 56, 91, 103, 120, 141, 286; *ibid.,* V, 56-57; *ibid.,* VI, 68, 163, 176, 180, 192; *ibid.,* VII, 34, 37, 68, 116, 162, 167; *ibid.,* VIII, 25, 96, 134, 143-44, 222; *ibid.,* IX, 33, 41, 64, 132, 185, 200, 206, 302; *ibid.,* X, 19, 239; *ibid.,* XI, 7, 14, 44, 138; *ibid.,* XII, 36-37, 237, 242, 265; *Works of Nashe* (McKerrow), I, 126; *ibid.,* II, 169; *Works of Deloney* (Mann), p. 160.

10. John Lyly, *Euphues and His England* (Arber), p. 327.

11. *Works of Lodge* (Hunterian Club), I, v, 37; *Works of Greene* (Grosart), II, 31, 226; *ibid.,* III, 86; *ibid.,* IX, 8; *ibid.,* X, 225.

12. *Works of Lodge* (Hunterian Club), I, v, 71; *ibid.,* II, ii, 29; *Works of Deloney* (Mann), p. 269.

13. *Works of Greene* (Grosart), II, 63; *ibid.,* IV, 106, 108-109; *ibid.,* IX, 76.

14. *Works of Nashe* (McKerrow), I, 114.

15. *Works of Greene* (Grosart), II, 153; *ibid.,* III, 25; *ibid.,* IV, 132; *ibid.,* VIII, 153-54; *Works of Nashe* (McKerrow), II, 263; Riche, *op. cit.,* p. 39.

16. John Lyly, *Euphues* (Arber), p. 157; *Wilson's Arte of Rhetorique* (Mair), p. 151; *A Petite Pallace of Pettie His Pleasure* (Hartman), p. 75; *Works of Lodge* (Hunterian Club), II, iii, 20; *Works of Greene* (Grosart), XII, 111.

17. Stephen Gosson, *The Ephemerides of Phialo* (Huntington Library facsimile), p. 72 *verso; Works of Lodge* (Hunterian Club), I, v, 16; *Works of Greene* (Grosart), VI, 57.

18. *Works of Sidney* (Feuillerat), I, 25.

19. *Works of Lodge* (Hunterian Club), I, iii, 51; *Works of Deloney* (Mann), p. 199.
20. Joseph Jacobs (ed.), *The Fables of AEsop,* p. xx.
21. Charles Dudley Warner (ed.), *Library of the World's Best Literature, Ancient and Modern,* XXIX, 11485.
22. Thomas North (trans.), *The Morall Philosophie of Doni* (Huntington Library facsimile), pp. 51-52, 111.
23. *Ibid.,* pp. 78-80.
24. E. K. Chambers, *The Mediaeval Stage,* I, 166.
25. *Ibid.,* I, 221-24.
26. Enid Welsford, *The Court Masque,* pp. 42-43; Chambers, *op. cit.,* I, 275, 391-92.
27. *Ibid.,* I, 384-87.
28. Welsford, *op. cit., pp.* 71-72.
29. *Ibid.,* pp. 106-109.
30. Arthur B. Leible, *Conventions of Animal Symbolism and Satire in Spenser's Mother Hubberds Tale* (Dissertation), p. 19.
31. Thomas Wright, *A History of Caricature and Grotesque in Literature and Art,* pp. 106-109.
32. Leible, *op. cit.,* p. 27.
33. William Caxton (trans.), *The History of Reynard the Fox* (Edited by Edward Arber), p. 83.
34. Caxton, *op. cit.,* pp. 84-89.
35. Wright, *History of Caricature and Grotesque,* pp. 78-80.
36. *Ibid.,* p. 81.
37. Leible, *op. cit.,* pp. 35-36.
38. Thomas Wright and James Orchard Halliwell (eds.), *Reliquiae Antiquae,* I, 65-66.
39. Eugen Kölbing (ed.), *The Romance of Sir Beues of Hamtoun* (Early English Text Society), pp. 115-18.
40. Kölbing, *op. cit.,* p. 115.
41. *Ibid.,* p. 129.
42. *Ibid.,* pp. 127-31.
43. *Ibid.,* p. 198.
44. *Ibid.,* p. 129.
45. William J. Thoms (ed.), *Early English Prose Romances,* p. 27. The earliest edition of the romance in English prose was printed by William Copland before 1570.
46. Julius Zupitza (ed.), *The Romance of Guy of Warwick* (Early English Text Society Publications, Extra Series, No. 25), I, 110-12; Thoms, *op. cit.,* pp. 368-69.
47. In the prose version (Thoms, *op. cit.,* pp. 368-69), the incident

is told in a Homeric simile, Guy and the lion being compared to Andronicus (Androcles) and the lion.

48. Zupitza, *op. cit.*, I, 195-99; Thoms, *op. cit.*, pp. 378-79.
49. *Ibid.*, p. 378.
50. Henrietta Raymer Palmer, *List of English Editions and Translations of Greek and Latin Classics Printed Before 1641* (Bibliographical Society), p. 87. A copy of this summary of Pliny's work is in the British Museum (433. a. 4.).
51. All footnote references to the Old Testament are to the Authorized Version; references to the New Testament are to the Greek text: Brooke Foss Westcott and Fenton John Anthony Hort (eds.), *The New Testament in the Original Greek.*
52. Deut. 33:17; Job 39:9-12; Ps. 92:10.
53. Isa. 14:29; Isa. 59:5. The terms *basilisk* and *cockatrice* are used synonymously.
54. Isa. 13:21.
55. Robin, *op. cit.*, pp. 6, 74, 85.
56. Gen. 49:9; Judg. 14:5-9; Job 4:10; Prov. 28:1; Prov. 30:30; Isa. 31:4; Ezek. 19:6.
57. Gen. 49:27; Matt. 7:15; Matt. 10:16; Luke 10:3.
58. Judg. 15:4-5; Song of Sol. 2:15; Luke 13:32.
59. Job 39:12-18.
60. Gen. 3:1; Gen. 49:17; Ps. 140:3; Isa. 14:29; Matt. 10:16; II Cor. 11:3; Rev. 12:9; Rev. 20:2.
61. Prov. 30:25.
62. Ps. 105:34-35; Isa. 33:4; Matt. 6:19-20.
63. Isa. 13:21; Isa. 34:11, 13-15.
64. I Kings 12:11, 14; Rev. 9:5, 10.
65. Ps. 58:4-5.
66. Eccles. 10:20. Thomas Nashe's (Pasquil's) statement "I heard a bird sing more than I mean to say" (*Works of Nashe* (McKerrow), I (*The First Parte of Pasquils Apologie*), 114) is reminiscent of the Biblical passage, as also is the well-known saying "A little bird told me."
67. Num. 22:21-35; II Pet. 2:15-16.
68. Jer. 13:23.
69. Matt. 23:24.
70. Matt. 23:27; Luke 13:34.
71. Matt. 24:28; Luke 17:37.
72. Mark 9:48.
73. Prov. 26:11; II Pet. 2:22.
74. II Pet. 2:22.
75. Isa. 11:6; Isa. 65:25.

76. Matt. 10:16; Luke 10:3.
77. Matt. 7:15.

CHAPTER THREE:

1. Wright, *History of Caricature and Grotesque,* p. 49.
2. See above, p. 25.
3. Wright, *History of Caricature and Grotesque,* pp. 78-80.
4. *Ibid.,* pp. 88-91.
5. *Ibid.,* p. 92.
6. Thomas Wilson, in his *Arte of Rhetorique* (1553), writes as follows: "By the signe wee vnderstand the thing signified: as by an Iuie garland, we iudge there is wine to sel. By the signe of a Beare, Bull, Lyon, or any such, we take any house to be an Inne." (*Wilson's Arte of Rhetorique 1560* (Mair), p. 174.)
7. Leible, *op. cit.,* pp. 36-37.
8. Leible, *op. cit.,* pp. 37-38.
9. *The Blazon of Gentrie,* title page. A copy of this work is in the rare book collection of the Harper Library at the University of Chicago.
10. *The Blazon of Gentrie,* II, 40-41. This sixteenth-century explanation, of course, is not the one offered by students in our time. (See S. T. Aveling, *Heraldry: Ancient and Modern,* pp. 1-3.)
11. Leible, *op. cit.,* p. 39.
12. *The Blazon of Gentrie,* II, 21.
13. See Ferne's dedication to his *Blazon of Gentrie.*
14. I have used the copy of this work (printed in 1591) which is in the rare book collection of the Harper Library at the University of Chicago.
15. *The Accedence of Armorie,* fol. 1 *recto*-fol. 12 *recto.*
16. *Ibid.,* fol. 42 *recto*-fol. 43 *recto.*
17. *Ibid.,* fol. 80 *verso.*
18. *Ibid.,* fol. 52 *recto*-fol. 52 *verso.*
19. *The Blazon of Gentrie.*
20. *Ibid.,* I, 30.
21. Henry Green (ed.), *Whitney's "Choice of Emblemes"* (facsimile reprint), p. 2.
22. *Ibid.,* p. xxiv.
23. A Spanish version, *Las Emblemas de Andres Alciato* (1684), in the Indiana University Library, Bloomington, contains 211 emblems with the mottoes and verses in Latin. A number of these emblems employ conventional ideas about animals, as the

following selected list shows: One emblem (p. 82, not num-
bered) has the motto *"Consilio, et [virtute] Chimaeram su-
perari"* and a picture of Bellerophon, mounted upon Pegasus,
slaying the Chimera with his lance; *Emblema* 137, a picture of
Hercules slaying the Lernean Hydra; *Emblema* 145, the motto
"Consiliarii Principum" and a picture of Chiron the Centaur
instructing Achilles and Patroclus; and *Emblema* 178, the
motto *"Ex Pace Ubertas"* and a picture of a halcyon on its nest
in the sea.

24. Green, *op. cit.*, p. xvi.
25. Leible, *op. cit.*, pp. 60-61.
26. Green, *op. cit.*, p. xiv.
27. I have used a Dutch translation of this work, *Princeliicke
    Deviisen* (1635), which contains 217 emblems: 180 by Paradin
    and 37 by Gabriel Simeon (*Les Devises et Emblèmes héroïques
    et Morales*, 1559). In this collection, Emblem VIII has the
    motto *"Nutrisco & extinguo"* and a picture of a salamander in
    the fire; Emblem XVI, the motto *"Inextricabilis error"* and a
    picture of a sphinx; Emblem CCVI, the motto *"Esto tiene su
    remedio, y non jo"* and a picture of a hart eating dittany to
    extract an arrow.
28. The following is a list of the mottoes and pictorial devices of
    some of the emblems in Whitney's collection that employ con-
    ventional ideas about animals: *"Turpibus exitium"* — a scarab
    beetle in the center of a rose, which he despises because he pre-
    fers to dwell in dung, p. 21; *"Latet anguis in herba"* — a snake
    climbing a strawberry plant, p. 24; *"Vitae, aut morit"* — a bee
    and a spider, sucking honey and poison, respectively, from the
    same flower, p. 51; *"Non dolo, sed vi"* — an ape making a dog
    pull chestnuts out of the fire, p. 58; *"Homines voluptatibus
    transformantur"* — Circe touching with her wand Ulysses' men,
    whom she has transformed into ass, goat, dog, and swine, p. 82;
    "Quod in te est, prome" — a pelican nourishing her brood
    with the blood of her own breast, p. 87; *"Inuidiae descriptio"*
    —envy, an ugly hag eating a viper and tearing her own heart,
    p. 94; *"Ex Bello, pax"* — bees hiving in a helmet, p. 138;
    "Homo homini lupus" — Arion, thrown overboard at sea, be-
    ing borne by a dolphin to Corinth, p. 144; *"Dum aetatis ver
    agitur: consule brumae"* — Aesop's ant and grasshopper, p. 159;
    "Vnica semper auis" — the phoenix with wings spread, fanning
    the flames that consume her, p. 177; *"Caecus amor prolis"* —
    a she-ape killing her babe by hugging it, p. 188; *"Victoria cru-
    enta"* — an elephant, killed by a serpent, kills the serpent by

falling on it, p. 195; *"Inanis impetus"* — a dog foolishly barking at the moon, p. 213.

29. Green, *op. cit.*, p. xviii. Whitney borrowed 202 of his 248 emblems, particularly the pictorial devices, from Paradin (*op. cit.*), Gabriel Faerni (*Fabulae*), Sambucus (*Emblemata*), Hadrian Junius (*Hadriani Iunii Medici Emblemata*, 1565), and Alciat (*op. cit.*): eighty-six emblem devices (more than a third of Whitney's collection) from Alciat and forty-eight from Sambucus. Whitney's devices, moreover, were struck off from the same wood blocks that had been used by Alciat and the other emblem writers. These blocks were available in the establishment of his printer, Christopher Plantyn, at Leyden, the chief publisher of emblem books in the period. It was the custom among printers in the sixteenth century to buy up the old wood blocks which had been cut for other books and to introduce them into their own publications. Plantyn possessed abundant stores of pictorial embellishments for books of many kinds; and when woodcuts or engravings had served for a work in Latin or French, he freely employed them for similar works in Flemish, Dutch, or English, and perhaps in Spanish and Italian. (Green, *op. cit.*, pp. 234, 236, 252.)

30. See above, p. 130, n. 30.
31. *Op. cit.*, pp. 4-5.
32. *Op. cit.*, p. 5.
33. Samuel Marion Tucker, *Verse Satire in England Before the Renaissance* (Columbia University Studies in English and Comparative Literature, No. 20), pp. 43-46.
34. Leible, *op. cit.*, p. 51.
35. Thomas Wright (ed.), *Political Poems and Songs Relating to English History, Composed During the Period from the Accession of Edward III to That of Richard III* (Rolls Series), I, 1-25.
36. *Ibid.*, I, 26-40.
37. *Ibid.*, I, 72-83.
38. *Political Poems and Songs* (Wright), I, 417-54.
39. Walter W. Skeat (ed.), *The Vision of William Concerning Piers the Plowman Together with Richard the Redeless*, I, 603-28.
40. *Ibid.*, I, 615-16. Skeat (*ibid.*, II, xcii) states the contents of this parable of how the King's harts (retainers wearing the badge of the white hart, which Richard II had dispersed too widely) came to misfortune as follows: "The worst of all faults are those committed against nature. . . . When a hart comes to be a hun-

dred years old, he adopts this plan for renewing his youth. It is his wont to catch and kill an adder, and to feed upon his venom, by which means he succeeds in renewing his skin. It is natural, then, for the hart to prey upon the adder; but it is unnatural for him to attack a Colt [Thomas Fitz-alan], or a Horse [the earl of Arundel], or a Swan [the duke of Gloucester], or a Bear [the earl of Warwick]. It is therefore because of their unnatural conduct that the harts failed of success."

41. *Ibid.*, I, 616-17.
42. *Ibid.*, I, 617.
43. Skeat, *op. cit.*, I, 609-26.
44. Tucker, *op. cit.*, p. 97.
45. *Political Poems and Songs* (Wright), I, 363-66.
46. Frederick J. Furnivall (ed.), *Political, Religious, and Love Poems* (Early English Text Society), pp. 6-11.
47. *Political Poems and Songs* (Wright), II, 221-23.
48. *Political Poems and Songs* (Wright), II, 224-25.
49. *The Political Prophecy in England* (Columbia University Studies in English and Comparative Literature, No. 37), p. 2.
50. Taylor, *op. cit.*, p. 4.
51. John Allen Giles (ed.), *Galfredi Monumetensis Historia Britonum* (Publications of the Caxton Society), p. 124.
52. *Ibid.*, pp. 119-24; Taylor, *op. cit.*, pp. 7-10.
53. Taylor, *op. cit.*, pp. 48-50.
54. See above, p. 38.
55. Leible, *op. cit.*, p. 49. A stock example of the Elizabethan dramatists' attitude toward the prophecies is Hotspur's ridicule of "the dreamer Merlin and his prophecies, . . . of a dragon and a finless fish, . . . clip-wing'd griffin and . . . moulten raven, . . . couching lion and . . . ramping cat, . . . such a deal of skimble-skamble stuff." (*1 Henry IV*, iii, 1, 147-55.) Taylor, p. 105f.
56. Leible, *op. cit.*, p. 50. Taylor, pp. 113-14.
57. Francis Oscar Mann (ed.), *The Works of Thomas Deloney*, p. xxi.
58. Anatole de Montaiglon et Gaston Raynaud (eds.) *Recueil Général et Complet des Fabliaux des XIIIe et XIVe Siècles* (Imprimés ou inédits), I, 11 (*Des Deux Bordéors*) ; III, 283 (*Des Braies au Cordelier*, which has these lines: "La dame sot mout de renart; Engigneuse fu de toz tors.").
59. *Ibid.*, III, 223. *De Charlot le Juif.*
60. *Ibid.*, III, 217-18. *Le Testament de l'Asne* (par Rutebeuf).
61. William Carew Hazlitt (ed.), *Shakespeare Jest-Books* (Re-

prints of the early and very rare Jest-books supposed to have been used by Shakespeare), II, 222. Hazlitt says (*ibid.*, II, 190) that although "the edition of 1611 is the earliest now known," it is "beyond doubt that Tarlton's Jests were in print before 1600" and that "the first part indeed is mentioned in one of Nash's tracts as in existence prior to 1592, and was probably committed to the press not long after the death of Tarlton, which happened in Sept. 1588."

62. *Ibid.*, II, 198.
63. *Ibid.*, II, 203.
64. *Ibid.*, I, ii, 45-46.
65. Hazlitt, *op. cit.*, I, ii, 149.
66. *Ibid.*, II, 288. Hazlitt expresses some doubt (*ibid.*, II, 262) that the *Merrie Conceited Jests of George Peele* had appeared in print before 1607, "although the dramatist was dead without doubt before 1598."
67. Kenneth Robert Henderson Mackenzie (trans.), *Master Tyll Owlglass His Marvellous Adventures and Rare Conceits,* p. 103.
68. Mackenzie, *op. cit.*, p. 257.
69. Arthur B. Leible, "The Philosophical Background of *King Lear*" (unpublished paper), pp. 7-8.
70. William W. Goodwin (ed.), *Plutarch's Morals* (Translated from the Greek by Several Hands), V, 218-33. In the same work (IV, 192), Plutarch writes that beasts, in their obedience to nature, are for an example to man.
71. Leible, "Background of *Lear*," p. 6.
72. Charles Frederick Tucker Brooke (ed.), *Shakespeare's Plutarch* (The Shakespeare Classics), I, ix-x.
73. William Harrison Woodward, *Vittorino da Feltre and Other Humanist Educators,* p. 222 and n. 1.
74. William Harrison Woodward, *Desiderius Erasmus Concerning the Aim and Method of Education,* p. 139.
75. *Ibid.*, p. 167.
76. *Ibid.*, pp. 186-87, 192.
77. Foster Watson (trans.), *Vives: On Education* (A translation of the *De Tradendis Disciplinis* of Juan Luis Vives), pp. 250-51.
78. Maurice Adams (ed.), *The "Utopia" and the "History of Edward V," by Sir Thomas More,* pp. 145, 155.
79. Sir Thomas Elyot, *The Gouernour* (Everyman's Library ed.), pp. 204-205.
80. Leible, "Background of *Lear*," p. 20.
81. John Keble (ed.), *The Works of That Learned and Judicious*

Divine, Mr. Richard Hooker, I, 163-84.
82. *Ibid.,* I, 158-61.
83. Foster Watson, *The English Grammar Schools to 1660: their Curriculum and Practice,* p. 440.
84. Watson, *op. cit.,* pp. 5-6.
85. *Ibid.,* p. 440; Francis R. Johnson, "Two Renaissance Textbooks of Rhetoric: Aphthonius' *Progymnasmata* and Rainolde's *A booke called the Foundacion of Rhetorike,*" *The Huntington Library Quarterly,* VI (1942-1943), 427-44. Richard Rainolde's *Foundacion of Rhetorike* (1563) is an adaptation in English of Aphthonius' *Progymnasmata* (fourth century). Four other leading treatises on rhetoric in England before 1600 are Thomas Wilson's *Arte of Rhetorique* (1553), which went through at least eight editions; Ramus' edition (1579) of Andomarus Talaeus' *Rhetoric* (1547); Peacham's *Garden of Eloquence* (1577); and Abraham Fraunce's *Arcadian Rhetoric* (1588).
86. *Desiderius Erasmus Concerning the Aim and Method of Education* (Woodward), p. 143. Woodward quotes Erasmus.
87. *Wilson's Arte of Rhetorique 1560* (Mair), pp. 188-89.
88. *Wilson's Arte of Rhetorique 1560* (Mair), p. 191.
89. *Ibid.,* pp. 192-94.
90. *Ibid.,* pp. 197-98.

CHAPTER FOUR:

1. John Lyly, *Euphues* (Arber), pp. 98, 129, 153, 190; John Lyly, *Euphues and His England* (Arber), pp. 226, 315, 395; *Works of Ascham* (Giles), III, 213, 236; *Wilson's Arte of Rhetorique* (Mair), pp. 1-3 (preface), 11, 19, 26, 46-49, 76-77, 83, 93, 102, 109, 111, 116-17, 150, 173, 192, 194-95, 206-207; *A Petite Pallace of Pettie His Pleasure* (Hartman), pp. 18, 40, 64, 93, 122, 154, 162, 171, 201, 225-26, 234; John Grange, *The Golden Aphroditis* (facsimile), pp. E ii *verso,* K ii *recto;* Stephen Gosson, *The School of Abuse* (Shakespeare Society), p. 22; Stephen Gosson, *The Ephemerides of Phialo* (Huntington Library facsimile), pp. 8 *verso,* 10 *recto,* 33 *verso,* 34 *rector-34 verso,* 46 *recto,* 65 *recto,* 68 *recto-68 verso,* 69 *recto-69 verso,* 84 *recto,* 85 *recto;* *Works of Sidney* (Feuillerat), I, 39, 113, 146, 179, 311, 322, 364, 403, 409, 459, 472, 507; *ibid.,* II, 11, 119, 198; *ibid.,* III, 4, 16, 30; *Works of Lodge* (Hunterian Club), I, ii, 30; *ibid.,* I, iii, 19; *ibid.,* II, i, 3, 21, 28, 30; *ibid.,* II, ii, 27, 48, 57-58; *ibid.,* II, iii, 13, 28, 48, 56, 65, 91; *ibid.,* III, iii ,15, 60-61;

ibid., III, iv, 27; *ibid.,* IV, i, 24, 50-51, 58, 96-98, 101, 105, 110-11, 114; *Works of Greene* (Grosart), II, 21, 40, 83, 285; *ibid.,* III, 19-20, 92; *ibid.,* IV, 16, 40, 81, 86, 117, 135-36, 190, 262, 314; *ibid.,* V, 17, 131, 134-35, 282; *ibid.,* VI, 76, 187, 205; *ibid.,* VII, 28, 185, 209; *ibid.,* VIII, 80, 141; *ibid.,* IX, 289-90, 310, 346; *ibid.,* X, 233, 237-38, 269; *ibid.,* XI, 131, 219; *ibid.,* XII, 60, 145, 162; *Works of Nashe* (McKerrow), I, 40, 98, 205, 209, 345; *ibid.,* II, 70, 112-13, 153, 171, 237, 290; *ibid.,* III, 36, 215; *Works of Deloney* (Mann), pp. 7, 17, 61, 63, 229; Riche, *op. cit.,* pp. 143, 175.

2. *Works of Sidney* (Feuillerat), I *(Arcadia)*, 113.
3. *Wilson's Arte of Rhetorique* (Mair), pp. 1-3 (preface).
4. *Ibid.,* p. 46.
5. *Ibid.,* p. 48.
6. *Wilson's Arte of Rhetorique* (Mair), p. 191.
7. *Ibid.,* p. 48.
8. *Ibid.,* p. 116.
9. *Ibid.,* p. 26.
10. *Ibid.,* p. 125.
11. *Wilson's Arte of Rhetorique* (Mair), pp. 76-77.
12. *Ibid.,* p. 191.
13. *Ibid.,* p. 117.
14. *Ibid.,* p. 195.
15. *Wilson's Arte of Rhetorique* (Mair), p. 171.
16. *Ibid.,* p. 173.
17. *Ibid.,* p. 199.
18. *Ibid.,* p. 207.
19. *Ibid.,* p. 208.
20. *Ibid.,* p. 219.
21. *Wilson's Arte of Rhetorique* (Mair), p. 220.
22. *Ibid.,* pp. 219-20.
23. *Works of Ascham* (Giles), III, 153.
24. *Ibid.,* III, 154.
25. *Works of Ascham* (Giles), III, 156.
26. *Ibid.,* III, 164.
27. *Ibid.,* III, 205, 213.
28. *Works of Ascham* (Giles), III, 236.
29. *Ibid.,* III, 201.
30. *Ibid.,* III, 250.
31. *Works of Ascham* (Giles), III, 225.
32. *Ibid.,* III, 226.
33. William Painter, *The Palace of Pleasure* (edited by Joseph Jacobs), I, 89-90.

34. *Ibid.,* I, 86-87.
35. *Ibid.,* III, 250.
36. *Ibid.,* I, 112-13.
37. *Ibid.,* I, 198.
38. Painter, *op. cit.,* I, 204, 213-14.
39. *Ibid.,* I, 203.
40. *Ibid.,* I, 205.
41. *Ibid.,* II, 211.
42. *Ibid.,* II, 239.
43. *Ibid.,* II, 288.
44. Painter, *op. cit.,* III, 54.
45. *Ibid.,* III, 48.
46. *Ibid.,* I, 245.
47. *Ibid.,* III, 17.
48. *Ibid.,* III, 212.
49. Painter, *op. cit.,* III, 160.
50. *Ibid.,* III, 171.
51. *Ibid.,* I, 199.
52. *Ibid.,* II, 36-37.
53. *Ibid.,* III, 154.
54. *Ibid.,* III, 141.
55. Painter, *op. cit.,* III, 10.
56. *A Petite Pallace of Pettie His Pleasure* (Hartman), p. 6.
57. *Ibid.,* p. 203.
58. *Ibid.,* p. 241.
59. *A Petite Pallace of Pettie His Pleasure* (Hartman), p. 168.
60. *Ibid.,* pp. 16-17.
61. *Ibid.,* p. 18.
62. *A Petite Pallace of Pettie His Pleasure* (Hartman), p. 48.
63. *Ibid.,* p. 124.
64. *Ibid.,* p. 165.
65. *A Petite Pallace of Pettie His Pleasure* (Hartman), p. 257.
66. *Ibid.,* p. 48.
67. *Ibid.,* p. 51.
68. *Ibid.,* p. 93.
69. *Ibid.*
70. *A Petite Pallace of Pettie His Pleasure* (Hartman), p. 97.
71. *Ibid.,* pp. 186, 206.
72. *Ibid.,* p. 207.
73. *Ibid.,* p. 187.
74. *Ibid.,* p. 204.
75. *Ibid.,* p. 207.
76. *A Petite Pallace of Pettie His Pleasure* (Hartman), p. 216.

77. *Ibid.*, pp. 219, 225.
78. *Ibid.*, p. 211.
79. *Ibid.*, p. 240.
80. *Ibid.*, p. 263.
81. *Ibid.*, p. 270.
82. *A Petite Pallace of Pettie His Pleasure* (Hartman), p. 21.
83. *Ibid.*, p. 24.
84. *A Petite Pallace of Pettie His Pleasure* (Hartman), p. 64.
85. *Ibid.*, p. 69.
86. *Ibid.*, p. 75.
87. *Ibid.*, p. 113.
88. *Ibid.*, p. 154.
89. *A Petite Pallace of Pettie His Pleasure* (Hartman), p. 231.
90. *Ibid.*, p. 239.
91. *A Petite Pallace of Pettie His Pleasure* (Hartman), p. 104.
92. *Ibid.*, pp. 139-40.
93. *Ibid.*, p. 226.
94. *Ibid.*, p. 261.
95. *A Petite Pallace of Pettie His Pleasure* (Hartman), p. 148.
96. *Ibid.*, pp. 14-15.
97. *Ibid.*, p. 15.
98. *Ibid.*, p. 40.
99. *A Petite Pallace of Pettie His Pleasure* (Hartman), p. 148.
100. *Ibid.*, pp. 269-70.
101. *Ibid.*, p. 188.
102. *Ibid.*, p. 26.
103. *Ibid.*, p. 168.
104. *Ibid.*, p. 190.
105. *A Petite Pallace of Pettie His Pleasure* (Hartman), p. 237.
106. *Ibid.*, p. 240.
107. *Ibid.*, p. 250.
108. Riche, *op. cit.*, p. 79.
109. Riche, *op. cit.*, p. 142.
110. *Ibid.*, p. 139.
111. *Ibid.*, p. 128.
112. *Ibid.*, p. 145.
113. *Ibid.*, p. 213.
114. *Ibid.*, p. 219.
115. *Ibid.*, p. 39.
116. Riche, *op. cit.*, p. 63.
117. *Ibid.*, pp. 34-35.
118. Stephen Gosson, *The School of Abuse* (Shakespeare Society), pp. 22-23.

119. *Ibid.*, p. 7.
120. *The School of Abuse* (Shakespeare Society), p. 9.
121. *Ibid.*, pp. 10-11.
122. *Ibid.*, p. 9.
123. *Ibid.*, p. 10.
124. *Ibid.*, p. 11.
125. *Ibid.*, p. 17.
126. *Ibid.*, pp. 19-20.
127. *Ibid.*, p. 25.
128. *Ibid.*, pp. 48-49.
129. *The School of Abuse* (Shakespeare Society), pp. 27-28.
130. *Ibid.*, p. 27.
131. *Ibid.*, p. 13.
132. *Ibid.*, p. 37.
133. *Ibid.*, p. 35.
134. *The School of Abuse* (Shakespeare Society), pp. 45-46.
135. *The School of Abuse* (Shakespeare Society), p. 46.
136. *Ibid.*, pp. 33-34.
137. *Ibid.*, p. 36.
138. *The School of Abuse* (Shakespeare Society), p. 40.
139. *The Ephemerides of Phialo* (Huntington Library facsimile), p. 1.
140. *Ibid.*, p. 3 *recto*.
141. *Ibid.*, p. 2.
142. *Ibid.*, p. 2.
143. *Ibid.*, p. 1 *recto*.
144. *The Ephemerides of Phialo* (Huntington Library facsimile), pp. 1 *verso*-2 *recto*.
145. *Ibid.*, p. 41 *verso*.
146. *Ibid.*, p. 42 *recto*.
147. *Ibid.*, pp. 48 *recto*-48 *verso*.
148. *Ibid.*, p. 40 *recto*.
149. *Ibid.*, p. 56 *recto*.
150. *Ibid.*, p. 62 *recto*.
151. *The Euphemerides of Phialo* (Huntington Library facsimile), p. 62 *verso*.
152. *Ibid.*, p. 65 *verso*.
153. *Ibid.*, p. 1 *verso*.
154. *Ibid.*, p. 2 *verso*.
155. *Ibid.*, p. 11 *verso*.
156. *Ibid.*, pp. 13 *recto*-13 *verso*.
157. *Ibid.*, pp. 13 *verso*-14 *recto*.
158. *Ibid.*, p. 19 *recto*.

159. *The Ephemerides of Phialo* (Huntington Library facsimile), p. 50 *recto.*
160. *Ibid.,* p. 64 *verso.*
161. *Ibid.,* p. 53 *recto.*
162. *Ibid.,* p. 26 *recto.*
163. *Ibid.,* p. 32 *verso.*
164. *Ibid.,* p. 38 *recto.*
165. *Ibid.,* p. 36 *verso.*
166. *Works of Lodge* (Hunterian Club), I, ii, 9-10.
167. *Ibid.,* I, ii, 31-32.
168. *Ibid.,* I, ii, 1.
169. *Ibid.,* I, ii, 25.
170. *Works of Lodge* (Hunterian Club), I, ii, 32.
171. *Ibid.,* I, ii, 35.
172. *Ibid.,* I, iii, 15.
173. *Ibid.,* I, iii, 49.
174. *Ibid.,* I, iii, 24.
175. *Ibid.,* I, iii, 31.
176. *Ibid.,* I, iii, 43.
177. *Works of Lodge* (Hunterian Club), I, iii, 50.
178. *Ibid.,* I, iii, 23-24.
179. *Ibid.,* I, iii, 14.
180. *Ibid.,* I, iii, 16.
181. *Ibid.,* I, iii, 17.
182. *Ibid.,* I, iii, 23, 43.
183. *Ibid.,* I, iii, 51.
184. *Works of Lodge* (Hunterian Club), II, ii, 61.
185. *Ibid.,* II, ii, 6.
186. *Ibid.,* II, ii, 15, 17-18.
187. *Ibid.,* II, ii, 20.
188. *Ibid.,* II, ii, 19.
189. *Works of Lodge* (Hunterian Club), II, ii, 20-22.
190. *Works of Lodge* (Hunterian Club), II, ii, 27-28.
191. *Ibid.,* II, ii, 24-25.
192. *Works of Lodge* (Hunterian Club), II, ii, 28-29.
193. *Ibid.,* II, ii, 31.
194. *Ibid.,* II, ii, 38-39.
195. *Ibid.,* II, ii, 38.
196. *Ibid.,* II, ii, 33.
197. *Works of Lodge* (Hunterian Club), II, ii, 53.
198. *Ibid.,* II, ii, 61.
199. Leible, *Conventions of Animal Symbolism and Satire,* pp. 195-96. Probably the conception of the "satyr-ape," who expressed

disapproval of certain aspects of man's conduct, stemmed from the Aesopic fable of "The Man and the Satyr" (Jacobs, *op. cit.*, pp. 131-32), in which a satyr, an ape-like creature, is represented as being at dinner with a man who had invited him to share the meal and as saying, "I will have nought to do with a man who can blow hot [to warm his hands] and cold [to cool his porridge] with the same breath." To this fable has been assigned also the origin of the proverbial saying about "blowing hot and cold."

200. Leible, *Conventions of Animal Symbolism and Satire*, p. 97.

201. *Works of Lyly* (Bond), III, 412.

202. *Ibid.*, III, 395.

203. Alexander B. Grosart (ed.), *The Complete Works of Thomas Nashe* (Huth Library), I, 143-205.

204. *Works of Nashe* (McKerrow), III, 352.

205. *Ibid.*, I, 207.

206. *Ibid.*, I, 260.

207. *Ibid.*, I, 268.

208. *Ibid.*, I, 290.

209. *Works of Nashe* (McKerrow), I, 306.

210. *Ibid.*, I, 385.

211. *Works of Lyly* (Bond), III, 400-402; *Works of Nashe* (McKerrow), I, 90, 102, 134; *ibid.*, III, 341-42, 351, 368.

212. *Works of Greene* (Grosart), XI, 211, 238, 288, 292.

213. *Works of Nashe* (McKerrow), I, 161, 196, 199, 207, 240, 242.

214. *Ibid.*, I, 282, 288, 290, 314, 328-29, 333; *ibid.*, III, 38, 54, 85, 112, 128, 130.

215. *Works of Nashe* (McKerrow), I, 288.

216. *Ibid.*, I, 290.

217. *Works of Greene* (Grosart), X, 99, 223; *ibid.*, XI, 7, 27.

218. Alexander B. Grosart (ed.), *The Works of Gabriel Harvey, D.C.L.* (Huth Library), I, 233-34; *ibid.*, II, 23, 34, 37, 39-43, 52, 59, 69, 73, 79, 82, 90-91, 113-14, 236-38, 245-65, 292, 294, 322, 331; *ibid.*, III, 10-11, 14, 29, 32-33, 35, 61-62.

219. *Ibid.*, I, 189, 233-34; *ibid.*, II, 7, 82, 222-24.

220. *Ibid.*, II, 245-65.

221. *Works of Harvey* (Grosart), I, 233-34.

222. *Ibid.*, II, 238.

223. *Ibid.*, II, 237.

224. *Ibid.*, II, 292.

225. *Ibid.*, II, 222.

226. *Ibid.*, I, 205.

227. *Works of Greene* (Grosart), V, 248.

228. *Works of Greene* (Grosart), V. 249.
229. *Works of Lyly* (Bond), III, 401; *Works of Nashe* (McKerrow), I, 62, 93; *ibid,* III, 376.
230. *Works of Lyly* (Bond), III, 401; *Works of Nashe* (McKerrow), I, 62, 93, 125, 134.
231. *Works of Nashe* (McKerrow), I, 333. The expression "*Wolfes print*" is, of course, a pun on the name of the contemporary printer John Wolfe.
232. Leible, *Conventions of Animal Symbolism and Satire,* p. 192.
233. *Works of Nashe* (McKerrow), I, 93, 95; *ibid.,* III, 362.
234. *Works of Nashe* (McKerrow), I, 221-26.
235. *Ibid.,* II, 99.
236. *Works of Greene* (Grosart), XI, 13.
237. *Works of Harvey* (Grosart), I, 179.
238. *Ibid.,* II, 302.
239. *Works of Harvey* (Grosart), II, 306.
240. *Works of Nashe* (McKerrow), I, 216.
241. *Works of Greene* (Grosart), VI, 266.
242. *Ibid.,* X, 9.
243. *Works of Greene* (Grosart), X, 72.
244. *Ibid.,* X, 201.
245. *Ibid.,* XI, 47.
246. *Ibid.,* XI, 51-52.
247. *Works of Nashe* (McKerrow), II, 97.
248. *Works of Nashe* (McKerrow), III, 382.
249. *Ibid.,* III, 391.
250. *Works of Greene* (Grosart), X, 18, 90; *ibid.,* XI, 50, 243.
251. *Ibid.,* X, 90.
252. *Ibid.,* XI, 29.
253. *Works of Greene* (Grosart), XI, 50.
254. *Ibid.,* XI, 285.
255. *Ibid.,* XI, 283.
256. *Works of Nashe* (McKerrow), I, 36.
257. *Works of Greene* (Grosart), X, 8-9, 17-18; *ibid.,* XI, 53.
258. *Works of Lodge* (Hunterian Club), II, ii, 33, 61-62; *Works of Greene* (Grosart), X, 44, 70, 96, 268; *ibid.,* XI, 52; *Works of Nashe* (McKerrow), I, 20.
259. Stephen Gosson, *The School of Abuse* (Shakespeare Society), pp. 33-34; Stephen Gosson, *The Ephemerides of Phialo* (Huntington Library facsimile), p. 89 *recto; Works of Lodge* (Hunterian Club), II, ii, 20; *Works of Greene* (Grosart), X, 212; *Works of Nashe* (McKerrow), I, 83, 167; *ibid.,* III, 17, 373.
260. *Works of Greene* (Grosart), X, 9, 29, 33, 39, 72-73, 97, 144;

ibid., XI, 53; *Works of Nashe* (McKerrow), I, 93.

261. Stephen Gosson, *The Ephemerides of Phialo* (Huntington Library facsimile), p. 40 *recto; Works of Greene* (Grosart), XI, 76.

262. *Works of Greene* (Grosart), X, 199, 235, 268; *ibid.*, XI, 35, 217-18; *Works of Nashe* (McKerrow), II, 136.

263. *Works of Greene* (Grosart), XI, 243; *Works of Nashe* (McKerrow), II, 93; *ibid.*, III, 349.

264. *Works of Lyly* (Bond), III, 404.

265. Title page.

266. The Argument.

267. Title page.

268. Title page.

269. Title page.

270. Title page.

271. Title page.

272. Title page.

273. *Works of Greene* (Grosart), IV, 218-19; *ibid.*, VI, 258; *ibid.*, VII, 53-54; *ibid.*, IX, 269.

274. *Ibid.*, III, 16; *ibid.*, V, 49, 85; *ibid.*, VII, 22; *ibid.*, VIII, 44, 58; *ibid.*, IX, 228; *ibid.*, XII, 120-21, 227; *Works of Lodge* (Hunterian Club), IV, i, 8.

275. *Works of Greene* (Grosart), III, 58, 83; *ibid.*, VII, 8; *ibid.*, VIII, 186, 192, 204, 220; *ibid.*, IX, 230, 232-33, 243; *ibid.*, XII, 42, 68; *Works of Lodge* (Hunterian Club), IV, i, 10.

276. *Works of Greene* (Grosart), III, 48, 83, 88; *ibid.*, VIII, 26, 186; *ibid.*, IX, 333; *ibid.*, XII, 144; *Works of Lodge* (Hunterian Club), IV, i, 8, 14, 16, 33, 90.

277. *Works of Greene* (Grosart), III, 11, 17-18, 42; *ibid.*, V, 43; *ibid.*, XII, 120-21, 174.

278. *Ibid.*, V, 97; *ibid.*, IX, 275; *ibid.*, XII, 23.

279. *Ibid.*, XII, 101.

280. *Ibid.*, III, 79, 102, 181; *ibid.*, V, 83; *Works of Lodge* (Hunterian Club), IV, i, 70.

281. *Works of Greene* (Grosart), VIII, 82; *Works of Lodge* (Hunterian Club), IV, i, 108-109.

282. *Works of Greene* (Grosart), XII, 229; *Works of Lodge* (Hunterian Club), IV, i, 6, 17, 92.

283. *Works of Greene* (Grosart), III, 62, 101; *ibid.*, IX, 240; *ibid.*, XII, 17, 221.

284. *Ibid.*, VIII, 219; *ibid.*, XII, 118, 128; *Works of Lodge* (Hunterian Club), IV, i, 38.

285. *Works of Greene* (Grosart), III, 153; *ibid.*, V, 49; *ibid.*, VII,

60; *Works of Lodge* (Hunterian Club), IV, i, 27.

286. *Works of Greene* (Grosart), III, 75; *ibid.*, V, 229; *ibid.*, VIII, 22, 194; *Works of Lodge* (Hunterian Club), IV, i, 26, 30-31.

287. *Works of Greene* (Grosart), XII, 101.

288. *Works of Lodge* (Hunterian Club), IV, i, 5, 10.

289. *Works of Greene* (Grosart), III, 19-20, 26, 83; *ibid.*, IV, 202, *ibid.*, VIII, 143, 149; *ibid.*, XII, 111, 202, 220, 253-54; *Works of Lodge* (Hunterian Club), III, iii, 15, 71; *ibid.*, IV, i, 7-9, 22, 24-25, 36, 47.

290. *Works of Greene* (Grosart), III, 148; *ibid.*, IV, 202; *ibid.*, VIII, 22; *ibid.*, XII, 28; *Works of Lodge* (Hunterian Club), IV, i, 10.

291. *Works of Greene* (Grosart), V, 71, 94, 155; *ibid.*, VIII, 138, 142; *ibid.*, IX, 297; *Works of Lodge* (Hunterian Club), III, iii, 71; *ibid.*, IV, i, 29, 52.

292. *Works of Greene* (Grosart), V, 84-85.

293. *Ibid.*, III, 157; *ibid.*, XII, 68, 79; *Works of Lodge* (Hunterian Club), III, iii, 68.

294. *Works of Greene* (Grosart), V, 53; *ibid.*, VII, 63; *ibid.*, VIII, 138; *ibid.*, XII, 114.

295. *Ibid.*, XII, 144.

296. *Ibid.*, III, 11.

297. *Ibid.*, V, 43.

298. *Ibid.*, III, 11; *ibid.*, V, 86.

299. *Ibid.*, III, 14.

300. *Ibid.*, V, 203.

301. *Ibid.*, III, 36-37; *ibid.*, VIII, 140.

302. *Works of Greene* (Grosart), III, 23; *ibid.*, VIII, 44, 59, 152-53.

303. *Ibid.*, III, 39; *ibid.*, VIII, 141; *ibid.*, IX, 310; *Works of Lodge* (Hunterian Club), IV, i, 113.

304. *Works of Greene* (Grosart), V, 55; *ibid.*, VII, 67.

305. *Ibid.*, V, 57; *ibid.*, VII, 68.

306. *Ibid.*, V, 56-57; *ibid.*, VII, 68.

307. *Ibid.*, V, 57; *ibid.*, VII, 69.

308. *Ibid.*, III, 86; *ibid.*, V, 58; *ibid.*, VII, 69; *ibid.*, IX, 259.

309. *Ibid.*, IX, 289.

310. *Ibid.*, V, 62, 115; *ibid.*, VII, 73; *ibid.*, VIII, 81.

311. *Works of Greene* (Grosart), V, 115.

312. *Ibid.*, V, 84-85.

313. *Ibid.*, V, 49-50, 89; *ibid.*, IX, 261.

314. *Ibid.*, VII, 62; *ibid.*, VIII, 219.

315. *Ibid.*, XII, 235-36.

316. *Ibid.*, V, 170.

317. *Ibid.*, V, 147; *ibid.*, XII, 7.
318. *Ibid.*, V, 233.
319. *Ibid.*, VII, 22; *ibid.*, IX, 269.
320. *Ibid.*, VI, 179; *ibid.*, VII, 35.
321. *Works of Greene* (Grosart), XII, 146-48; *Works of Lodge* (Hunterian Club), IV, i, 114.
322. *Works of Lodge* (Hunterian Club), IV, i, 22.
323. *Works of Greene* (Grosart), XII, 158.
324. *Ibid.*, V, 152; *ibid.*, XII, 158, 270-71. Professor Archer Taylor, in his article "The Proverb 'The Black Ox Has not Trod on His Foot' in Renaissance Literature," *Philological Quarterly*, XX (October, 1941), 266-78, calls attention (p. 278) to a probable connection between the proverbial black ox of Renaissance literature, English and Continental, and "a literary and iconographic tradition of Death riding a black ox," a tradition which, he says, was well established in late medieval Christian use. According to Professor Taylor, "the Albanian proverb 'The black ox has not yet mounted on you,' which is said to mean 'Death has not yet taken away your parents and consequently you have not known suffering,' suggests how readily an allusion to Death can pass into a more general allusion to sorrow, care, and poverty."
325. *Works of Greene* (Grosart), VIII, 94, 138; *ibid.*, XII, 163, 176, 251.
326. *Ibid.*, III, 14; *ibid.*, VIII, 139; *ibid.*, XII, 163.
327. *Ibid.*, III, 12; *ibid.*, VIII, 146; *ibid.*, XII, 206.
328. *Works of Greene* (Grosart), III, 12; *ibid.*, VIII, 146.
329. *Ibid.*, V, 16, 203; *ibid.*, VII, 48, 59; *ibid.*, XII, 251.
330. *Ibid.*, V, 16.
331. *Ibid.*, XII, 23.
332. *Ibid.*, V, 60; *ibid.*, VII, 72.
333. *Ibid.*, III, 127; *ibid.*, VIII, 180; *ibid.*, XII, 28, 70, 133; *Works of Lodge* (Hunterian Club), IV, i, 10.
334. *Works of Greene* (Grosart), V, 60; *ibid.*, VII, 72.
335. *Ibid.*, VIII, 68, 71, 223; *ibid.*, XII, 28.
336. *Ibid.*, XII, 37.
337. *Works of Greene* (Grosart), XII, 271.
338. *Ibid.*
339. *Ibid.*, VI, 183-84; *ibid.*, VII, 37.
340. *Ibid.*, IX, 228.
341. *Ibid.*, III, 27; *ibid.*, VIII, 155; *ibid.*, IX, 273.
342. *Ibid.*, XII, 180.
343. *Works of Lodge* (Hunterian Club), IV, i, 26, 30-31.

344. *Works of Greene* (Grosart), VII, 12; *ibid.*, IX, 263.
345. *Ibid.*, XII, 254; *Works of Lodge* (Hunterian Club), III, iii, 12; *ibid.*, IV, i, 8.
346. *Works of Greene* (Grosart), VII, 48, 59.
347. *Works of Lodge* (Hunterian Club), IV, i, 83.
348. *Works of Greene* (Grosart), IX, 333.
349. *Ibid.*, XII, 159.
350. *Ibid.*, XII, 174.
351. *Ibid.*, IV, 198; *Works of Lodge* (Hunterian Club), IV, i, 112.
352. *Works of Greene* (Grosart), VII, 11-12.
353. *Ibid.*, XII, 28.
354. *Ibid.*, V, 70.
355. *Ibid.*, III, 78; *ibid.*, V, 192-93.
356. *Works of Greene* (Grosart), VI, 180.
357. *Ibid.*, VI, 184; *ibid.*, VII, 37, 72; *Works of Lodge* (Hunterian Club), IV, i, 30.
358. *Works of Greene* (Grosart), IX, 239-40.
359. *Ibid.*, XII, 24.
360. *Ibid.*, VIII, 25; *ibid.*, XII, 265.
361. *Ibid.*, XII, 241.
362. *Ibid.*, VI, 187, 195; *ibid.*, VIII, 164; *ibid.*, XII, 109, 138, 165, 174, 205; *Works of Lodge* (Hunterian Club), IV, i, 112.
363. *Works of Greene* (Grosart), VIII, 210; *ibid.*, XII, 9.
364. *Works of Greene* (Grosart), VIII, 103-104; *ibid.*, XII, 9.
365. John Lyly, *Euphues* (Arber), pp. 135, 153; John Lyly, *Euphues and His England* (Arber), pp. 256, 331, 337, 379, 454; *Works of Greene* (Grosart), II, 49, 82, 90, 132, 155, 255, 263; *ibid.*, IV, 68-69, 242, 286; *ibid.*, VI, 36, 47; *ibid.*, IX, 38, 43, 79, 96, 155, 174; *Works of Lodge* (Hunterian Club), I, v, 15, 112; *ibid.*, II, iii, 55; *ibid.*, II, iv, 60; *ibid.*, III, iv, 67; *Works of Sidney* (Feuillerat), I, 167, 300, 390, 460; *ibid.*, II, 90, 137; *Works of Deloney* (Mann), pp. 27-28, 80, 100, 251, 268; *Works of Nashe* (McKerrow), II, 210, 221, 275; *ibid.*, III, 188, 196.
366. John Grange, *The Golden Aphroditis* (facsimile), p. G iv *recto;* John Lyly, *Euphues* (Arber), pp. 35, 41, 75, 87; John Lyly, *Euphues and His England* (Arber), pp. 260-61, 313, 319, 322, 327, 337, 364, 475; *Works of Greene* (Grosart), II, 27, 52, 63, 93, 108, 111, 118-19, 132, 163, 263; *ibid.*, III, 198, 208-209; *ibid.*, IV, 108-109, 130, 242; *ibid.*, VI, 119; *ibid.*, IX, 33, 43, 65; *Works of Lodge* (Hunterian Club), I, v, 105; *ibid.*, III, iv, 30, 70; *Works of Deloney* (Mann), p. 29; *Works of Nashe* (McKerrow), II, 210, 259-60; *ibid.*, III, 191, 214.
367. John Grange, *The Golden Aphroditis* (facsimile), pp. A iv

verso, L ii *recto,* N *recto;* John Lyly, *Euphues* (Arber), pp. 75, 87; John Lyly, *Euphues and His England* (Arber), pp. 215, 280, 282, 321, 458; *Works of Greene* (Grosart), II, 186, 190; *ibid.,* III, 198; *ibid.,* IV, 18, 36; *ibid.,* VI, 115; *ibid.,* IX, 33, 163-64, 167; *Works of Lodge* (Hunterian Club), II, iii, 44, 57, 59; *Works of Sidney* (Feuillerat), I, 87; *Works of Deloney* (Mann), p. 208; *Works of Nashe* (McKerrow), II, 269, 277, 301.

368. John Grange, *The Golden Aphroditis* (facsimile), p. M ii *verso;* John Lyly, *Euphues* (Arber), pp. 145, 203; John Lyly, *Euphues and His England* (Arber), p. 239; *Works of Greene* (Grosart), II, 92, 106-107, 122, 156, 186; *ibid.,* IV, 63; *ibid.,* VI, 70; *ibid.,* IX, 163, 200, 221; *Works of Lodge* (Hunterian Club), I, v, 8; *ibid.,* II, iii, 32, 53, 103; *Works of Sidney* (Feuillerat), II, 83; *Works of Deloney* (Mann), pp. 14, 17, 28, 61, 126, 217; *Works of Nashe* (McKerrow), II, 216, 220, 229, 233, 259, 297, 299; *ibid.,* III, 193.

369. *Works of Greene* (Grosart), II, 55, 117; *ibid.,* III, 182; *ibid.,* IV, 96; *ibid.,* VI, 119; *ibid.,* XI, 160; *Works of Nashe* (McKerrow), II, 221.

370. John Lyly, *Euphues* (Arber), pp. 54, 149; *Works of Greene* (Grosart), II, 20, 44-45, 51, 60, 207, 232, 255, 279; *ibid.,* III, 239; *ibid.,* IV, 82, 115-16; *ibid.,* IX, 74, 129, 138, 190, 207; *Works of Lodge* (Hunterian Club), I, v, 69; *Works of Deloney* (Mann), p. 121; *Works of Nashe* (McKerrow), II, 284.

371. John Grange, *The Golden Aphroditis* (facsimile) p. A iii *verso;* John Lyly, *Euphues and His England* (Arber), pp. 273, 474; *Works of Greene* (Grosart), II, 28, 62, 167, 188, 235, 261, 229; *ibid.,* III, 205-206, 233; *ibid.,* IX, 52, 66, 96; *Works of Lodge* (Hunterian Club), I, iii, 81; *ibid.,* I, v, 15; *ibid.,* II, iii, 35, 40; *Works of Sidney* (Feuillerat), I, 300, 388; *ibid.,* II, 12, 27, 182; *Works of Deloney* (Mann), p. 90.

372. John Grange, *The Golden Aphroditis* (facsimile), p. L ii *recto;* John Lyly, *Euphues* (Arber), p. 78; John Lyly, *Euphues and His England* (Arber), pp. 256, 260-61, 316, 435, 462, 475; *Works of Greene* (Grosart), II, 20, 65, 118-19, 132, 163, 257; *ibid.,* IX, 76; *Works of Lodge* (Hunterian Club), II, iii, 10, 12, 14; *ibid.,* III, iv, 50; *Works of Sidney* (Feuillerat), I, 7, 388; *ibid.,* II, 12, 134, 137, 191; *Works of Deloney* (Mann), pp. 82, 112; *Works of Nashe* (McKerrow), II, 214, 219, 240, 260, 284, 302; *ibid.,* III, 214.

373. John Grange, *The Golden Aphroditis* (facsimile), p. D *recto;* John Lyly, *Euphues* (Arber), pp. 35, 78, 177; John Lyly, *Eu-*

phues and His England (Arber), pp. 273, 320, 322, 363, 435, 453, 461-62, 472; *Works of Greene* (Grosart), II, 20, 27, 62, 65, 93, 154-55, 163, 167, 188, 235, 255; *ibid.,* III, 198; *ibid.,* IV, 130, 263; *ibid.,* VI, 49, 61, 75, 119; *ibid.,* IX, 33, 65, 76, 96; *Works of Lodge* (Hunterian Club), II, iii, 12, 32, 44, 73; *Works of Sidney* (Feuillerat), I, 7, 56, 157; *ibid.,* II, 119, 137; *Works of Deloney* (Mann), pp. 7, 27-28, 61, 85, 90, 155, 217; *Works of Nashe* (McKerrow), II, 214, 240, 302; *ibid.,* III, 188.

374. John Grange, *The Golden Aphroditis* (facsimile), p. K iii verso; John Lyly, *Euphues* (Arber), pp. 44, 107; John Lyly, *Euphues and His England* (Arber), pp. 273, 327, 394, 419-21; *Works of Greene* (Grosart), II, 62, 87, 131; *Works of Lodge* (Hunterian Club), I, v, 69; *ibid.,* II, iii, 25; *Works of Nashe* (McKerrow), II, 219).

375. John Lyly, *Euphues* (Arber), p. 55; *Works of Greene* (Grosart), II, 15, 31, 92, 154, 264; *ibid.,* III, 181, 222, 236; *ibid.,* IV, 17, 39-40, 57, 61, 122, 229; *Works of Lodge* (Hunterian Club), III, iv, 52; *Works of Sidney* (Feuillerat), II, 115, 119; *Works of Deloney* (Mann), pp. 24-25, 121, 127; *Works of Nashe* (McKerrow), II, 240, 290.

376. John Lyly, *Euphues* (Arber), p. 55; *Works of Greene* (Grosart), IX, 135, 180; *Works of Lodge* (Hunterian Club), I, v, 36; *ibid.,* II, iii, 12.

377. John Lyly, *Euphues and His England* (Arber), pp. 471-72; *Works of Greene* (Grosart), II, 107; *ibid.,* IX, 37-38; *Works of Lodge* (Hunterian Club), II, iii, 44, 55; *Works of Sidney* (Feuillerat), I, 309; *Works of Deloney* (Mann) pp. 19, 152, 217, 253; *Works of Nashe* (McKerrow), III, 200.

378. John Lyly, *Euphues* (Arber), pp. 42, 202; John Lyly, *Euphues and His England* (Arber), pp. 232, 239; *Works of Greene* (Grosart), IX, 22; *Works of Lodge* (Hunterian Club), II, iii, 13, 51; *ibid.,* III, iv, 67.

379. John Grange, *The Golden Aphroditis* (facsimile), p. D iii recto; *Works of Sidney* (Feuillerat), II, 201; *Works of Nashe* (McKerrow), III, 218.

380. John Lyly, *Euphues* (Arber), p. 110; John Lyly, *Euphues and His England* (Arber), pp. 287-88, 346; *Works of Greene* (Grosart), II, 263; *ibid.,* III, 204-205; *ibid.,* IX, 191, 200; *Works of Lodge* (Hunterian Club), I, v, 15; *Works of Nashe* (McKerrow), II, 284.

381. John Lyly, *Euphues* (Arber), pp. 71, 127; *Works of Greene* (Grosart), II, 49, 208, 263; *ibid.,* IV, 125-26; *Works of Lodge* (Hunterian Club), III, iv, 46.

382. John Lyly, *Euphues and His England* (Arber), p. 282; *Works of Greene* (Grosart), II, 263; *Works of Lodge* (Hunterian Club), II, iii, 15, 43, 63; *ibid.*, III, iv, 56; *Works of Sidney* (Feuillerat), I, 108.

383. *Works of Sidney* (Feuillerat), I, 237; *Works of Deloney* (Mann), p. 174.

384. John Lyly, *Euphues* (Arber), p. 135; John Lyly, *Euphues and His England* (Arber), pp. 347, 372, 462, 474; *Works of Greene* (Grosart), IV, 36; *ibid.*, VII, 201; *ibid.*, IX, 96, 104, 132; *Works of Lodge* (Hunterian Club), II, iii, 35, 56; *ibid.*, III, iv, 54, 73; *Works of Sidney* (Feuillerat), I, 300; *Works of Deloney* (Mann), pp. 40, 81; *Works of Nashe* (McKerrow), II, 285.

385. John Lyly, *Euphues and His England* (Arber), pp. 378, 380; *Works of Nashe* (McKerrow), II, 226.

386. *Works of Greene* (Grosart), III, 184.

387. John Lyly, *Euphues and His England* (Arber), p. 350; *Works of Deloney* (Mann), p. 50.

388. John Grange, *The Golden Aphroditis* (facsimile), pp. D *verso*, L ii *recto;* John Lyly, *Euphues* (Arber), pp. 78, 87, 153; John Lyly, *Euphues and His England* (Arber), pp. 214, 256, 301, 390, 454, 462; *Works of Greene* (Grosart), III, 198; *ibid.*, IV, 68-69, 242, 279-80, 306; *ibid.*, VI, 36, 60-61, 110, 115; *ibid.*, VII, 155; *ibid.*, IX, 30, 33, 38, 96, 104, 157, 174; *Works of Lodge* (Hunterian Club), I, v, 11, 61, 63, 128; *ibid.*, II, iii, 14, 32, 37; *Works of Sidney* (Feuillerat), I, 311.

389. John Grange, *The Golden Aphroditis* (facsimile), p. S iv *recto;* John Lyly, *Euphues and His England* (Arber), pp. 312, 443; *Works of Greene* (Grosart), II, 232-33; *ibid.*, IV, 152; *ibid.*, IX, 25, 50, 163-64; *Works of Lodge* (Hunterian Club), II, iii, 27, 75; *Works of Sidney* (Feuillerat), I, 98, 238; *Works of Deloney* (Mann), pp. 29, 238.

390. John Lyly, *Euphues* (Arber), p. 124; John Lyly, *Euphues and His England* (Arber), p. 341; *Works of Deloney* (Mann), p. 19.

391. John Lyly, *Euphues* (Arber), p. 106; John Lyly, *Euphues and His England* (Arber), pp. 331, 366, 397, 473; *Works of Greene* (Grosart), II, 285, 295; *ibid.*, III, 222; *ibid.*, IV, 133; *Works of Lodge* (Hunterian Club), I, v, 8; *ibid.*, II, iii, 43; *Works of Deloney* (Mann), pp. 28, 155, 162, 170.

392. John Lyly, *Euphues and His England* (Arber), pp. 312, 390, 432; *Works of Greene* (Grosart), II, 43, 49; *ibid.*, IV, 36, 231; *ibid.*, VII, 192; *ibid.*, IX, 128-29, 207; *ibid.*, XI, 156; *Works of Lodge* (Hunterian Club), I, v, 10, 63; *Works of Sidney* (Feuil-

lerat) , I, 286; *Works of Nashe* (McKerrow) , II, 243.

393. John Lyly, *Euphues* (Arber) , p. 44; *Works of Lodge* (Hunterian Club) , III, iv, 48.

394. John Lyly, *Euphues and His England* (Arber) , p. 341; *Works of Greene* (Grosart) , IV, 165; *ibid.,* IX, 145-46.

395. *Works of Greene* (Grosart) , XI, 143; *Works of Lodge* (Hunterian Club) , III, iv, 61; *Works of Sidney* (Feuillerat) , I, 155; *ibid.,* II, 89.

396. John Lyly, *Euphues and His England* (Arber) , p. 215; *Works of Greene* (Grosart) , II, 30; *ibid.,* III, 205-206; *ibid.,* XI, 156; *Works of Lodge* (Hunterian Club) , I, v, 4, 11; *Works of Nashe* (McKerrow) , III, 182.

397. John Lyly, *Euphues and His England* (Arber) , p. 366.

398. *Ibid.,* p. 229; *Works of Greene* (Grosart) , IX, 147-48.

399. John Grange, *The Golden Aphroditis* (facsimile) , p. H ii *verso; Works of Greene* (Grosart) , IV, 244; *Works of Lodge* (Hunterian Club) , I, v, 10; *Works of Sidney* (Feuillerat) , II, 166.

400. John Grange, *The Golden Aphroditis* (facsimile) , pp. K ii *verso,* L iv *verso;* John Lyly, *Euphues* (Arber) , pp. 35, 153; John Lyly, *Euphues and His England* (Arber) , pp. 273, 312, 333, 335, 454; *Works of Greene* (Grosart) , II, 35, 87, 90-91, 119, 188, 257, 275-76; *ibid.,* IV, 109; *ibid.,* VII, 129; *ibid.,* IX, 32, 79-80; *Works of Lodge* (Hunterian Club) , I, v, 95; *ibid.,* III, iv, 27; *Works of Sidney* (Feuillerat) , II, 100; *Works of Deloney* (Mann) , pp. 8-9, 95, 187, 250.

401. John Lyly, *Euphues* (Arber) , pp. 75, 109; John Lyly, *Euphues and His England* (Arber) , pp. 319, 327; *Works of Sidney* (Feuillerat) , I, 363-64.

402. *Works of Greene* (Grosart) , II, 25; *Works of Deloney* (Mann) , p. 258.

403. *Works of Lodge* (Hunterian Club) , II, iii, 10; *ibid.,* III, iv, 17; *Works of Deloney* (Mann) , p. 182; *Works of Nashe* (McKerrow) , II, 232.

404. John Grange, *The Golden Aphroditis* (facsimile) , pp. E ii *verso,* K ii *recto; Works of Greene* (Grosart) , II, 230; *ibid.,* IV, 44, 61, 132, 314; *ibid.,* IX, 96; *Works of Lodge* (Hunterian Club) , I, v, 72; *Works of Sidney* (Feuillerat) , I, 79, 96, 311, 470-71.

405. John Lyly, *Euphues* (Arber) , p. 124; *Works of Nashe* (McKerrow) , II, 272-73.

406. John Grange, *The Golden Aphroditis* (facsimile) , pp. C ii *verso,* N *verso;* John Lyly, *Euphues* (Arber) , p. 75; John Lyly,

Euphues and His England (Arber), pp. 364, 379, 462; *Works of Greene* (Grosart), II, 228, 257, 259-60; *ibid.,* IX, 47, 191, 199; *Works of Lodge* (Hunterian Club), II, iii, 15, 35; *Works of Sidney* (Feuillerat), II, 186; *Works of Deloney* (Mann), pp. 24, 232; *Works of Nashe* (McKerrow), II, 307.

407. John Lyly, *Euphues* (Arber), p. 45; *Works of Greene* (Grosart), II, 24, 120-21, 156, 225, 261, 263; *ibid.,* III, 179, 184; *ibid.,* VI, 57; *ibid.,* VII, 107, 196; *ibid.,* IX, 63, 79; *Works of Lodge* (Hunterian Club), I, v, 54; *Works of Sidney* (Feuillerat), II, 27; *Works of Nashe* (McKerrow), III, 204.

408. John Grange, *The Golden Aphroditis* (facsimile), pp. H iv *verso,* O iii *verso;* John Lyly, *Euphues* (Arber), pp. 54, 99, 116, 196; John Lyly, *Euphues and His England* (Arber), pp. 224, 235, 286, 372, 376, 381, 384, 401; *Works of Greene* (Grosart), II, 119, 175, 182, 187, 192, 205-206, 222-23, 236, 257, 261, 279-80, 284; *ibid.,* III, 196, 208-209, 220, 240; *ibid.,* IV, 51, 54, 159, 242; *ibid.,* VI, 84; *ibid.,* VII, 202-204; *ibid.,* IX, 47, 75, 189, 190; *ibid.,* XI, 146; *Works of Lodge* (Hunterian Club), I, v, 63; *ibid.,* II, iii, 11, 13, 26, 36, 51, 63, 67, 71; *ibid.,* III, iv, 34, 49; *Works of Sidney* (Feuillerat), I, 210; *ibid.,* II, 96, 179, 181; *Works of Deloney* (Mann), pp. 29, 77, 225, 267; *Works of Nashe* (McKerrow), II, 221, 284, 293; *ibid.,* III, 195.

409. John Grange, *The Golden Aphroditis* (facsimile), p. H iii *recto;* John Lyly, *Euphues and His England* (Arber), pp. 363, 409; *Works of Greene* (Grosart), II, 74, 228, 233, 262; *ibid.,* III, 194, 239, 251; *ibid.,* IV, 37, 65, 72, 278; *ibid.,* VI, 45; *ibid.,* VII, 123; *ibid.,* IX, 27-28, 60, 189, 200; *ibid.,* XI, 152; *Works of Lodge* (Hunterian Club), I, v, 68; *ibid.,* II, iii, 43; *Works of Deloney* (Mann), p. 24.

410. John Lyly, *Euphues* (Arber), p. 73; John Lyly, *Euphues and His England* (Arber), p. 298; *Works of Greene* (Grosart), II, 61; *ibid.,* III, 192-93; *ibid.,* IV, 54; *ibid.,* VI, 57; *ibid.,* VII, 205; *ibid.,* IX, 31, 75, 149-50, 180; *ibid.,* XI, 119; *Works of Deloney* (Mann), p. 4; *Works of Nashe* (McKerrow), III, 223.

411. John Lyly, *Euphues* (Arber), p. 129; John Lyly, *Euphues and His England* (Arber), pp. 215, 269, 417; *Works of Greene* (Grosart), IV, 46; *Works of Lodge* (Hunterian Club), II, iii, 33; *ibid.,* III, iv, 41, 71, 90; *Works of Sidney* (Feuillerat), I, 289.

412. John Lyly, *Euphues and His England* (Arber), p. 347.

413. *Works of Greene* (Grosart), IX, 42, 178, 199.

414. *Ibid.,* IX, 95; *ibid.,* XI, 169.

415. John Grange, *The Golden Aphroditis* (facsimile), p. N iii

verso; John Lyly, *Euphues* (Arber), pp. 35, 58, 100, 107; John Lyly, *Euphues and His England* (Arber), pp. 356, 360; *Works of Greene* (Grosart), IV, 112; *ibid.,* VI, 45; *ibid.,* IX, 42, 185, 207; *ibid.,* XI, 175; *Works of Lodge* (Hunterian Club), I, v, 129; *Works of Sidney* (Feuillerat), I, 58; *ibid.,* II, 185; *Works of Deloney* (Mann), p. 19.

416. John Grange, *The Golden Aphroditis* (facsimile), p. H *verso;* John Lyly, *Euphues* (Arber), pp. 68-69, 107, 123; John Lyly, *Euphues and His England* (Arber), pp. 356, 381, 411; *Works of Greene* (Grosart), II, 59, 74, 188, 228, 260-61; *ibid.,* IV, 51, 96; *ibid.,* IX, 60, 74; *ibid.,* XI, 119, 141; *Works of Lodge* (Hunterian Club), I, v, 54, 120; *ibid.,* III, iv, 49.

417. John Lyly, *Euphues* (Arber), pp. 35, 58, 153, 157, 182, 187; John Lyly, *Euphues and His England* (Arber), pp. 252, 261-65; *Works of Lodge* (Hunterian Club), I, v, 111, 128; *ibid.,* II, iii, 8, 10; *ibid.,* III, iv, 17; *Works of Sidney* (Feuillerat), I, 94; *ibid.,* II, 20; *Works of Deloney* (Mann), pp. 27-29, 38, 204; *Works of Nashe* (McKerrow), II, 285.

418. John Lyly, *Euphues* (Arber), pp. 39, 100-101, 109, 111; John Lyly, *Euphues and His England* (Arber), p. 315; *Works of Greene* (Grosart), II, 129; *ibid.,* IV, 22, 120; *ibid.,* VII, 122; *ibid.,* IX, 29, 171, 218; *Works of Lodge* (Hunterian Club), I, v, 34; *ibid.,* II, iii, 15, 67; *Works of Sidney* (Feuillerat), II, 102; *Works of Deloney* (Mann), p. 28; *Works of Nashe* (McKerrow), II, 284.

419. *Works of Greene* (Grosart), IV, 242; *ibid.,* XI, 168, 190, 193; *Works of Lodge* (Hunterian Club), I, v, 60; *Works of Nashe* (McKerrow), II, 322.

420. John Grange, *The Golden Aphroditis* (facsimile), p. A ii *recto;* John Lyly, *Euphues* (Arber), p. 79; John Lyly, *Euphues and His England* (Arber), p. 419; *Works of Greene* (Grosart), II, 28; *ibid.,* VI, 63; *ibid.,* IX, 66, 91; *Works of Lodge* (Hunterian Club), I, v, 123; *Works of Nashe* (McKerrow), II, 221.

421. John Lyly, *Euphues* (Arber), pp. 44, 53; John Lyly *Euphues and His England* (Arber), p. 327; *Works of Greene* (Grosart), III, 209; *Works of Lodge* (Hunterian Club), II, iii, 103; *Works of Sidney* (Feuillerat), I, 196; *Works of Nashe* (McKerrow), II, 266, 275-76, 325-26.

422. John Lyly, *Euphues* (Arber), p. 73; John Lyly, *Euphues and His England* (Arber), p. 320; *Works of Greene* (Grosart), II, 17, 61, 77, 222, 257, 261; *ibid.,* III, 179, 184; *ibid.,* IX, 75, 82, 85; *Works of Lodge* (Hunterian Club), I, v, 12, 108.

423. John Grange, *The Golden Aphroditis* (facsimile), p. K iii

verso; John Lyly, *Euphues and His England* (Arber), p. 326; *Works of Greene* (Grosart), II, 65; *ibid.,* VI, 63; *ibid.,* IX, 133.

424. John Lyly, *Euphues* (Arber), pp. 35, 63, 97; John Lyly, *Euphues and His England* (Arber), pp. 353, 392, 469; *Works of Greene* (Grosart), II, 18, 27, 38, 63, 93, 108, 113-14, 129, 292; *ibid.,* III, 208-209, 251; *ibid.,* IV, 67, 106, 120; *ibid.,* IX, 29, 65-66, 76; *Works of Lodge* (Hunterian Club), I, v, 72, 111; *Works of Sidney* (Feuillerat), I, 244, 279, 300; *Works of Deloney* (Mann), p. 152; *Works of Nashe* (McKerrow), II, 299.

425. John Lyly, *Euphues* (Arber), p. 61; *Works of Greene* (Grosart), II, 28, 30, 178, 199, 264; *ibid.,* III, 192, 204; *ibid.,* IV, 15, 17, 86; *ibid.,* VII, 203; *ibid.,* IX, 32, 60-61, 66, 221; *Works of Lodge* (Hunterian Club), I, v, 60, 119; *ibid.,* II, iii, 44, 63; *Works of Sidney* (Feuillerat), I, 164-65; *Works of Deloney* (Mann), pp. 163, 234-35, 260-61; *Works of Nashe* (McKerrow), II, 275.

426. *Works of Greene* (Grosart), II, 175, 228; *ibid.,* IV, 20-21; *Works of Lodge* (Hunterian Club), II, iii, 36; *Works of Sidney* (Feuillerat), I, 415.

427. *Works of Sidney* (Feuillerat), I, 107.

428. John Lyly, *Euphues* (Arber), pp. 66, 78-79, 93; *Works of Greene* (Grosart), IV, 81, 84-85; *ibid.,* VI, 36-37; *Works of Lodge* (Hunterian Club), II, iii, 25.

429. See above, p. 129, n. 9.

430. See above, p. 128, n. 6. It would be extremely difficult not to say impossible, to determine the actual origin of the many allusions in English and Continental literature to horns as the symbol of cuckoldry; but three passages in particular seem to suggest the nature of the ideas behind these allusions. In Greene's *Mamillia* (*Works of Greene* (Grosart), II, 229), Pharicles asks Clarynda these questions in a letter: "Shall I hold the net and others catch the fish? yea, shall euery man get his fee of the Deare, and I get nothing but the hornes?" The implication in this reference to the hunters' custom of dividing the venison is obvious. In the *Carde of Fancie* (*ibid.,* IV, 88-89), Castania's words addressed to Gwydonius suggest a possible connection between the proverbial horns and the Greek myth in which Diana is said to have transformed Actaeon into a stag: "Yes but you would respect Diana . . . if she pinched you but with *Acteons* plague, to pester your head with as many hornes as a Hart." In *A Disputation Betweene a Hee Conny-Catcher and a Shee Conny-Catcher* (*ibid.,* X, 260), Greene tells about a husband who discovered that "in his absence"

he had been cuckolded by his friend, who "had been grafting hornes in the Chimnies." The idea of grafting horns in chimneys seems to be reminiscent of Plutarch's mention in the "Roman Questions" of his *Morals* (Goodwin, *op. cit.*, II, 205-206) of the Roman practice of nailing up stags' horns against the walls in the temples of Diana after making sacrifices to this goddess.

431. See above, p. 128, n. 3.
432. See above, p. 128, n. 4.
433. See above, p. 128, n. 2.
434. *Works of Sidney* (Feuillerat), I, 119-24.
435. *Ibid.*, I, 124.
436. *Works of Lodge* (Hunterian Club), I, v, 83-86.
437. *Ibid.*, II, iii, 39.
438. *Works of Lodge* (Hunterian Club), II, iii, 41.
439. *Ibid.*, III, iv, 81-82.
440. *Works of Greene* (Grosart), II, 15, 17, 33, 39, 187; *ibid.*, IV, 12, 77, 234; *Works of Lodge* (Hunterian Club), I, v, 9-13, 15-16, 19-20, 24, 27, 29, 32, 34, 55, 60, 63, 68, 73, 83-88, 90, 92-93, 138-39; *ibid.*, II, iii, 12, 14-15, 29, 36, 43, 51, 79, 82, 91, 101, 103; *ibid.*, III, iv, 29, 81; *Works of Sidney* (Feuillerat), I, 24-25, 79-80, 82, 193-94, 255, 264, 283, 293, 301, 330, 332, 339-44, 383-84, 392, 426; *ibid.*, II, 107, 109, 111, 115, 122-23, 125, 148, 157, 163, 197.
441. *Desiderius Erasmus Concerning the Aim and Method of Education* (Woodward), p. 42.
442. *Ibid.*, p. 40.
443. See above, pp. 26-27.
444. *Works of Lodge* (Hunterian Club), I, v, 59-60.
445. *Ibid.*, III, iv, 81.
446. See above, pp. 23-24.
447. *Works of Lodge* (Hunterian Club), III, iv, 81.
448. *Works of Sidney* (Feuillerat), I, 107-108, 285-86, 415-16, 422-23, 430, 445, 455, 462.
449. *Works of Lodge* (Hunterian Club), III, iv, 45-46.
450. *Works of Sidney* (Feuillerat), I, 455.
451. *Works of Lodge* (Hunterian Club), III, iv, 46.
452. *Works of Greene* (Grosart), II, 6; *ibid.*, VI, 264; *ibid.*, VII, 102; *ibid.*, IX, 182, 221; *ibid.*, XI, 223; *ibid.*, XII, 5, 212; *Works of Deloney* (Mann), p. 183; *Works of Nashe* (McKerrow), III, 220; *Works of Harvey* (Grosart), I, 67, 161; *ibid.*, II, 82, 237, 311.
453. *Works of Nashe* (McKerrow), III, 201-12.

454. *Ibid.*, III, 201-202.
455. *Works of Nashe* (McKerrow) , III, 202-203.
456. *Ibid.*, III, 203-204.
457. *Works of Nashe* (McKerrow) , III, 206.
458. *Ibid.*, III, 207.
459. *Ibid.*, III, 208-209.
460. *Ibid.*, III, 209-10.
461. *Works of Nashe* (McKerrow) , III, 210.
462. *Works of Nashe* (McKerrow) , III, 211.
463. *Ibid.*, III, 214.

Index